George Garrett: The Elizabethan Trilogy

D1194306

George Garrett: The Elizabethan Trilogy

Edited

by

Brooke Horvath

and

Irving Malin

Texas Review Press
Huntsville, Texas

Texas Review Press, Huntsville, TX 77341
©1998 by *Texas Review* Press
Printed in the United States of America
All rights reserved

Requests for permission to reproduce material from this work should be sent to:

Permissions
Texas Review Press
English Department
Sam Houston State University
Huntsville, TX 77341

Gratitude is due *South Carolina Review*, *Texas Review*, and *Virginia Quarterly Review* for material that initially appeared in them.

Library of Congress Cataloging-in-Publication Data

George Garrett : the Elizabethan trilogy / edited by Brooke Horvath and Irving Malin.

p.   cm.

Includes bibliographical references and index.
ISBN 1-881515-13-3 (cloth). — ISBN 1-881515-14-1 (pbk.)
1. Garrett, George P., 1929—Death of the fox. 2. Great
Britain—History—Elizabeth, 1558-1603—Historiography.
3. Elizabeth I, Queen of England, 1533-1603—In literature.
4. Biographical fiction, American—History and criticism.
5. Historical fiction, American—History and criticism.
6. James I, King of England, 1566-1625—In literature.
7. Garrett, George P., 1929—Entered from the Sun.
8. Raleigh, Walter, Sir, 1552?-1618—In literature.
9. Marlowe, Christopher, 1564-1593—In literature.
10. Garrett, George P., 1929—Succession.   I. Horvath, Brooke.
II. Malin, Irving.
PS3557.A72D435   1998
813'.54--dc21

                                                    98-26217
                                                       CIP

This book is dedicated to

George Garrett

Editors' Note on Documentation

The gathering of these essays was begun in the spirit of a festschrift, and contributors were encouraged to document or not, as they saw fit. Although a scholarly collection of essays has been the result of our desire to pay tribute to George Garrett, we have left each essay's documentation as its author wished it to be.

Contents

Introduction

Once, in an introduction to a poetry anthology, George Garrett remarked that he would much rather be among the unbuttoned company of poets in the hinder pages than up front in jacket and tie as master of ceremonies. These are my feelings too on this occasion. For a long time I have planned an elaborate essay on Mr. Garrett's work and I wish fervently that I had gotten it done so it might find a place in this book.

I won't bore you with my excuses except to say that my ambition overmastered me. It was to be a searching effort, this essay, examining the Elizabethan trilogy thoroughly and relating those pages to Garrett's other novels and his poems and short stories and his genial but acute criticism. A great deal of reading would be required, not only in the familiar Garrett volumes, but also in Elizabethan history, of which I know so little.

Well, maybe I am beginning to parade my excuses—so please let me, if you will, describe what my essay was to be about. When you see what I desired to attempt, perhaps you will understand my difficulties.

I would begin by proposing that every seriously intended historical novel (in this case, three novels) implies or contains or asserts a theory of history. Most of them imply rather than containing or asserting since it is the novelist's business to illuminate while entertaining. His or her first goal must be to produce a work of literary art that holds the reader's emotionally engaged attention in a way that lectures and intricate theories rarely do. But if the subject of the literary work is history, then that work becomes a species of meta-history because it sets up an inevitable comparison between the methods of fiction and those of formal history; it avers, if not the ascendancy of fictive imagination over historical method, certain notions about the shortcomings of formal history: lack of full sympathy, deficiency of color and warmth, inadmissibility of the author's personal experiences which can rarely be brought to bear upon the subject of Napoleon or Phoenician shipbuilding in the time of Cyrus. The novelist, however, recognizes these methods, and others, as legitimate means to artistic truth, and so do most historians as well, though the severities of their discipline usually forbid their employing such means.

But when the usages and methods of one intellectual endeavor are conjoined with those of another, a criticism of both endeavors results, and this is true no matter what those endeavors are. History—that is, the documented facts of the case as they can best be resurrected—is never unmixed in its writing; it is always aided (or polluted, as some would have it) by other kinds of thought: the sciences of geology, psychology, archeology, meteorology, physics, chemistry, statistics, astronomy, and so forth; and it is always found in the company of some school or other of philosophy, whether by design or by accident. It would be difficult for their partisans to prove that the methods of these disciplines furnish more practical aid to the historian than the methods of poetry and fiction. For, after all, history too is a literary art and Clio shows more sisterly feeling to Calliope and Melpomene than to Urania.

Most of the theories implied in works of fiction are confused and flimsy and haphazard because the novelist has undertaken too lightly the concomitant role of meta-historian or has failed to recognize it as a proper duty. But historians generate jerry-built theories too and I would be glad—given world enough and time—to try to demonstrate that the theory of history Marguerite Yourçenar implies in *Hadrian's Memoirs* is at least as valid as the one Oswald Spengler asseverates in *The Decline of the West*. Actually, it is probably more valid for being implied rather than stated. Historical statement is forever subject to revision, but artistic implication is unrevisable and always capable of suggesting fresh aspects of truth or new ways to approach the truth.

There are certain works of fiction that contain theories of history and discuss them openly. Most famous, perhaps, is *War and Peace*, in which Tolstoy advances certain conclusions that seem at variance with the several stories we follow with his characters. For me, Thomas Mann's *Doctor Faustus* is more successful in this regard, embodying its theory of a tragic national destiny in the destiny of a single unhappy composer of music.

Usually, though, the historical fiction writer is not concerned to promulgate a large-scale theory of history but only to advance speculations in the form of dramatic presentation about a limited number of events and personages within a circumscribed stretch of time. I might suggest that the more circumscribed a novel's scope is, the less it suggests a theory of history. Shelby Foote's brilliant novel *Shiloh* takes place over only a few days and implies little theoretical framework; Olaf Stapledon's future-history epic, *Starmaker*, takes place over billions of eons and implies a complex and profoundly mystical historical theory.

But many more examples would be needed to shore up my supposition.

And of course my essay would display these titles and describe their contents perceptively and then move on to its next preliminary point. I would posit the notion that most historical fiction sets out to illuminate certain aspects of history generally regarded as settled fact. It may reinterpret the facts in a new and unexpected fashion—this is but normal for the genre—but it does not deny the existence of the facts and does not demur from their importance. Fiction usually accepts historical facts as givens and then goes on to dramatize, and sometimes to explain, how and why they happened. This is done by drawing minutely the personalities of historical personages or in creating personalities for them, by supplying both quotidian and psychological detail for the events that took place, by furnishing atmosphere, moral tone, and political climate with the observation of a thousand small incidents and gestures, and with the inclusion of every sort of little particular: clothing, hair styles, slang and dialect, houses and mansions and palaces, wagons and carriages and broughams—even belt buckles, doorknobs, wallpaper, and chamber pots.

All this earnest bric-a-brac is necessary to convince readers of what they already know: that Daniel Boone did indeed exist, that he explored and traced great areas of wilderness, that he was a cunning woodsman and an upright person, and that he ended his days as a revered judge in Missouri. A novelist's readers know these facts about Boone from their classes in high school or from works of formal history or from folklore. Yet Elizabeth Madox Roberts must have rested steadfast in her faith that her readers didn't really *know* this hero, could not truly recognize the man or understand his trials and achievements, until her novel, *The Great Meadow*, presented him as a figure strongly a part of his milieu and, at the same time, strikingly apart from it.

The historical novelist has to rely upon readers to know something about the subject matter before they open the book.

Otherwise, the story must be told from the beginning of the world almost, and this fact might account for the sleepy length of novels that deal with times and places unfamiliar to most of us. Historical novels about China or India or even Russia are usually weighty objects— or if they are normal in size come in series.

Without some background knowledge, however vague and inaccurate, on the part of readers, two kinds of historical novel could not be viable. I speak first of the popular "costume" novel, the sort invented by Sir Walter Scott and carried on by such nimble or clumsy practitioners as Rafael Sabattini, Samuel Shellabarger, Frank Yerby, and Inglis Fletcher. The purpose of these writers was to tell light romantic stories set against the backdrops—often onion-skin thin—of historical milieus. Even though the stories are detachable from their backgrounds—their invented incidents being common to most times and places—it is history that gives them flavor and just enough grounding in a reader's imagination to add the perfume of the sachet to their atmospheres.

The other novel for which some preknowledge of background is necessary is the "alternate history," the fantasia on historical themes. Here the purpose of settled history is not to convince us that the incidents of the fiction take place—we understand that they could not possibly take place—but that our prior knowledge of historical facts will be changed, enlarged or brought round to new perspectives, by the author's addition of fantasy or whimsy. The career of Virginia Woolf's Orlando is hardly realistic, but the author's vision of history is made clear, given firm outlines, by the fantasy. The events and details of Michael Moorcock's *Gloriana* can have no basis in the physical world we know, but its whimsies are in service of a happy celebration of the Elizabethan imagination. In the novel of "alternate history," the settled facts that serve as sometimes misty backgrounds in costume novels are brought to the forefront of the reader's attention by the author's departure from these facts. This procedure is like musical theme-and-variation; the composer causes us to concentrate on the intricacy of his variations while the unplayed theme continually sounds in the mind's ear.

But costume novels and alternate histories can be set apart from the mainstream historical novel whose purposes are (so my essay would reiterate) the illumination and dramatization of the history most of us regard as the truth.

Perhaps it would not have seemed to the readers of my projected essay that I was closing in on George Garrett, but they would be misled, for I would have only a couple of preliminary points still to make before venturing some generalizations about his trilogy and *Death of the Fox* in particular. I would try to find some way to placate their patience while I made my final preparatory observations.

Primary among these would be that historical fiction usually derives its action from deterministic premises. It takes for granted that the most important events of history (excluding natural disasters like Vesuvius and the Potato Famine) proceed from human actions, that these actions proceed from motives, and that the motives are generated by the fixed characters of the actors. A historical agent's character is fixed because the results of his or her actions are known, they are history-book facts, and the nature of the character must be drawn up with regard to these facts, these results of those actions. We will allow a novelist to portray a Julius Caesar who suffers—as all humans must—moments or hours of self-doubt, but we will not accept indecisiveness as a dominant part of his character. The fact that Caesar crossed the Rubicon insures that the novelist who portrays him must show him as having superlative confidence in his own judgments. To this degree—and it is a large one—his character is cast in stone before the novelist ever sets ballpoint to notepad.

So then, actions proceed from character, and the characters of well-known historical personages are fixed. It will also be a tenet held by most fiction writers that the motives of characters are those of self-interest. Fictional characters act so as to further their own interests or causes, though some of these may seem to be altruistic. This means that any large-scale historical event, whether it be the battle of Actium, the succession of James I to the throne, or the dispatch of Russian missiles to Cuba, is made up of a tangle of interlocking self-interests. The events may be highly complex, grand in importance and even in dignity when considered as wholes, but at bottom they are composed of a jigsaw puzzle of self-interested motives pretty simple in nature, easy to comprehend and sympathize with, and usually selfish and ignoble. A character may act upon his or her ideals, those interests may be good for the nation or for some special cause, but in the end they are primarily good for that character.

This rationale of the fiction writers may finally be only a superstition based upon the biases of determinism, but in my essay I would demonstrate with well-chosen examples like *The Heart of Midlothian, Henry Esmond, I, Claudius, Lonesome Dove* and others, that novelists adhere to this notion like egg wash to puff pastry.

Then, having shown all these things to be indubitable (at least until strongly challenged), I would submit, with all due and becoming modesty, my final preliminary proposition: that almost all historical fiction is reductive in nature, whittling the giants of history down to size, showing that even the greatest movements and events must march on feet of clay, making the humble and even the flawed character equal with the most luminous, and casting a cold skeptical eye upon its own purview, whether this is a vast panorama or an intimate fictional diary. Because history, as it is given us in fiction, is grounded in that most plebeian of materials, personal self-interest, it is knowable mostly in a mode recognizable by a reader's knowledge of his or her own weakness. All is diminished, all is leveled, all is commonplace. We are Mme Curie; Bolingbroke is we.

Now my essay would turn at last to the works of George Garrett with the aim of showing that this novelist's work and concomitant implied theory of history differ from those received ideas I have outlined. Garrett's historical novels are reductive too—but in a different way from those of other writers. Some of his characters act from sheer self-interest, but many pursue nobler designs, directing their actions by the best notions they have of the greater good of their societies. His Ralegh, his Elizabeth, his Robert Cecil are examples of leaders whose motives, though not completely altruistic, are not generated wholly by self-interest.

What makes Garrett's pages wryly reductive, humbling the great personages and diminishing the grandeur of certain events, is his comic vision. Motives may be predominantly altruistic, or at least civic-minded, but they are not unalloyed; self-interest is usually a factor, even though the characters may not always recognize this fact. It is the usual case in fiction that dramatic irony obtains when the reader recognizes the self-interested motives of a character while the other characters do not; they fall victim to stratagems invisible to them because they are unaware of the motives that concoct them.

Consider, for example, the fall of Sir Francis Bacon as it is analyzed in *Death of the Fox*. Bacon is being set up to take the blame for some of King James's more unsavory but necessary actions. (They are necessary in James's view, at least.) He is an ideal sacrificial victim because he has blind faith in the King. But the King "needs neither faith nor love from his politic servants" (504); the King, the novel tells us, needs only "pure service." When it is politic for Bacon to be sacrificed, James will offer him up—as Bacon himself well knows. His motive for being so willing a victim is—so the philosopher tells himself—love and devotion to James. But he is deceived. His only motive is weakness of character. After analyzing at some length the relationship between Bacon and his King, the chapter concludes with an anecdote that serves as parable: A distinguished visitor comes to Bacon and is made to wait in an anteroom. As he sits watching, servants come in one by one and openly steal money from their master, taking it from a chest "without bolt or lock on it" (505). When Bacon appears, his visitor describes what has been happening and is startled to learn that his host knows all about it. But why not put a stop to it?

Here is the conclusion of the episode, and it emblemizes the darkly comic view of motive that underlies almost all of Garrett's fiction, but especially his historical work: "'Because . . .' replied Francis Bacon, Lord Verulam, Lord Chancellor of England. 'Because I cannot help myself'" (506).

It would be dignifying Bacon's motive here to call it self-interested since it is actually a self-destructive compulsion, but I have chosen the most extreme example so as to show what dire skepticism immerses Garrett's idea of motive and of the bleak comedy that hangs upon the realization of such motives. More characteristic are the strands of self-interest that Garrett discovers in the motives of Sir Edward Coke and Henry Yelverton.

But one of the things that marks Garrett's Elizabethan trilogy apart from other historical fiction is the transcendence of self-interest in the characters. They may often be—as Bacon is—swayed by fancies of personal gain or influenced by uncontrollable obsessions, yet they are equally ruled by their civic responsibilities and once having taken on public roles can never step back from them, can never shed the burdens of duty. They become what they had imagined they would only have to seem; they are role-players trapped in their roles.

Ralegh himself is a player with many roles, so many in fact that he is not drawn in a single portrait but in a series or gallery of portraits, all of them likenesses but none of them defining him completely. Part Three of *Death of the Fox* is prefaced by a quotation from Ralegh's speech of October 29, 1618: "For I have been a soldier, a courtier, and a seafaring man" (147). There follows, then, beginning at chapter two of the Third Part, a series of "types," generalized portraits of professionals of the time; the purpose is to give readers some notion of what it was like to follow these trades, what craft and art, what disciplines and knowledge, what strength and courage and stamina and cunning were required to fill these several roles, any one of which would occupy the whole lifetime of an ordinary person.

The first portrait is of the man at arms, and after a brief visual sketch of this soldier, the chapter leaps into dramatic monologue:

> "Well, now, I'd talk to you the same as I would to any man .... I'll treat you with the same respect I would any green, whey-faced, knock-kneed, rope-backed bumpkin fresh from country muster; or some pale-faced, weasel-eyed sneak of a rogue pressed out of prison to be a soldier." (257)

The opening of his prologue is brusque and does not soften even at its conclusion: "Your soul belongs to the preacher and God. It's the skin of your ass that's all mine . . ." (258).

This portrait is so thoroughly characteristic of the profession that it is valid for soldiers of every age and nation. This is the sound of the drill sergeant then, now, and forever, and it is no accident that his tone closely resembles the voice of the sergeant in Garrett's masterly short story, "The Old Army Game," as he introduces himself: "'You are all about to begin the life of a soldier. My name is Sergeant Quince. Your name is Shit'" (149).

But the portrait in *Fox* is not so generalized that it can be lifted from context. Garrett uses the portrait of his soldier for other purposes too—to sketch in a thumbnail history of Queen Elizabeth after her accession, to give an account of the recent wars, to characterize the Queen and Essex and Lord Grey and others as an old soldier would judge of them. The sentence that tells worlds about the Queen, the historical situation, and the speaker himself is this one: "I believe the Queen at heart was a good English captain" (267).

Next comes a picture of the courtier. Like the soldier he is introduced in visual terms with a description of his finery and a refined physical appearance that shows him so perfect in self-presentation that "he seems to have been created all at once as he is." Here Garrett adds an important motivic phrase: "By a portrait painter perhaps" (299).

The delineation of the courtier as a type proceeds in different fashion from that of the soldier. The introduction is longer and contains a fullblown satiric scene, and then when the dramatic monologue begins there is an uneasy ambiguity about whose voice we are hearing. The soldier spoke as himself, for though he is a composite figure in Ralegh's memory and imagination, he is presented as an independent entity. The courtier, however, is presented in time-lapse, so that we see him in the various stages of a conventional career. Like the soldier, he is a representative of his trade, broadly generalized. But little by little, this voice metamorphizes. When the courtier says that there were periods in his life when he thought of nothing else but fashion, he adds, "And, considering all, those times were, if I may say so, among my most memorable"(316). Then there is a comment not in the courtier's voice— "It is possible to believe him"—and it has to be spoken by Ralegh himself, intruding into the dramatic monologue.

After a while it becomes apparent that Ralegh is merely imitating the voice of a representative courtier (as he mimicked a soldier's voice, only not making the fact evident) partly in order to tell his own story in third person. For the representative type transforms to an individual, with a phrase about Elizabeth's court pets: "—All of which leads, as if by a winding stair, to the subject of her favorites . . ." (334).

At this point, the story of Ralegh at court, his progress and intrigues, the shinings and darkenings of his career, his successes and failures, is recounted. From the soldier we get military history, served up in a rude wooden bowl; from the courtier we get a history of internal affairs combined with the biography-autobiography of Ralegh. Ralegh reveals himself as the voice he has been ventriloquizing.

Then he retreats, steps back, and the episode ends with the courtier puppet in dumb show: "This ghost, an ageless young man, ever idle and restless, courteous and cruel, unchanging child of change, this man will say no more. He touches his lips to signal silence. He smiles and, miming the blowing out of a candle, he takes a thief's farewell, first the color fading, then the sad cold light of his eyes gone, and one last blinking of something—a jewel, a coin cupped in his palm, and darkness comes between us and is final" (373).

The final vocation drawn is the sailor's, and here Garrett varies his method. Chapter four of Part Three begins with the dramatic monologue that by now we are accustomed to. The voice that was used for introduction of the soldier and courtier does not enter until we have heard the sailor's own words for five pages. The seaman is a rugged blunt sort, forthright in his "lifelong habit of speaking loud and clear to be heard above wind and slapping waves" (380). He talks directly to us, the readers, determined that we shall understand: "I will be invisible until you have some picture of the ships we sailed, lived in, and died on" (382).

The sailor's chapter presents perhaps the most curious of Garrett's uses of voice. The seaman is still a projection of Ralegh's voice, as were soldier and courtier, but in these pages this projection achieves such measure of independence that it can engage with Ralegh's other voice, his own proper voice which sets the stage for his representative types and comments upon their physical appearances and biographical backgrounds. There is give-and-take between the two voices in some places, rather like operatic duets. As the sailor leaves off describing the vessels of his time, he remarks that "ships are no better or worse than the men who handle them" (386). Ralegh then interrupts to interpolate his own longish description of sailors: *"High time to think of the men who sailed and handled the ships, hauling ropes and lines and spars,"* he begins. When he quotes a source to give information about the dreadful diet at sea, the sailor breaks in: "Amen to that. It is the God's truth" (391). At a later point, the voice of Ralegh once more interrupts the sailor with an ominous surmise: *"Think: if the King knew his plan from the beginning, if the King is partner to the secret . . ."* (428).

It becomes very difficult to keep the voices separate. Both voices are those of Ralegh, in whose mind most of the action is taking place. The sailor, soldier, and courtier should have no existence apart from the speaker's attempt to delineate them as types representative of their trades. When Ralegh describes, or creates, these types he is only trying to make clear the things necessary to know and do in order to pursue them. He himself has managed to master all three, so that none defines him entirely. He is more than a courtier, more than a sailor, more than a soldier—more than all three together.

It is almost as if these complex, life-engulfing vocations are but poses for him, roles that he plays in carrying out a large design he has in mind. If he needs a sailor or courtier, he makes himself into one, instead of hiring another man as his agent. A passage in the courtier's chapter furnishes a clue about how Ralegh can be in these professions, and even be master of them, without being delimited by them: "He has never posed for his own portrait; though he has sat in a stiff pose for another, a great man, after the features and lines of the true model were drawn from the quick. Such men are busy with affairs and cannot keep still for picture-makers" (305).

Such an interplay of voices—though we have been led to assume that one man, Ralegh, was speaking all the parts—is complex enough. But Garrett further complicates the issue when the sailor begins to tell the story of Ralegh's career as a seaman. Being a projected type, he has to speak of Ralegh in the third person ("In the time between the voyage of the *Falcon* and the Armada, Ralegh was not idle"[411]), but a reader does not fail to recall that it is Ralegh speaking through him; he is but the ventriloquist's dummy.

Yet he is not.

I spoke above of Ralegh's taking on various roles without being defined by them because he had a large design in mind, a secret plan, as it were. That was what his contemporaries conjectured about him and what they could not find out; that is one reason they called him Fox. Ralegh's hidden purposes seemed to be connected to his Virginia colony and the sailor has his own theory about this subject:

> . . . Myself, I don't believe his true purpose in Virginia, or Guiana either, was to raise up new English villages and counties. It looks to me like he was aiming to make ports for English ships at both places and then bottlecork the Indies and the Main: Guiana at the end of the tradewinds crossing, Virginia where the Gulf Stream meets with the easterlies. Together they could have ruined the Spaniard. (411)

Well, that is a plan worthy of the Fox. But who, actually, is telling us of it? Is it a surmise on the part of an old tar, a real sailor we might meet in a tavern in Plymouth, taking hot rum while a cold rain whips streets and harbor? Or is it Ralegh speaking in the guise of a sailor, letting us in on his true intent? But why is he telling us now and who, exactly, does he imagine us to be? Who are the *we* that overhear these whispers, echoes, murmurs, guesses, thoughts, and half-thoughts of four centuries gone?

George Garrett has said that one of the reasons he undertook the enormous Elizabethan sequence was to try to escape the preoccupation with self that stains so much of our contemporary literature. Friends and critics, though, have discerned in the figure of Ralegh lineaments of the author, chief among which might be his many-mindedness, his pursuit of several disciplines and professions at once. Another strong similarity would be his sense of responsibility toward literature and education and the many secret plans, stratagems, and cunning tactics he has devised to further these responsibilities.

It is silly to read authorial autobiography into all fiction; it is a pernicious habit at last. But I will state what I believe to be a fact: any careful analysis of the interplay of voices, and the number of them, in *Death of the Fox* will always discover the voice of the author. George Garrett is present as a ghost among these other lively ghosts. Only he is an avatar of the future instead of the past.

Now my essay would glance back at itself and underscore the qualities of thought and the innovations in technique that set the Elizabethan trilogy apart from all other historical fiction of my acquaintance—even from works like Hermann Broch's *The Death of Virgil*, which it resembles in some technical aspects and Bryher's *The Player's Boy*, with which it shares subject matter and a part of its outlook.

Most historical fiction, like formal history, must forego the advantages of the writer's identification with its main characters, so that authorial engagement is mostly on an intellectual level and emotional closeness is lacking. But Garrett identifies—at first tentatively, then with increasing willingness—with certain of his subjects, with Robert Cecil in *The Succession*, with Captain Barfoot in *Entered from the Sun*, with Ralegh and even Elizabeth in *Death of the Fox* and this makes his historical characters vivid as personalities while making them ambiguous as historical figures. They inhabit that ambivalent region of behavior which so exercises this novelist in books like *Poison Pen* and *The King of Babylon Shall Not Come Against*

You; they are both private and public figures at the same time, swayed by the exigencies and temptations of private life while bowing to the responsibilities of public duty. Their motives are rarely reducible to simple self-interest though they may be tinted with it. The history these characters create amounts to conscious design, however confusingly the design is executed. Purpose triumphs over a welter of conflicting motives.

Yet the novels expend most of their time and energy upon these conflicts of motive, interest, and social philosophy. So that while the settled facts of history remain inviolate in Garrett's work, as they do in that of most writers, the ways they come into being are not illuminated nor finally explained; the facts retain an aura of uncertainty and circumstantial accident in their processes no matter how firm they stand as results.

Which is to say they give the impression of having been lived through in the way that the events of our daily lives are lived through: plans are formulated and largely but never completely carried out, partly because of our best efforts and partly despite them. The moment in Garrett's fiction that crystallizes this idea about purpose and accident in history occurs at the end of *The Succession* when it is revealed that all the plottings, intrigues, machinations, and accidents that make the accession of James possible are as yet only the imaginative extrapolations of a courier setting out on his journey.

The facts of the case are settled, interred in books and shrouded in footnotes. The events that brought these facts into being the novelist has unsettled a thousand times over, casting wry comic doubt upon their origins, motives, purposes, and uses. The more the personal voice of Garrett is heard in the pages of his historical fiction, the more the characters' voices play off each other and themselves; the more dialogue there is between the Renaissance and the contemporary eras, the more commanding the vision of these many-stranded, many-hued tapestries with their jostling crowds of figures.

These are the conclusions my essay would attempt, positing the idea that George Garrett has broken new ground, not with radical revisions of the facts, not with a wild theory of historiography, not with a rejection of the traditions of fiction. Yet the simultaneity of his vision in which the pattern of the completed whole and the muddle of ambiguous process are held before us in a single framework is sufficiently distinctive to make his work original, very different from that of the general class of historical novelists.

Had time and circumstance been on my side, I might have written a piece to bring this author some of the credit he deserves. But we shall have to turn to the genuine essays that follow my inchoate notes here to find that level of achievement. My friends and colleagues have been able to do what I could not. I envy them their successes.

—*Fred Chappell*

Death of the Fox

R. H. W. Dillard

The Destiny at Plymouth: 21 June 1618

A meditation for George Garrett

We die in earnest, no jest,
Rawly like a bruise, flesh
From the withered tree, fruit
Of decay hung on the bone.

Wood and weed mark out the way,
Wag's way from sea to land,
Sheets wet, dust on the tongue,
And always dust to sea to dust.

The story of a day shut up,
Earth, grave and dust, a rattle
Like knuckles of a broken fist,
One last tattoo, no last delay.

So only trust remains, a dance
On sawdust, a way that times
Day to dusk to the edge of days
Where soil breaks green as a sea.

David R. Slavitt

A Twentieth Century Fox—
in the Warner Brothers' Chicken Coop

Garrett had told me once that there was a screenplay of *Death of the Fox*, but you never know with him whether or not he's joking. Often, he is joking but has conspired and agreed to play stooge to the world so that the most far-fetched claims he makes turn out to be the plain (if there is such a thing) truth. In context—and the con-man usually has a text, doesn't he?—the proposition certainly seemed less than plausible. In our conversation about the first novel of his Elizabethan trilogy he had described its opening action as, "basically, three guys in various places in London who are having trouble falling asleep."

Which is true, actually. And it was entertaining to imagine some poor son-of-a-bitch screenwriter in his Malibu slum with the semis roaring along the Pacific Coast Highway in front of the house and the ocean out in back flushing constantly like a broken toilet. Some problem! I mean, these guys are in their beds alone and just thinking, which is exactly the thing that movies can't do unless you have an actor do a take or you draw in a glowing lightbulb over the head of your cartoon duck.

Not a lot of action. The opening paragraph of the novel gives him a detail or two, but it isn't exactly what the Panavision camera hungers for:

Sir Henry Yelverton lies warm in a great curtained bed, half awake, hearing the sound of breathing, the rustling of his servant, Peter, who, just or unjust, can sleep like a dog at any time, content in the trundle bed set at the foot of his own. It is past one o'clock. He has heard the sound of chimes and bells, near and far, and in far from perfect agreement, announcing the new day. Bells and the hoarse barking of a dog in the court beyond the chambers.

I assume that there might have been some talk about a movie, an inquiry, maybe, some Hollywood shuffle a producer might have contrived as a part of the industry's campaign to raise and then dash the hopes of American writers, a way of adding insult to the injuries done them by their publishers. He lets the reference pass, and I don't pursue it. End of story.

Except, of course, that it isn't. It's only the set-up. "Years Later" as they say on the screen when they can't think of a more graceful way to indicate the passage of time, I am rounding up the usual suspects for another classical gang-bang (The Complete Greek Drama, no less!) and I mention to Garrett, who is doing the *Frogs* for me, that I've managed to recruit Frederic Raphael for the *Ajax*. I am feeling quite pleased with myself, now that I've got an Oscar winner to decorate the roster. Pulitzers and Bollingens are okay, but their award ceremonies don't get a night on TV. Raphael wrote *Darling* and *Two for the Road* and *Glittering Prizes* and some splendid and woefully under-appreciated novels, and I feel entitled to brag a little. And Garrett is good to brag to because unlike some of the classicists I deal with, he's likely actually to have heard of these things.

"Well, he's the one," Garrett tells me, "who wrote that screenplay of *Death of the Fox*. And made more money from it than I did, I expect," he says with a grin, because how could it happen to him any other way? And he adds quickly, "It's supposed to be a fine screenplay. I've never seen it, but I hear it's just great."

So I write to Raphael and ask him if it's true, and whether he might have a copy of it still that I could send on to Garrett who has heard good things about it.

A month or so later, because word has to get from me to someplace in the Dordogne and from there to the London office of William Morris, a package arrives, compliments of Mr. Raphael. It's it. Eureka! (Greek for: you never can tell what the vacuum cleaner will pick up, can you?)

There was also a note with some explanation of what happened:

I agreed to do the job very reluctantly, because I did not see Garrett's "literary" book as the source of an easy buck. However, vanity and greed worked their usual persuasion and I went to work. The script was greeted with a long telegram, in which John Calley [producer of *Postcards from the Edge* and *Remains of the Day*] said that it was the best script that had ever been received at the studio. He must have liked it a bit. He also said that he was not going to press for any revisions until we had recruited "the best director in the world" who, alone, was worthy of the material. After which, nothing. Six, seven months later I was asked, again by Warner Brothers, to do a screenplay about a French bank raid, based on a much more—let's say—*accessible* book. I went to L.A. to discuss the approach (work and the annual holiday converge sometimes) and while I was there I took the chance to ask Calley—still a player—what had happened on *The Death of the Fox*. In the usual way, I said that I had taken my wages and had no grievance, but . . . "Freddie," he said, "that was a great script. A terrific script. I don't retract one word of what I said in my telegram. You did get my telegram, didn't you? I meant every word. But you know something? Who the fuck is Sir Walter Ralegh?" They didn't make the one about the bank raid either.

It's that last sentence I especially like, the topper, the kind of thing Garrett himself would do.

I made a photocopy of the script before I sent it down to Charlottesville for Garrett's inspection, and the praising rumors all turned out to be correct. From the first page, it is an extraordinary piece of work, not faithful to the book, maybe, but never betraying its spirit, and sometimes finding ways to convey something of Garrett's vision of the Fox. It starts out like this:

1. CREDITS.
The first titles appear in silence. The silence is bruised by a faint, intermittent grinding sound. The sound grows louder, harsher. An axe is being sharpened on a grindstone. The main title appears: DEATH OF THE FOX.

CUT TO

2. C.U.: SIR WALTER RALEGH.
A shock close-up, from a low angle. A pair of dark eyes, unblinking, looking directly at the audience, but at a strange and unnerving angle. The man whose eyes are so keen, so commanding, so proud is kneeling at the block. The eyes are looking down at the crowd who have come to see him die—at

us. The shot is held long enough to unnerve us, long enough to make us keyed up for the blow which will serve to sever this haughty head. The eyes hold ours. Then there is a movement. SIR WALTER stretches his arms. The signal for the EXECUTIONER, though we do not know it. The eyes continue to stare into ours. After these interminable few seconds . . .

CUT TO

3. CREDITS.
The last credits. And just as we relax, the tension of the execution scene almost forgotten—the axe falls. A terrible crunching clunk. Another silence. The last credit. A pause. Another crunching clunk. Followed by a slow and terrible groaning noise.

CUT TO

4. EXT. THE ENGLAND-SCOTLAND BORDER. DAWN.
The last credits have been against a dark, dawn sky, shot with red. The dawn of the day when the new King of England, JAMES THE SIXTH OF SCOTLAND, is crossing the border to take charge of his new kingdom as JAMES THE FIRST.

The explanation of the terrible groaning: a tree creaks and falls heavily into camera. The place where the axe has fallen gapes like a great white, bloodless wound. The branches crash on the hard ground . . . .

That this is awfully good hardly needs to be pointed out. But it is perhaps worth observing that there are very few people in the world who are likely to read this prose. The producers and the money people don't read actual scripts. They read digests and reports from underlings. The director reads the script, and the actors read at least those parts where their characters' names are in caps. The careful elegance of "the blow which will serve to sever this haughty head" is an *acte gratuit*, a craftsman's pride expressing itself in a place where nobody will ever look.

This, too, strikes me as quixotic and . . . Garrett-like. But then the fact that there are similarities in the ways these two writers respond to the stresses high-brows have to expect in middle- and low-brow culture ought not be surprising. They both do what they have to do, and they don't complain or grump, but they keep their own counsel and maintain their own private standards.

This quality they share of private craftsmanly dedication is what makes the screenplay so uncanny an adaptation of the novel. There are spiritual affinities that allow Raphael a remarkable freedom of means because of his intuitive understanding of what the ends ought to be—of an episode, a scene, even a single shot. Consider, for example, the appearance in the novel (619-22) of "Mr. Gregory Brandon, Gent., hangman and executioner, and his young son Richard, who is learning his father's trade." What Garrett does is to enlarge the figure by giving him a scene and a touch of life before the encounter with Ralegh on the scaffold to which the book is inexorably moving. They are on their way to that appointment, and the son asks whether the father thinks Ralegh will give them some reward. The father "looks ahead along the narrow street. Nothing moves except his lips. 'It is the custom. And I know him to be a most gracious and generous gentleman, a true gentleman . . . .'"

That repeated "gentleman" is the cue for Garrett to work in one of those bits of information his research had produced—that King James found a way to make money by selling knighthoods and even peerages, of which he created an enormous number. He lets us know that Brandon was one of the purchasers of those clearance-sale honors and lets him have a degree of wry awareness of the value of what he has paid his money to get because "he is capable of making distinctions between gentlemen of this age and the last."

If Brandon shares the writer's view—which, by this time, is the reader's, too—that Elizabeth's time was wonderful and that James' was a great falling-off from that moment of splendor, then Brandon becomes oddly sympathetic. A good-guy executioner, almost.

But for a movie? There's no way to do a whole sequence about Brandon's purchase of his knighthood. It doesn't really have anything to do with Ralegh's story. If Brandon is worth a few seconds and a few frames, they have to show something of his human dimension—indeed any human dimension other than that *guignol* figure he is about to become. What can Raphael do in a blink or two to accomplish this? He ignores the novel's discussion of the knighthoods and discards the scene in the cart with the son. Instead, he invents:

214. EXT. A FARM YARD. DAY.
A man is chopping up mangelwurzels for the cattle. A simple
country activity. But the chopping is very deliberate. The axe
descends right across the middle of the thick neck of the beet.
On closer inspection, we see that the man is the
EXECUTIONER. Practicing his art.

We saw him briefly during the opening credits. We saw him again
at the execution of Essex, where he had a couple of lines, asking
Essex's forgiveness. He has been established just enough so that
this moment of our recognition is a payoff as well as a set-up for the
final scenes of the film. When we get to that point, we will have seen
him on his farm, where he leads his other life, chopping
mangelwurzels. He will be, at least minimally, a rounded character
who does his duty, however difficult or unappealing that may be.

There are differences of course, between the novel and the
screenplay. Garrett's vision of Ralegh, I am persuaded, is funda-
mentally religious. Ralegh is a man of destiny, or at least that is the
way I read that peculiar foreshadowing at the execution scene where
Ralegh's death prefigures that of Charles I. As an Anglican, Garrett
takes the reign of Elizabeth I with great seriousness. Ralegh's death
is the end of the memory of great events, a second-hand, smaller, but
more approachable termination—like that, say, of St. Peter. Raphael's Ralegh is rather different, a man of honor, a splendid but secular being without any supernatural overtones. It may be only that
Raphael found it technically impossible to convey in a movie that
Brandon's son Richard is one day going to be Charles's executioner.

Still, the similarities are greater than the differences. For Garrett's compelling prose, so rich in reference that it is all but a hyp-
notic induction, Raphael finds a sophisticated cinematic syntax of
accumulating cross-references, a brilliant scries of moves that have
engendered that rumor about this being one of the greatest screen-
plays never to have been filmed. Back at the beginning, the tree has
fallen down. That scene continues:

A fox, flushed out by the falling tree, goes springing away from
where the WOODMAN is working. The clatter of alarmed
hooves and the exclamation of men: the KING's party is riding
south. The WOODMAN leans for a moment on his axe and
watches.

C.U. : JAMES. His eyes roll as he fights to control his frightened horse. JAMES is a good horseman, a keen— addicted—huntsman. He is afraid only of steel. Yet his expression now, of mock alarm, warns of the real fear which is always in him. He is relieved to be able to show that, this time at least, he is not truly afraid. And his present lack of real terror draws attention to, rather than hides, his habitual cowardice.

> JAMES: (with all uneasy laugh) Have they sent someone to trip us up so soon?

They watch the fox scamper into cover.

> HAY: (one of the escort of NOBLES, and an old favorite of the KING) Does your majesty imagine the beast to be one of Ralegh's familiars?

It is a wonderful series of moves at the beginning of an amazing screenplay. That the movie has never been made and that the book has had only a small and cultish readership is unfathomable, but much of life is unfathomable. But Ralegh's lesson, whether we see him as a religious figure or as a stoical man of honor, is one of fortitude and acceptance. As Garrett writes in the first couple of pages after Sir Walter's appearance:

The man regrets. Complains and rails against necessity. Yet comes to live with it, lawfully wedded. And comes, perhaps, to add the grace of some style to his complaints. Sternly suppresses rebellion of foolish wishes. Puts down the idle desire to be restored and to live wasted time again, or to suffer his losses and wounds twice over. Time offers neither pardon, mercy, nor reprieve. And to live dead time again would be to suffer the same gnawings, tossings, and turnings, if not worse.

Irving Malin

Hermetic Fox-Hunting

Although *Death of the Fox* is a long, admirable novel about the Renaissance, it—as well as *The Succession* and *Entered from the Sun*—has not received the critical discussion it deserves. The trilogy is one of the significant achievements of modern (American) literature. I want here to pursue a somewhat radical way of interpreting the text; I recognize that my pursuit, *any* critical discussion, necessarily "deforms" the text because it cannot offer a full picture; it is skewed, limited, perverse.

Although Spears and Dillard have recognized that *Death of the Fox* is, in part, a meditation on "history," they have not seen that the text questions the very notion of "history" and/or "narrative." I believe that Garrett recognizes that historical novels must, in effect, assume that language itself is always the ghostly subject. When I read *Death of the Fox*, I "see" the glorious, diverse manners and rituals of the Renaissance, but I recognize that the text is *written* and, furthermore, that the Renaissance—any "historical" period (or "event")—is a *linguistic creation*. Garrett is fortunate that he is writing about a "period" which was a time of the greatest English writers. The novel, then, is a mirror; it attempts to explore the *dimensions of language*.

I want, at first, to read the title and subtitle. *Death of the Fox* is surely metaphorical and obscure. "Fox" can mean, among other things, an animal or a human being who acts like a fox. Although I have not troubled to refer to the *OED*, I still assume that one of the recognized qualities of a fox is its ability to *hunt* for food. It seeks *prey*.

If Garrett had simply used the title, he would have raised the questions of signifier (or signified). He uses as a subtitle "a novel of Elizabeth and Ralegh." I am puzzled. Is Elizabeth a "fox"? Is Ralegh? In *what ways* are they foxes? And to complicate matters, "of" troubles me. Don't we usually write that a novel—whatever this word means!—is *about* a subject? Why, then, does Garrett use "of" rather than "about"? Perhaps he is playing; he is "outfoxing" me. I will assume that "Elizabeth" and "Ralegh" are words, not "real" people. But why should "Elizabeth" *precede* "Ralegh"? And isn't the novel about many other "people"?

I usually worry about the design—the appearance—of a cover. Here I see a painting (reproduced) of a man. I guess this "portrait" of "Ralegh" has not been examined. If the "novel" is *of* "Elizabeth" *and* "Ralegh," why don't I see a portrait of "Elizabeth"? Thus Garrett "displaces" me. Although "Elizabeth" precedes "Ralegh" as a word, "she" *disappears* on the cover. Portrait clashes with text. *Image fights word.* What is the exact *relation* of portrait and word? Should I use the word "iconography" here?

When I turn to the text, the first thing I read is a "note" by Garrett. It begins with this sentence: "First of all, and finally I hope, this is a work of fiction." The sentence (re)introduces ideas of "beginnings and ends." And the note then tells me that the novel—"the work of fiction"—is not in any *sense* a "biography" of Ralegh. Garrett opposes "biography" and "fiction"; he subtly implies that one *genre* is *different* from another. But isn't any "biography" a "fiction"? A "biography" of Ralegh must *omit* elements of his life, must *shape* them in some pattern. Garrett is already questioning—and asking me to question—the "sense" of things: words, character, life. He is trying to "outfox" me or, at least, to make me *hunt* for clear sense.

And then he informs me that scholars have helped to create a dense description of the period. But he refers to the "fact" that their "biographies," although "rooted in fact," are "failures." But what does he mean by "failure"? Is Ralegh a failure? Is Garrett a "failure"? Am I? I am struck by the fact that Garrett refers to *distortion* in his note. Surely this text, although a distortion, is not a failure. It is a glorious achievement because it slyly explores the ambiguities of life and (as) text, success and failure, truth and lie.

After the "note" I am given the words "Part One." I immediately wonder about the *number* of *parts* in the text. I turn the pages and see that the text has nine parts. Why nine?

Certainly I am suffering from "referential mania" (a phrase from Nabokov's story "Signs and Symbols"). But Garrett, I insist, has provoked me. In fact, I'm beginning to believe that he is a fellow "patient" because he has already shaped his words carefully and suggestively.

Part One begins with lines from a Ralegh text entitled "Farewell to the Court." What is going on here? The "beginning" has as epigraph lines of "farewell." Again origins and ends! And farewell disturbs me because it almost echoes failure (those "f" and "l" sounds). Now I begin to think that Garrett's text begins with Ralegh's words! Or does it begin with Garrett's title? What is "beginning"? Of a text, a life, a critical explication? I don't know!

There are four lines from Ralegh. These have references to "sight," "lost," "unknowne waies," "minde to woe," "past," "staies." Ralegh—or the "I" writing the lines—seems to reflect (upon) all the words which I have introduced. Am I reading "correctly"? Am I reading "obsessively"? Am I *hunting* for *sense* or *creating non-sense*? My mind is filled with "woe." But I'm pleased by my perversities because I have "deliberately" outfoxed the reader—*you*. Or have I just bored *you*? Surely I can't read the entire text of *Death of the Fox* in this way. I'll see! I have nothing to lose!

Section One begins with a description of Yelverton lying warm in a "great curtained" bed. He is "half awake." His servant, Peter, can "sleep like a dog at any time." This is "just or unjust." Although taking only a few lines of the beginning paragraph, I am drowning in details. I see a reference to "half awake," "just or unjust." "Any time" bothers me. Why has Garrett used *these* words? Does he expect me to *relate* them to previous ones? I know that if I start to explicate them—to read them closely—I will upset *you*. I'll just write that the text begins with questions of lie, hidden (curtained) meaning, dream, animal/human. No! I must mention a possible pun on "curtain"/ "certain." I must note that "fox" has been replaced by "dog." I must emphasize *displacement*—the beginning *is* darkness (evening). I must haunt you with the perception that I may be the only "correct" reader of Garrett's selection of words.

Do I dare continue? I will look at the other lines in the paragraph. Yelverton has heard the "sound of chimes and bells, near and far, and in far from perfect agreement announcing the new day." Consider these words. "Near and far" are ambiguous—especially if Yelverton is "half awake." There is "far from perfect agreement." Distance! Distance from time meaning sense! Distance implies "imperfect agreement." The "new day" is "announced." But when has it begun? When will it end? Why is one day different from another?

Why is an announcement *announced*? Garrett can't be playing when creating such meanings. I must be misreading his words, but the very fact that I'm a "distant" reader supports my contention about distance. And I know that I have *alienated* you. But isn't the novel itself about alienation (alien nation)? Isn't it about disagreement?

I could easily support my contention that the entire text is filled with texts—proverbs, riddles, biblical quotations, legal definitions. I need only to point to some of these. On page sixty-five Elizabeth once renamed him; she called him "water" not Walter: "To water ... And isn't that the name the Queen gave him. Who gave a name to all she loved. She called him Water." She has a private language. On page sixty-one I find the beginning of a religious, traditional (not private!) saying: *"Naked we entered into this world . . . ."* On page forty-five I see the Bible in King James's hand: "He has been preparing a book of meditations on the Bible." On page thirteen James's words on the divine right of kings are quoted. On page thirty-seven Coke explicates legalities, "old statutes." All of these quotations—and there are many more—are *texts within the text* by Garrett. But they are not intrusive because they mirror the linguistic ambiguities I have cited (sighted) previously. Thus Garrett suggests that words dominate the period, the "interpretive" communities.

Now I could move *conventionally* into description of plots (double meaning) and characters and events, but I choose instead to follow another path—a risky one!—and turn to Part Two and study the quotation from Ralegh as epigraph and the opening paragraph. I guess that I am following the occult secrets of a Dee or Bruno (see Frances Yates). I make much of the *alchemy* of language, the transformations it creates.

Part Two has an epigraph from Ralegh's *History of the World*:

> But what of *all this*? And to what *end* do we *lay* before the *living* the *fall and fortunes* of the dead, *seeing* that the world is the *same* that it hath been and the children of the *present time* will *still obey* their parents? It is in the *present time* that all the *wits* of the *world* are *exercised*. (my italics)

The epigraph is like a *curtain*, a *frame of reference*. It begins—

appropriately enough for my purpose—with a *question,* a question within the *big* questions posed by the entire text. "Of," "all," and "this" are simple words, but I am not sure of their meaning. Nouns are, after all, missing. Again I must hunt for meaning. Notice Ralegh's alliterations: "lay" and "living," "fall" and "fortune," "wits and world." Time dominates the statement— I am moved back to questions of beginnings and ends mentioned in the previous epigraph and first paragraph. And I am told somewhat easily that "the present time" exercises our wits. Isn't it ironic or playful that Ralegh's "history" is mutilated by Garrett? He has cut Ralegh's text for his own ends; he has, in a metaphorical sense, executed Ralegh's words. Therefore he has fought the "fox," revelled against him, despite the fact that Ralegh assumes *obedience* to parents, to Queen Elizabeth, to the Father. Garrett has rebelled against Law—the very crime for which Ralegh is being punished by Elizabeth and James!

The first paragraph of Part Two starts with the reading of documents, with interpretation by the Lieutenant of the Tower. The meaning is clear *after three readings*! But the fact that Apsley must "exercise" his wits suggests that interpretation is a demanding *task.* Apsley "descends" from the "upper chambers" of his house to where the others are waiting for meaning, for rigorous, "correct" significance. He moves down (as has Ralegh); the downward movement mirrors, in an oblique way, Ralegh's *fall.*

The words Garrett uses are interesting: "word by word," "weighling," "waiting," "warmed against the weather." There is subtle play with the "w"; there are possible puns on "weather" and "weigh." Again the language *dominates* "character"; it rules the world. And doesn't the "*world*" contain "*word*"?

I am not surprised that the epigraph and first paragraph reflect the ones I have seen in Part One. Garrett has constructed his textual "chamber" so carefully that the recurrence of words is bound to appear. My risky hunt is, after all, not at all dangerous.

Before I continue to the Part Three epigraph and first paragraph, I must cite two passages. On page 143 there are these sentences: "Then how what *we explicate Wilson's* fear that Ralegh would take his own life? Can Wilson, has he *imagined* yet what Apsley first *sensed,* then was *certain* of—that *not then and not now* will Ralegh take his own life?" (my italics) Who is "we"?

Is "we" Garrett and his reader? "Explicate"—the text is an "explication" of the nature of "explication." It is a "*meta-explication.*" Wilson, a representative of James, has, by *chance*, a wonderful name—at least for my purpose. "Will" and "son" and "soon" and "sun" are *possible* puns which echo previous words. I am using my playful imagination here. Please be *unsure* about whether I am wrong, outrageous, mad or not. Give me the *proof,* the *evidence* for my "crime." Notice that "certain" and "sense" are mentioned again. Why? I insist that the entire text is a hunt for the *sense* of history, for the *certainties* which may sustain us in our lives. "Not then and not now"—the emphasis is upon Time. What is it? How do we *know* it? Do our minds know it? Or do our decaying bodies?

Here's a passage from page 173:

> There is a pattern and design in any man's action, in the chronicle of his words, thoughts and deeds, which is an image, apelike, of the larger sum and total of the acts, the thoughts and deeds of all men. Which we call history. What was, is, will be. And its secret design is Providence which we can come to know only by and through contraries and paradoxes.

I am almost tempted to rest my case here. The passage implies that there is a "*secret design*" in all things, but how do we know something which is *secret*? Notice that knowledge is gained "*by and through contraries and paradoxes.*" Don't you find it alarming that my wild explication is *in* the text? The correspondence is "uncanny," except if you believe in some "*secret design*" which has compelled me to reflect the text. Am I creating the reflections in a deliberate way? Or have I been "moved" by something called "*Providence*"?

I'm now ready for Part Three; I'm confident that my irrational tracks have led me to the "truth."

The epigraph for Part Three—again it is from "Ralegh"—is the shortest one so far: "For I have been a soldier, a courtier, and a seafaring man. And the temptations of the least of these are able to overthrow a good mind and a good man." I don't see much ambiguity here, but I feel that you want me to demonstrate that I can misread anything. I'll rise to the bait. Why is "good mind" separated from "good man"? Is it necessary to imply that *mind* seems to stand as the dominant part of man? I guess so. Doesn't *mind make sense of the nature of man*? How else does a man *know* that he is a man? And how does mind recognize "goodness"? How does mind give *just* meaning? I like the word "overthrow." Isn't the text, in part, about "overthrows," turns of Fortune?

The first paragraph of this Part is too long to be quoted. You'll have to look at the actual text. "Weather" (and its possible pun) has "turned foul." The text so far has been a series of turns and counter-turns. The second sentence suggests torture, prepares us for many other tortures. I must mention that this sentence, like so many in the text, is a *fragment*. Where are the subject and verb? (Missing in action?) The third sentence is simple; I assume that there is no pun on "pane." The fourth sentence uses the word "placed." Perhaps "Ralegh" has been placed physically; "he" has surely been *dis-placed*. As have we. (I'm starting to use *fragments* because I have been "overthrown," seduced by the text.) The "upper chamber." Haven't I mentioned the chamber before? I think so. But I have not dared until now to equate "chamber" with *body*, with *textual structure*. Is the "upper chamber" an *occult, secret metaphor for mind?*

The next two sentences imply that "he" has "more space and comfort." "He" has his own kingdom. "He" is solitary, but "he" has the freedom to think without noise from others. It *seems* that "he" is really *not* a prisoner. "And he *knew* that his purse and former position would give him this very freedom." And the paragraph ends with the paradoxical position. Is "Ralegh" a prisoner or a "free" man? The answer depends on interpretation, on the name (word) you give "him."

Garrett, for the first time, uses on page 298 (not numbered) in this Part a page of "Ralegh's" words. Why? No reader has noted this "insertion." I note it but I'm uncertain about its duplicitous function. The page contains two passages from "Ralegh." One is from "The Lie": "Say to the Court it glowes and shines like rotten wood." The Court prepares us for the description in Chapter Three, which starts on the facing page of 299. The Court may be linked to a special prison. The line from "Ralegh" is *paradoxical: rotten wood shines.* And I have already indicated that the entire text is paradoxical. I like the fact that the paradox here comes from a text called "The Lie." Isn't the novel full of lies? (Was it Picasso who said that art is "a lie like truth"?)

The second passage comes from "Ralegh's" "dedicatory poem" for Gascoigne's *The Steel Glass* (an *oxymoron* perhaps linked to the paradoxes already mentioned): "For whoso reaps renown above the rest, / with heaps of hate shall surely be opprest." I don't want to linger on these lines, but I must note the alliterations, the possible puns on "renown" and "noun" and "known" and the *hidden now*. And I must note the linkage of *fame as imprisonment*. Certainly "Ralegh" suffered imprisonment because "he" ironically "stood out." And wasn't "Elizabeth" also imprisoned by "her" position?

On page 374 (again unnumbered) facing page 375, Garrett suddenly stops the action. He offers another written passage from "Ralegh": "To seeke new worlds, for golde, for prayse, for glory, / To try desire, to try love severed farr, / When I was gonne she sent her memory / More stronge than weare ten thowsand shipps of warr." The Elizabethan words are emphasized; history is, in part, mystical orthography. The words spelled here are fruitful especially for my punning text. "Prayse," for example, hides "pray"; and pray hides "prey." "Try" means to strive or test; but it puns—or suggests—"trial"; "trial" suggests "trail" (voyage). "Weare" is "were," but it also suggests "where" or "wear" (as in wear and tear). Notice that "warr" suggests "where." The individual examples whirl us on a *verbal voyage*; we are in the whirlwind of transformation, of changes, of (over)determination. And our textual voyage resembles "Ralegh's" physical voyages in chapter four. Readers, I must stress, are (see) seafaring men.

The lines are also about memory. "She—Elizabeth?—is there and *not* there; all memories are, in a sense, half-awake and ghostly." (See St. Augustine.) And the memory in "Ralegh's" poem suggests that this entire text is a memory (memorial). History, in another paradoxical way, is memory of the past; it exists *only in the present*. Therefore, a historical novel, written in the present about the past, is a risky voyage of the mind.

I'm still troubled by Garrett's insertions in the middle of the Part. I can interpret the insertions—if only in a fanciful way—as devices to slow the action (as well as to introduce themes in the following chapters). Perhaps they are also time-devices designed to make me aware of reading activity? They are not only frames; they are *moving* frames. Perhaps they metaphorically hint that the text is a moving structure (a ship?).

I move now to Part Four. The "Ralegh" epigraph is from "his" translation of Ovid's *Metamorphoses*. I seize this fact because I can use it for my purposes. Garrett's text is about the metamorphoses of Fortune's slaves. Men rise and fall; they turn into foxes or apes or dogs; they become animals (already mentioned in the text). And isn't Garrett's novel a philosophical (philogical) exploration of the nature of change? Time is, oddly, a *translation*, a translation of the past into the present. (James Merrill has a poem entitled "Lost in Translation"—dedicated to the translator Richard Howard—in which translation is both memory and memorial.) Here are "Ralegh's" words: "The world discernes it selfe, while I / the world behold, / By me the longest years and other times are told. / I the world's eye."

Consider these words: "I the world's eye." "Ralegh" puns (as do I and Garrett). I see the world; I perceive it. And the way I perceive it is a different "translation" from yours. There is then no *stable* world, no *stable* text (including critical essays!). And, to play with instability (as it plays with us), I maintain that a *pun* is a word in *transit*, a *sailing* word. Now I can understand why Garrett continually uses puns in the novel.

The first paragraph in Part Four is relatively short. I notice the words "swimming," "reading," "misting," "blurring," "going," and "coming." Each word grammatically suggests movement. (Indeed, the novel is built with the *verbal*, not the *verb*.) And I see familiar words: "panes," "figures." These words—puns!—together with the verbals—stress the fact that the text is moving more *rapidly* now as "Ralegh" watches for the hour of execution.

Part Five soon races toward the reader because Part Four is brief. (All the parts, like "Ralegh's life, *hasten toward conclusion*"). The epigraph is a passage from "Ralegh" to "his" son:

Marke well deare boy whilest theise assemble not, / Green springs the tree, hempe growes, the wagg is wilde / But when they meet, it makes the timber rott, / It fretts the halter and it choakes the childe. / Then bless thee and beware, and let us praye / Wee part not with the at this meeting day.

The passage begins with a possible pun on "marke"—the book itself consists of markings (and remarkings); it stresses future meetings which cannot be *avoided* by "Ralegh's" (man's) thoughts, by "his" mental activities. And the meetings lead necessarily to final encounters, to various kinds of death. Birth "springs" us into death—nature propels us into non-nature or unnature (death). These reasons *fret* and *choke* us. "Ralegh," like any man (including his son), has a concluding encounter with death. The growth of grass cannot continue *forever*. Therefore, "Ralegh" asks for blessing when bliss disappears. And may I note that the very Parts of the text, although they seem to increase, are not the complete story? There is a final "parting" and after this one there cannot be any written Part. (Thus Part itself is in relation to impart, import, depart, deport.)

The first paragraph of this section is short, but it, nevertheless, repeats such words as "darkness," "fallen," and "son." It also introduces, at least for me, the notion that "Bess," "Ralegh's" wife, shares the name of the queen. Is Garrett suggesting that the wife—in this, or any decent marriage, a queen—that marriage itself is a kind of Court? The paragraph ends with "one way or the other." Look closely at the phrase. Life itself moves "one way or the other." There is the notion of "forked paths," of the other, shadowy path we have *not* chosen. The Other—isn't the unknown path the one we fear? Almost more than we fear *ourselves*? But Garrett also has given us splittings of self; the Other exists within us. We are, indeed, doubles, "halves," split (spilt) identities.

Part Six quickly reaches us. (The book, the life, seems to *race* now toward [in]conclusion.) The epigraph is from Ralegh's translation from Horace: "The thirsting Tantalus doth catch at streams that from him flee. / Why laughest thou? the name but changed, the tale is told of thee." The cruel, chilling passage underlines that, like "Ralegh," we are Tantalus; we seek *that which we cannot obtain, that which we cannot control*. We desire what we cannot have—"truth, "love," "perfection," the right word. We are tantalized by composing the "correct" pattern despite the dark knowledge that it eludes all of our deliberate *strategies*.

The opening paragraph is not very useful for my purpose. It

"merely" states that "Bess" comes to Westminster with a cousin, "Mary," and the polymath "Hariot." Perhaps their grouping is meant to be a contrast to solitary "Ralegh" in the chamber. I am taken by the phrase "to win at the world's game." The world is *serious play* (another paradox) and if we were to take (make) it as such, we would "win." But the victory cannot be "eternal"; we are ultimately losers. "Ralegh, is, in a perverse way, a "beautiful loser" (Leonard Cohen) because he *accepts* the devious cards dealt him. Perhaps he finds delight in the paradox of winning by/in losing.

"The world's game" reminds me of the cliché: "Life is a game." But what are the rules? How do the players *know* the score? Are the players really spectators? Who is the referee? It is interesting to note that Garrett's playing with pay makes his text so contemporary. Think of the ludic texts of Coover, Perec, Nabokov. Or, rather, call these playtexts (a wonderful play on words by the critic Warren Motte).

Part Seven again begins with the "Ralegh" text: the Preface to *History of the World*. Beginning with beginning! I must quote it in part because the entire passage is long. I'm interested in the phrase "subject to interchange." Is Garrett playing with the notion that underneath the royal titles, all men are equal in their lives of rise and fall, that Fortune has no favorites? There is no assurance, no certainty—the word "certain" is used at least twice in the passage—no *fixity*. "The very next hour or day to come" can *undo* the life we have led, can *overthrow* it. *Now*— the present moment—is the time. Not the past. Not the future. But, of course, now moves quickly, so quickly that it becomes the past. How frightening! How amusing! Garrett, as a Christian, wants an "eternal now," a "continuous present" (to use secular Gertrude Stein's phrase).

And I turn to the first paragraph. I note a "two-wheeled cart," "a boy and man." "The boy's the image of his father." The "two-ness" intrigues me as it did previously. The text itself is split. It is about the Renaissance—filled with texts, rituals, fashions—but it seems to be so contemporary. It is a "post-modernist" *performance* because it seems to recognize the instability of life. Christianity itself is patterned on two-ness: divine/human; good/evil; human/animal; virtue/vice. There is, we must remember, a "divine comedy" in which the uncertainty principle rules by certainty. We cannot know the Divine Plan, but is it possible that It is *based* on *turn and counter-turn*, on the certainty of our uncertainty? The theological principles enunciated by that critic Augustine—wasn't he "two?"—seems to resolve the notion of Time opposed to Eternity.

Part Eight contains another epigraph from Ralegh's *History of the World*; the repetition of one text in back-to-back Parts takes place here for the first time. It must be quoted:

> *For* in that we *foreknow* that the sun will rise and set, that all men in the world shall die again, that after winter spring will come, after the spring, summer and harvest, and that according to the several seeds that we sow, we shall reap several sorts of grain, *yet is not our foreknowledge the cause of this or any of these. Neither does the knowledge in us bend or constrain the sun to set, or men to die.* (my italics)

The passage affirms what I have stated. We may know the cycles, the seasons, but *our knowledge does not make the seasons change.* And our knowledge is severely limited. I, for example, know that "Ralegh" will die in this text, but I cannot force Garrett to write *his* text, to *rewrite* it in any different way. My commentary cannot change the text, except to compel *you* to see why the text is arranged in a certain way. This essay can, at best, force you to think about a *possible* design. I'm trapped in my chamber (mind); so is Garrett. So is the text (which almost "has a mind of its own"). Knowing that I will die, I cannot cause the death *not to occur.* I may, if you will, change the details, but I cannot *erase* it.

Chapter One has an italicized opening paragraph: *"Beginning of the second day."* The paragraph is surely odd, surely surprising. It consists of one italicized sentence. Is the paragraph "Ralegh's" thought? Is it Garrett's "preface" to the second paragraph? This paragraph is quite puzzling. Perhaps it underlines the *notion of origin.* The "beginning," as I have obsessively mentioned, is a question which has continually troubled me. I alluded to the title. *Is the title the beginning of a text*? I take it that Garrett asks the same kinds of questions. Even now we do not know the origin of *our lives* (our bodily texts). Nor do we know the cosmological beginning. At what point does "Ralegh" become "Ralegh"? At his birth? At his death? Identity of self and/as text, is problematic, tantalizing, unnerving. We—Garrett and I—*seem* to believe that identity is a shifting pattern *of parts*. Life and text move.

Part Nine—the final one—begins with "Ralegh's" lines from "The Passionate Man's Pilgrimage": "And this is my eternall plea/ To him that made Heaven, Earth, and *Sea*, / *Seeing* my flesh must die so soon/ And *want* a head to dine next noone / Just at the stroke when my vaines *start* and spred / Set on my soule an everlasting head" (my italics). The "pilgrimage" has occurred throughout the text; it has been suggested by the various movements (physical, linguistic) that I have mentioned. I have underlined "Sea" and "Seeing" to note that punning quality. To see is to travel mentally, to make "just" perceptions, to, in effect, construct worlds. The text unites physical and perceptual and linguistic *voyages of discovery*. And I note that "Ralegh" puns on "want," using the word in a double way. "Want" means to desire something, but it also suggests absence or lack. Does "Ralegh"—or Garrett—mean to remind us that *we want things that are "wanting,"* missing lost goals, completions, ends? "Start" takes us back to "beginnings." Only an *"everlasting"* heaven (haven?) lacks Time, beginnings and ends—and halts the pilgrimage.

And now the first paragraph. It is short. It is a description of the "Dean" walking to the gatehouse of Ralegh. The words "long journey" reinforce the long journey of text and subject "Ralegh." The "Dean" "ends" as the day "begins." Again "deep weariness" occurs because every pilgrimage (or a life, or a day, of a text) is a troublesome juncture, a paradoxical one of "origins" and "ends," especially since the clarity of movement is subverted by questions.

You may have wondered about my title and approach. I have wanted to take a *hermetic* voyage, to risk seeing whether or not I could travel through the text in a new (knew?) way. I think that I can now rest because I have achieved a "design" which reflects the risky voyage Garrett has tried. We are both hunters of signs and omens or, better yet, voyagers who recognized that Providence guides us, directs us in a secret manner. My essay is, thus, a pilgrimage in which I try to convey the *process of interpretation*. It is a mirror of shape and content—the *shape of content*. Have I outfoxed you?

R.H.W. Dillard

The Elizabethan Novels: Death of the Fox

According to Gertrude Stein, the only way that historical novels and plays or, for that matter, the writing of history itself can be literature is for the writer to imagine his or her characters so completely that "the only existing the character has is the character the writer has given to them" (61). She goes on to speak of the near impossibility of the task because of "all the audience that has known every one about whom he is writing . . . . It is worse than the wailing of the dead soldiers in L'Aiglon there are so many auditors . . . and how can he lose all of them and if he does not how can history be writing that is literature" (61). The writer's task, in other words, is to write about a subject everyone knows and to imagine that subject so fully that readers lose all sense of what they already know and discover the subject completely anew.

Death of the Fox is a novel in which George Garrett fulfills Stein's description of the writer's task, a novel in which the historical Sir Walter Ralegh and the fading Elizabethan world around him in his last days (28-29 October 1618) take on fictive life, become a living man and a living world, colorful, detailed, and exact. The Ralegh of history and legend is subsumed into the Ralegh on the page, the fully imagined and rendered interior Ralegh who takes life in the text and the reader's awakened imagination. But, perhaps more important, it is a novel of the present living moment, of that moment's flow into history as it transforms the future into itself. The past lives naturally as the texture from which the present shapes itself, and Garrett's novel is an expression not only of a dreamed and re-created past, but also of that act of creation itself, the imaginative moment that gives time conscious being.

"All memory," Ralegh thinks to himself as he sits in the Tower, musing on last things on his next-to-last day on this earth, "is vain and foolish and all history compounded of many memories, therefore all the more vain and foolish. Yet a man could do worse than remember such times" (Garrett, *Death* 555). Ralegh remembers those times, and Garrett builds a texture of the memories of others around him as well. The reader shares the thoughts, dreams, and memories of such historical figures as King James, Henry Yelverton, Sir Allan Apsley, Sir Francis Bacon, and many others, including Ralegh's executioner, Gregory Brandon. As Ralegh nods by the fire after hearing his death sentence, Garrett also calls upon the testimony of three "ghosts"— a soldier, a courtier, and a sailor—to present Ralegh's complex and multiform world and his place in it more fully:

> Time, while the old man dozes, to summon up ghosts, imagined and imaginary. Nameless except for their roles and stations.
>
> Perhaps he will not be offended if they are to be considered *characters* in the fashion of the types of Englishmen drawn by Sir Thomas Overbury. Who showed more wit in his book of *Characters* than he did in his appetite for sweet tarts.
>
> Perhaps Ralegh may ignore an interlude with imaginary ghosts, since they are nameless and of no more dimension than figures in tapestry or stained cloth. (254)

These imagined "ghosts" and imagined historical figures populate a world which is in part ghostly itself, for the lost Elizabethan world still casts its brightness over the faded luster of the Jacobean landscape and renders its reality suspect even in the minds of those who are shaping it. Ralegh is, in one sense, the last Elizabethan, and his death is intended to function as an exorcism to those of the new era who feel that they must lay all the Elizabethan ghosts in order to assert their own substantiality and worth.

The "ghosts" and Ralegh, however, remember that departed Elizabethan world and bring it back to life for the reader fully dimensioned. It was a "time of color and wonder in England from which even the poorest and most humble were not quite forbidden or spared," "a false garden, forever new and changing" (554). It was a time of poetry to be followed by a time of prose; it was a time seemingly out of time, freed of past and future in its own unbelievably bright presence:

> Time was as the tides of the river for us. We rode it, floated upon it like the Queen's barge. Her barge was a glorious thing with gleaming brightwork, awnings of cloth of gold, silken pillows and lacquered oars, and it was pulled steady and skilled by a crew in royal livery. Her barge moved down the river, fire-

works fountaining explosions overhead, kettledrums beating, trumpets sounding proud and clear across the river. Her barge in moonlight, riding the Thames, that is a proper figure for our time. (554-55)

This "false garden" was, according to Garrett, the product of Elizabeth's deep conservatism, her desire not to repeat the mistakes of Henry VIII in attempting to master the future nor those of Mary in attempting to restore the past:

Freed from concern about the future by circumstance and by choice, schooling herself in the past and aiming to recover rather than to restore, she found herself oddly free to live (dangerously) in a continual present. And so, ironically, possessed a longer future and a longer past than any other monarch before her. Yet while England burned with change, turn and counterturn for half a century, it was, we can see now, a time of relative sameness and stability. And with her death that inner quiet, persistent at the heart of outer clamor, died too. To be followed, as surely, by England's deluge. Which, if true, means finally that whether she wished it so or not, her refusal to commit herself to the future made that future inevitable. (Garrett, "Dreaming" 419)

Elizabeth created the "false garden" of peace and stability, one that could not, by the very nature of things, last; and yet by that illusion she gave the prosaic and unstable future a measure by which to understand and judge itself and created a truth through and beyond the illusion. The Elizabethans lived in that paradoxical context of truth and illusion completely; Garrett demonstrates how their extravagant clothes and manners, their homes and dinners and pompous displays, were all part and parcel of the larger creation of the world of the Queen. They created an illusion of a great England and thereby made England great. Able to tell truth from fancy, they were able to manipulate fancy toward the creation of truth. They were, in short, poets.

In the novel Ralegh remembers the living poetry of that world and identifies love—Elizabeth's love for her people and theirs for her—as the source of its poetry and its lasting qualities even in an age of prose:

We deprived her of her youth, forbade her from the life and natural joy of a woman, and in the end denied her even the privilege to be old.

That she loved us and this kingdom I find remarkable. Yet she did love us and even at the last when so few loved her.

And it is that love . . . all these years afterwards, which has the power to transform our memory of her, of the age, and therefore of ourselves. So that we view those times gone with and through the transforming power of love. And none of us who were witnesses in the flesh will ever again have the power to give true testimony.

We are all false witnesses. Yet the sum of our witnessing may be true. (529)

Ralegh at the end, Ralegh remembering the poetry and the truth of his time and times, that is the subject of the novel—an old and beaten man, the last Elizabethan, awaiting and experiencing his final hearing, his condemnation and his execution, realizing in the face of the end that his life was wasted and that the world he lived it in and for was "false, illusory, chimerical, bewitched, enchanted" (555). He thinks, "I could easily curse myself and my wasted days" (555), but he does not. He chooses to die as he lived, to act upon his values even as they ring false at the end, to recreate those values by his actions in the minds of those who will live after him, to make those false values true by the life which his death will give them.

That has long been the puzzle of Sir Walter Ralegh: why he chose to die the way he did at the hands of a king he loathed and with such Elizabethan style in a time without style or understanding of style. Garrett's Ralegh dies, not with the rational self-assurance of Socrates, but with the imaginative assurance of a poet. "True or false," he thinks, his time "was a glorious springtime" (555), and he will not allow himself to betray the aesthetic rightness of that springtime. With a poet's faith in his craft and art he chooses the truth that is beautiful, and with an artist's moral strength he alters the composition of the time beyond him to make that beauty true. With a Christian's faith he knows that the truth is beautiful and the composition true:

There is a pattern and design in any man's actions, in the chronicle of his words, thoughts and deeds, which is an

> *image, apelike, of the larger sum and total of the acts, the*
> *thoughts and deeds of all men. Which we call history. What*
> *was, is, will be. And its secret design is Providence. Which*
> *we can come to know only by and through contraries and*
> *paradoxes.*
>   *Intricate beyond comprehending, it speaks of a beautiful*
> *simplicity.* (173)

It is this faith, grounded both aesthetically and spiritually, that enables Ralegh to complete his life as he does, that enables him to bear what his old age has brought him, and to discover (and create) a victory in his defeat. Thinking of the old Queen's looking glasses—the mirrors which she ordered covered in all public rooms where she might pass and the mirrors with which she surrounded herself in her bath—he comes to an understanding of her private honesty with herself and a larger understanding of the human condition. Like Howie Loomis at the end of *Do, Lord, Remember Me*, he attains a vision of the beauty that is present in suffering and disfigurement, in life in the fallen world of lies, of the purity that exists in the desert:

> Still in all, I think no man is so loathsome that, even in self-disgust, he cannot cleave to the belief that in some way, magical, as in some myth or child's tale of transformation, toad into prince, sow's ear into silk purse and the like, that in some way he is far more beautiful than he seems or knows. I venture there is a hidden truth veiled behind this illusion. We are said to be in the image of God—which we take to be the soul eternal and not the corrupted and corruptible flesh—and to be in the image of God, is, therefore, to be beautiful. And therefore the naked truth of us, veiled though it is, is beautiful, and would be most beautiful if we could behold it. This illusion, then, though it be denied by every wrinkle and deformity of flesh, may be the one true apprehension of our true condition. It is a sad wish that is more than a wish, because what it asks for has already been granted. (526-27)

Secure in that vision, Ralegh, by his words and actions, participates in the creation of the world that will follow his own, and, in *Death of the Fox*, he creates the world around him as well. He makes it real by imagining it with an imagination honed by experience and fully grounded in fact; that imaginative creation of the present gives him the necessary depth of vision to set about creating the future. He is taken by way of the Thames to his final trial, and on the way he creates a London, the London he sees and hears and smells and the London he remembers and knows to be real beyond the reach of his senses. Memory and imagining mingle with the sensations of physical fact to create the mystery of the living moment:

> He sighs for the shimmering, evanescent, butterfly's wing of the present moment. Which reason again reminds him is his most precious possession. That moment, in purity, always threatened by memory and wishes. Or is that true? Why not call the present the sum of all?
>
> The trick of time lies in its deceptions. Pea in the pod, shell game, past, present, future, shift place in one instant and who can say which is which and be sure? (203-04)

The moment may be mystery, but people give it reality by daring to *see* it and to *imagine* it. They give it conscious reality; they make it fact, and fact is, as Einstein suggested, as subjective as fancy and as true.

Ralegh sees the world and dreams it; King James allows the world to dream him, and he crushes his glasses in his hand that he may not have to see the world that gives him his reality:

> Where he has been, what he has dreamed, he cannot remember. Some part of it seems to have been at the Tower, that fearful place whose first foundations were tempered by the clotted blood of slaughtered beasts. In the dream Henry was alive and well. Christian of Denmark was there too. The keeper was baiting one of the lions with bear hounds. But it was a sad lion that would not fight the dogs. The dogs were all snarls and teeth like knives. The sad lion looked at him. A lion with his own face . . .
>
> Then he was somewhere else. He cannot remember where. Only that, cold sweat on him, it was dreadful as hell itself. (103)

James forces himself awake, but his hand dreams on, acting on what he has allowed himself to become, and crushes his glasses. The

King, eased and comforted by his faithful Steenie, "feels light-headed, drunk with emptiness" (104). He disappears into emptiness; he becomes only what we will make of him. But Ralegh imagines himself fully into a substantial world of breath and fact; dream of him what we may, his own imagination imposes itself upon our dreams, the reality of his vision becomes our fact.

Some of the most vividly rendered scenes in the novel occur not at the level of narrative fact or in the narrative present, but are imagined by Ralegh; Ralegh, the man without a future, imagines the future of others, how they will behave in the days after his death. He pictures Sir Thomas Wilson's futile efforts to take possession of his valuable books and instruments, foiled by Apsley. He pictures his kinsman and betrayer, Stukely, eaten up by fear and guilt and finding no comfort in the King's bag of gold, staring at his own face reflected in a rain-washed window, weeping and thinking, "A man is drowning out there" (457). And he pictures Sir Francis Bacon hosting a dinner, surrounded with his fourteen-year-old bride by elaborate jeweled objects, his philosophical materialism reflected in his gadgets: a complicated clock with a combative Crusader and Saracen, and a cunningly contrived silver ship which moves by clockwork with each cannon firing a different-colored smoke.

Bacon, who lives in fear of providence and who has only "a faith of this world, faith in the King he serves and in those who serve him" with "no faith left for himself" (503), stands as Ralegh's mirror image, his Jacobean double, lost in materialism and fear, unable to face the future. Even as Ralegh imagines Bacon, he finds in himself his own vision of the future and of the Kingdom of Heaven, knowing "that we never left home but only dreamed a dream of faring forth and returning; that we shall not be welcomed as returning, but rather greeted as if waking from a sleep and a dream; and that we shall be greeted in a language we understand, having always known it" (501). Ralegh imagines Bacon and finds himself, just as he imagines the prosaic world around him and finds proof of the poetic world he has lost and must re-create in his death. Ralegh's imagination allows him to know himself and his future and to fear neither. Unlike King James or Bacon, he has nothing unknown to fear, nothing that he is unable to imagine and come to terms with in his faith; and unlike them, he is able to go peacefully to sleep unhaunted by nightmares. The man without a future has the richest future of them all.

Jorge Luis Borges remarks that "a man sets himself the task of portraying the world," but that "shortly before his death, he discovers that the patient labyrinth of lines traces the image of his face" (Borges, *Dreamtigers* 93). But he also says, in his essay on the mysterious collaboration across the centuries of Omar Khayyám and Edward FitzGerald, that "all collaboration is mysterious," and that "death and vicissitudes and time caused one to know of the other and made them into a single poet" (Borges, *Other Inquisitions* 78). The collaboration between Ralegh and George Garrett is as mysterious. Ralegh dreams his world and makes it real as he is himself being dreamed by Garrett, but in a dream shaped by Ralegh's words and deeds. Ralegh's London and its inhabitants bear the faces Ralegh gives them, but they also trace the face of Ralegh. And both that London and that Ralegh trace the face of Garrett. And, of course, Garrett does know the terms of this mysterious collaboration which is at the very heart of his exploration of the "larger imagination."

The early draft of the novel, "Stars Must Fall," has a modern narrator, a man sitting in a boathouse in Maine (where Garrett has a house and a boathouse) who is called only "the Professor." This character, the ostensible author of the book, stands "in a sense . . . between you and the tale. His shadow falls between you and the people, their actions, the events which, joined together, become a story." He is a man "alone with paper and pen and books, alone with his mind, with five senses and the steady rhythm of his pulse . . . *hoping to summon up a company of ghosts and strangers*" (Garrett, "Stars Must Fall" 2-3). Later in the novel the Professor admits that, in his imaginative struggle to imagine Ralegh and his time, "I wrestle ghosts and angels. They all have my own face" (2). His dilemma depends upon his attempt to imagine another time without imposing on it his modern face and his modern preoccupations, a task made especially difficult by his sense that the modern world has become so detached from reality that "we cannot now even imagine *ourselves*. Except in bits and pieces. . . . Do we dare even to imagine a wholeness or a dream of wholeness when our safety seems to lie in its absence? Absence of thought, absence of feeling" (1-2).

Garrett resolved the Professor's dilemma by removing him from the novel, removing his shadow from between the reader and the events, and by bringing the act of the imagination, the collaboration between

Ralegh and Garrett, to the very center and heart of the novel:

> I came to cling to the notion that the proper subject and theme
> of historical fiction is what it is—the human imagination in
> action, itself dramatized as it struggles with surfaces, builds
> structures with facts, deals out and plays a hand of ideas, and
> most of all, by conceiving of the imagination of others, wrestles
> with the angel (Wallace Stevens' "necessary angel") of the
> imagination. (Garrett, "Dreaming" 420)

The Professor disappears from the novel, but the angel of Garrett's
imagination (who has his face) takes an even more important role.
Garrett celebrates his own imagination even as he creates Ralegh on
the page, for what better celebration is there than the imaginative act itself? His celebration of the larger imagination is the
complex result of the fusion of Garrett's and Ralegh's sensibilities in the novel, in the imaginative fact of *Death of the Fox*.
Like FitzGerald and Khayyám, Garrett and Ralegh become a
single poet, Ralegh shaping the material that feeds Garrett's
imagination, which in turns reshapes that material into the novel.
W. R. Robinson pointed out the close relationship between
Ralegh and the central characters of Garrett's first three novels:
Mike Royle, the courtier; John Riche, the soldier; Big Red Smalley,
the believer and spiritual explorer. Robinson noted that

> actually, since the first three novels were written during the
> period during which Garrett was searching for the form for
> *Death of the Fox* they constitute exploratory efforts toward
> what is consummated, at least for the time being, there. And, in
> fact, Garrett does deliver the man that had been struggling to be
> born through his earlier novels . . . . He [Ralegh] is the whole
> man of which they were fragments. (8-9)

Ralegh is the fullest expression of Garrett's quest for the fully
imagined individual, giving him the opportunity to bring the central
concerns of his poetry and fiction together in a single culminating
work, and freeing him to do work of a very different kind in the years
to follow.

Ralegh writes one last long letter of advice to his son Carew in
part 5 of *Death of the Fox*, the substance of the historical Ralegh

shaped into imaginative fact. But it is more than the re-creation of an unsent and possibly even unwritten letter by Ralegh, for it is an open fusion on the page of Ralegh and Garrett, an explicit revelation of that fusion which is the novel as a whole. The letter winds through some forty-eight pages, a distillation of the historical Ralegh's writings and a summation of his imagined meditations in the novel. But its conclusion is a close paraphrase of Garrett's poem "For My Sons"—the poem filtered through Ralegh's imagined sensibility and emerging in Ralegh's prose, the shared advice of two fathers separated by centuries to their sons:

For the world, I leave you a small inheritance and less wisdom.

Do not think much on my own guilt or innocence or the justice of the world. Live and think only that justice is in the world. Believe that.

Small wisdom and that only in old words. Words no more than sweet comfits to lighten the taste of dust on the tongue.

Nothing stings like the serpent. No pain greater. Bear it.

If a bush should burn and the flames cry out, bow down.

If ever a stranger wrestle you, do not let go until you learn his name.

If after long voyages, tossing and fever, you find a new continent, plant your flags proudly. Stand tall. Send forth a dove.

Rarely the fruit you reach for shall return your love. (563)

Ralegh destroys the letter, but Garrett writes it for him again 350 years later. Ralegh and Garrett become in this passage more than mirrors set up each to each; they become a single poet, or at least sharers of a most mysterious and meaningful collaboration. And that collaboration and that unity are the fullest celebration of the larger imagination.

What allows Garrett the opportunity for this full collaboration with Ralegh across the centuries is their shared belief. Both Ralegh and Garrett are Christian artists: Ralegh in an overtly Christian age when the terms of Christian belief were inherent in the thought of the time; Garrett in (to use W.H. Auden's term) an age of anxiety, a secular age without shared belief.

Ralegh designs the end of his life, the manner of his leaving it, with the care of a poet finishing a poem. He finishes it in Christian terms, just as he had finished the night before an old poem, one years old which had been playing along the edges of his mind all day long, one which lacked a proper ending:

> Even such is time which takes in trust
> Our youth, our joys, our all we have
> And pays us but with age and dust;
> Who in the dark and silent grave
> When we have wandered all our ways
> Shuts up the story of our days.
> But from this earth, this grave, this dust,
> My God shall raise me up I trust. (611-12)

The poem ends with faith and hope, and Ralegh ends his life, as any Christian would hope to, in imitation of Christ. He chooses the cup that must come, and he forgives himself the sins of his past in the surety of the mercy to come. He does not curse himself and die; he dies at ease with himself and with God.

Garrett enriches the imitation of Christ of Ralegh's death with a pattern of Christian symbols and echoes. Ralegh faces his unfair last trial, he shares his last supper, he finds his Judas in his kinsman Stukely, and he speaks his own version of Christ's last words to his executioner: "What doest thou fear? Strike, man, strike!" (739). These are Ralegh's historical last words set in an imaginative and consciously Christian context by Ralegh's modern collaborator. Garrett, then, celebrates the imagination that shapes the whole of the living world, and his novel becomes a prayer of praise to that divine imagination.

Garrett's journey into the past frees him to the present; in the hard-earned recovery of spirit in lost and irrecoverable fact, he finds the wisdom (speaking through Ralegh) to believe in the future of humankind:

> The pagan poets and philosophers, perceiving that the world can only grow older in time, divided all time into four ages, each of a baser metal than the last. And there is much truth in the figure. Yet it can never be truly apt while the world still lives. For if the history of man has its ages like the seasons,

then, like the seasons, they must turn and return, be revived as well. (554)

Death of the Fox, an exploration and celebration of the larger imagination, renews as well the genre of historical fiction, gives it a life in American literature that it has seldom had. It is also a book with largeness of spirit in a time of spiritual exhaustion. Garrett's imaginative examination of the individual uncovered for him the possibilities of coherence and wholeness even as he was writing in an incoherent and fragmented time; it freed him to explore beyond the self in *The Succession* and *Poison Pen* into the web of consciousness that shapes all public life, secure in the ground he discovered in this novel, the ground of the believing and loving self, knowing with Ralegh that "so long as the heart is right, it is no matter which way the head lies" (738).

Works Cited

Stein, Gertrude. *Narration.* Chicago: U of Chicago P, 1935.

Borges, Jorge Luis. *Dreamtigers.* Austin: U of Texas P, 1964.

_____. *Other Inquisitions 1937-1952.* Austin: U of Texas P, 1964.

Garrett, George. *Death of the Fox.* Garden City: Doubleday, 1971.

_____. "Dreaming with Adam: Notes on Imaginary History." *New Literary History* 1 (1970): 407-21.

_____. "Stars Must Fall" (manuscript in the collection of R.H.W. Dillard).

Robinson, W.R. "Imagining the Individual: George Garrett's *Death of the Fox.*" *Hollins Critic* 8 (1971): 1-12.

W. R. Robinson

Imagining the Individual:
George Garrett's Death of the Fox

"What doest thou fear? Strike, man, strike!" These were Sir Walter Ralegh's last words. With them he commanded the termination of his life. And with them George Garrett closes his fourth novel, which he once descriptively subtitled "An Imaginary Version of the Last Days of Sir Walter Ralegh." But Ralegh's last words, of necessity, must be the writer's first ones. For whereas the man to die is at an end, facing death, and in Ralegh's case is ready to surrender up his individual existence, the man inspired to create is at a beginning. Thus when Garrett as artist-historian takes on the job of restoring Ralegh to life, he must strike too, but not for decapitation—except figuratively insofar as he must depose his rational faculty so that his aesthetic powers can assume command and act. He must strike, instead, to sever old habits of mind and feeling that obstruct his re-creation of the man through creation of an original narrative.

That is precisely what George Garrett is about in this novel. Ralegh's death is his subject, but he writes to turn that death into a new life. To do so, he strikes out to reconstruct in its living oneness what Ralegh by an act of reason wilfully set asunder and thereby removed from the created world of time and space. In taking this matter of life and death into his own hands Garrett ventures into life's central paradox and irony, that region where life feeds upon death with the intention of transmuting the past into the present, including historical figures into living presences, fact into life, and life into art. There is no chance that he or any other man can cut the Gordian knot of life's creative matrix, and Garrett, knowing that, does not write with it in mind. But he also knows that to strike for creation he must enter that no-man's land, and he explicitly designates this realm as the territory of his adventuring in a prefatory note to *Death of the Fox* with his statement, "I wanted to make a work of fiction, of the imagination, planted and rooted in fact. I wanted facts to feed and give strength to the truths of fiction."

Read from that perspective, *Death of the Fox* piles up through an array of extensive detail a richly textured historical soil not only for the planting and rooting of the narrative but of Ralegh as well. With the consequence that, as Garrett's narrative gets its substance from historical fact, so Ralegh gets his from the facts of his time. Allowed to go unchecked to its extreme, this perspective, rather than feed and give strength to the truths of fiction, would enforce the truths that the times are the man and history is our present. So *Death of the Fox* must be read, finally, as it is written, since it is a work of fiction, from another perspective. This other perspective, again in Garrett's own words, this time from his essay "Dreaming with Adam: Notes on Imaginary History," allows

> that the proper subject and theme of historical fiction is what it is—the human imagination in action, itself dramatized as it struggles with surfaces, builds structures with facts, deals out and plays a hand of ideas, and most of all, by conceiving of the imagination of others, wrestles with the angel (Wallace Stevens' "necessary angel") of the imagination.

This does not mean that the imagination has a license to fancify history so that, by selecting the facts to suit its purposes and making them up where they don't exist, ancestors can become the heroes of romantic legend or the good old times can be glorified for the indulgence of nostalgia. Quite the contrary. "To approach the renaissance-imagination requires a commitment of one's own imagination," Garrett further remarks in clarifying what is entailed in this second perspective. "The proper theme of the work, then, is the human imagination, the possibility, limits, and variety of imaginative experience." And implicit in that commitment is the simple but demanding moral condition that "to write imaginary history is to celebrate the human imagination."

Such are the subject and purpose of *Death of the Fox*. But in committing himself to the imagination Garrett commits himself to an art of life. He is well aware of and admits that inevitability in his observation that

> It may well be that the present (though it is the past by the time two words are on a page or, for that matter, one sequence of images flashes across the movie screen) is the most fitting place

to awaken the imagination with some hope of such a felicitous union. To live well in the present demands as much imagination as can be mustered. But to live in the present fully one preserves the possibility of exploring the past. One may choose to deny that one's present world is in any part fictitious. The past, however, is chiefly fiction and must be imagined before it can exist. But the past is forever in the present, even when it is forgotten, and the attempt to imagine it, whether as a writer or reader, requires a sacrifice, an expense of vanity (like the old Queen alone in her mirrored room) . . . . The present and living well and fully in it come first for him, while the past, crucial as it is, assumes value to the degree that it contributes to the enhancement of the present.

Now it is the human imagination that makes the enhancement of the present possible. For, as Garrett defines it, it is "an energy in motion and never abstract, [which] permits the wedding and intercourse of thought and feeling, each responsive to, respectful of the other." To carry out the enhancement of the present, the imagination, Garrett's definition implies, must elude the nemesis of abstraction. That nemesis is more explicitly identified in Garrett's response to the question regarding the value of the past in fiction:

> . . . I can answer only this much. We have no poverty of thinkers. If sages are few, honest intellectuals are plentiful, and their voices are heard. And there are plenty, a growing number, of course, equal or superior in intellectual power, who in reaction or revolution would cast aside the mind and follow feeling, sensation, impulse where they might lead. Too often both are abstractionists, peg-legged dancers, one-eyed princes (knaves?) in the kingdom of the blind.

These repudiations of abstraction reveal that Garrett understands that as part of his commitment to celebrating the imagination and enhancing the present he must not choose to try to create—even if he could—apart from his finite condition in the finite world. He knows that in giving himself to the aims and instruments of the imagination he commits himself to employing both the factual and fictional perspectives in their proper functional relationship.

That means for him that the imagination, properly valued, won't go berserk when turned loose on its own because its deepest concern is with creation, and creation, he is insisting, appears, and can appear, only in individuals who at their best are complexly compound creatures. Should one be tempted to hold to the conventional notion that what comes natural to the human imagination and what therefore it will celebrate when turned loose will be nothing more than irresponsible vaporous dreaming? Garrett dispels such a possibility by further qualifying the imagination's interest in other imaginations when he says that in *Death of the Fox* "The subject is the larger imagination, the possibility of imagining lives and spirits of other human beings, living or dead, without assaulting their essential and, anyway, ineffable mystery." In giving himself completely to it instead of cautiously checking and restraining his imagination, he not only puts himself in motion and avoids the death of abstraction but commits himself to grant freely the deepest respect and abiding love to Ralegh—actually to his world, man, himself, the past, and his medium of language: to all the elements that constitute *Death of the Fox*—at the same time that the end result of that loving relation is to transcend them into a new individuality beyond them.

Therefore, also implicit in Garrett's commitment to celebrating the imagination, by his own admission, is the further commitment to creating the individual. Indeed Garrett's commitment as an artist is, inescapably, to make an individual art object, an autonomous entity comprised of both a material and form that exists as a world unto itself connected somehow to other autonomous entities but not causally or determinately. The prerequisite of his doing so is that he appreciates the autonomous individuality of another. It is for this reason that the distance and difference between the 20th-century imagination and the Renaissance's, his own and Ralegh's, is of crucial importance for him. But at the same time Ralegh's splendid individuality has the power to flush out the individuality of Garrett's imagination as it repeatedly flushes the man out of his office in his encounters with his contemporaries. In this respect, *Death of the Fox* is a tribute of the highest order to Ralegh's power as a guru-midwife to call forth by means of his own rich humanity the human potential in others. His essential and ineffable mystery evokes theirs.

Garrett pays the expense of vanity required by the imagination in imagining Ralegh. He as an ego is obliterated—he submits to being an effaced narrator. His imagination thereby clarified, it cannot only imagine another human being; it is also equipped to serve as the transmutational agency between Ralegh and *Death of the Fox*. In paying tribute to Ralegh's individuality Garrett succeeds in preserving, perpetuating, and refining in an autonomous work of fiction the value of individuality exemplified by Ralegh for himself and us. What Garrett's imagination celebrates in celebrating itself, then, is the individual, and it celebrates the individual by creating the individual.

I

I have gone to the trouble of extensively quoting Garrett to this point to establish that his historical fiction issues from a seasoned, incisive intelligence and profound purpose as well as a vigorous imagination. With Garrett's words before him, the reader cannot lapse sleepily into a casual regard of his narrative and pass it over as just another historical fiction of the Frank Yerby or Lloyd Douglas variety.

But if the reader's own imagination has even the first stirrings of life in it, then he couldn't possibly be guilty of such a lapse. Especially if he keeps in mind that Garrett is a Southern writer and that *the* subject of the Southern imagination is history. In that context it should come as a startling surprise that Garrett, taking his narrative as seriously as he does, did not choose a Confederate Civil War hero as bearer of the life of his imagination. It is of crucial importance that he didn't. Once awakened to that strange departure, it should come as an even greater surprise to the reader that the present should ultimately have priority over the past in *Death of the Fox* and that fiction, hardnosed serious fiction dedicated to the whole truth, should prevail over fact. Then he cannot possibly miss at least one of the exciting new things that are happening in *Death of the Fox*, the revision of the Southern imagination's attitudes towards and use of the past. Nothing less than a new kind of Southerner and South is in the making in Garrett's narrative.

Even if that context should not occur to the reader or matter, still he should readily recognize, if the least alive imaginatively, that Garrett, in committing himself to imagining the individual, directly addresses himself to the overarching project of our time, to the enterprise we are all, will it or no, inescapably caught up in. That project has officially been dubbed Existentialism. But that simply means that we choose to regard existence—the fancy word for creation of life—as the supremely real and valuable. And since existence occurs only in the concrete, only in specific individuals, that means we have invested our energy in working out to the maximum realization within our power our potential for individual existence on earth. Given this additional context, it might be tempting to label _Death of the Fox_ a Southern Humanistic Existential novel. But that would be stupid. Not only because that would violate Ralegh's essential and ineffable mystery but the narrative's as well. Garrett's existential realism invites comparison with that of Sartre and Robbe-Grillet, but to go off on such tangents as tags and comparisons would simply be to lose the most important "existential" qualities of _Death of the Fox_, the factual thoroughness with which Ralegh's life is rendered without being violated. It is in the intactness of the man that Garrett has invested his imagination. Nevertheless, without being aware of its existential dimension, the reader will undoubtedly miss the excitement of exploring with Garrett's imagination the proper way to behold and realize our own individualized existences. And having missed this unique opportunity for having his own essential and ineffable mystery evoked, the reader will be a poorer individual for it.

Now undoubtedly more than mere stirrings of the imagination are required to detect and enjoy the subtlest thing that is happening in _Death of the Fox_. Yet it is there, and indeed, it is where the real excitement is to be found. For here is where the imagination really lives, and is truly alive. I am talking about the narrative's form. Garrett has testified that _Death of the Fox_ was "a long time finding its form and coming to be"—somewhere in the neighborhood of 20 years, to be a bit more exact. His writing of it over those years has, in other words, been a quest for the necessary form for man, and the finished version of the narrative stands as a solution to an enduring problem for his imagination.

Alert to its form and the life of form, the reader can readily behold the finer nuances of Garrett's artistry. He can even go, should he be so disposed, on a comparative romp. As he should. For the collective enterprise of the fictional narrative imagination of our time is to envision a viable form for man. It will be very instructive to compare his solution to those of the mockers and insulters, the ideologues and bellyachers, the exquisitely sensitive and morally outraged. It will be equally instructive to compare his solution with those of writers like Wright Morris and Saul Bellow, who are close to his in kind. My own preference is to start with a distinction between "mythic autobiography" and "mythic biography" as the two main genres being developed today in the search by fictional narrators for a viable form for man. ("Mythic" in these phrases means the release of the creative power to act in the world.) That distinction throws into sharp relief the difference between a first-person narrative in which the "I" imagines itself and a third-person one in which the indentity-less consciousness imagines another human being. While one is an inside and the other an outside narrative, both are devoted to imagining the autonomy and integrity of the individual and to releasing his potential life. The difference between the two is the same difference that set Hazlett and Keats off against Wordsworth. With the distinction between mythic auto-biography and biography in hand, while keeping close attention upon the formal qualities of *Death of the Fox*, it is possible to appreciate the full extent of Garrett's "negative capability" and the full stature of his achievement in so imagining Ralegh's individuality that Ralegh can provide both Garrett and ourselves with a basic model of the living man in our time and for all time.

II

Above all else the thing that is happening in *Death of the Fox* is that a new man is being formally composed. Garrett has been composing that man throughout his novels, beginning with *The Finished Man* and continuing through *Which Ones Are the Enemy?* and *Do, Lord, Remember Me* to *Death of the Fox*. Actually, since the first three novels were written within the period in which Garrett was searching for the form for *Death of the Fox*, they constitute exploratory efforts toward what is consummated, at least for the time being, there. And, in fact, Garrett does deliver the man who has been struggling to be born through his earlier novels in *Death of the Fox*.

That birth process entails a complicated formal context and development, but in general its formal texture and sweep comprise a central event during which an individual attempts to gain his autonomy from the circumstances of his existence—particularly the authority of father, society, and God. His extrication from his confining circumstances comes laboriously because of a deep bond of interdependence and affection between the two. In fact, in *The Finished Man*, where the birth process begins, Mike Royle, a Southerner who has made it out of his region, returns to his native land and eventually chooses to stay to defend, in a futile heroic gesture, a condemned Negro. Going back is a prerequisite of his going on. John Riche of *Which Ones Are the Enemy?* picks up where Royle left off. He, too, is a man alone but he begins already inside his engaging circumstances—the rigidly structured class and command society of the army, for which he has great respect. His attempt at autonomy in a personal life off the army base with an Italian girl named Angela implicates him in a web of evil and he loses everything but his will to survive. Big Red Smalley of *Do, Lord, Remember Me*, another man alone, expands Riche's predicament from a man-society to a man-God confrontation. He steps outside of Riche's limiting circumstances and, in effect, questions the ground of his own existence. That daring traps him in the middle between normally socialized human beings and God. There, having tried for too much on his own, he is destroyed by his own hand. Ralegh caps this progressive involvement, enlargement, and elaboration by including in himself the predicaments and impulsions of all his predecessors: a courtier like Royle, a soldier like Riche, and a man of God like Big Red Smalley, he returns inexplicably to England to face a certain death, enjoy England's earthly delights, and make his peace with God. In short, he is the whole man of which they are fragments. That inclusiveness is so encompassing it extends also to point of view. *Death of the Fox* incorporates the third-person objective point of view of the first novel, the first-person subjective point of view of the second, and the multiple diffracting points of view of the third.

What the form of Ralegh's life has most obviously in common with its predecessors is that at its end he, too, is a loser. But he loses with a difference. Though he dies in the end, he is in charge. Throughout his story he keeps coming on, emerging from behind the law, position, property, and even his own rational pride in every part of the narrative until he stands clear and free. He outwits all that would ignore or deny him or fix his image to become an exalted distillation of his time's essential life. Standing alone, just one man and his death at the end, he is the form, not simply of his own life, but of his time as well. Unlike Royle, Riche, and Smalley, all defeated by circumstances, Ralegh triumphs over his environment; he saves himself, and in doing that he saves the best of his world.

The form is the man, Garrett has told us, in effect. Through the first three novels that man was gathering his formal parts and strength to strike out on his own. In this latest novel that man comes forward in his full vital plumage. By his form—that is, the structure and style of the narrative—he is, in addition to those virtues just mentioned, a man of all seasons in the best sense: he contains, like the imagination, all the possibilities of life and time in him simultaneously and allows them their day when they are ripe. City, country, war, love, peace, high adventure on the seas; gold, poetry, religion; past, present, future—none of these is denied its due. Moreover, he is in the present tense and, though situated within an intricate design and capable of the most formal of reflections and debates, prefers to dwell among the vernacular, free of strict, stylized conventions, where he can be direct and literal rather than ornate and symbolic. He takes life as it comes, and as it comes in his form it is as subtle and crafty as anything a man can be asked to cope with. For his form unites life's antitheses in the infinite elusiveness and change-ability that goes with its inherent paradoxicality and double dealing.

All these talents add up to a man who is a master of the world and its ways, an authentic hero in an age of anti-heroes. He bears his rich contingent humanity with dignity and poise, not with awkward and foolish self-consciousness. That is made possible perhaps by Ralegh's historical remoteness. Yet the historical personage is not the whole form of *Death of the Fox*. He serves as the peg upon which the form is hung. An inevitable difference has to exist between Ralegh and Garrett's man. That difference presents itself succinctly in the contrast between Ralegh's joyously submerging into death at the end of his life and Garrett's narrative joyously ascending into life from the point of Ralegh's death.

That difference cannot be properly appreciated, however, unless it is seen that the historical personage and the form of Garrett's man share the twin faculties of reason and imagination. These are the powers respectively underlying fact and fiction and that must be, above all else, welded together in the creation of a viable form. The point of their meeting and mating is the precise locus where Ralegh and Garrett's man join like siamese twins. The statement by Garrett on the priority of the present quoted earlier ended with the claim that the reward for the expense of vanity was "a recollection, vague beyond imagining, shared by living and dead, of something beautiful, and forever, joyously new." This "recollection" is the very origin of the imagination's life, the eternal present where life is exchanged. It is innocence and wholeness regained, the source of existence and inspiration returned to. Ralegh and Garrett's man are indistinguishable at this still point where their lives link together; here during the transaction in which the heritage of life is passed from one man to another, their humanity is identical. The important detail is that this heritage is the property of and is passed down by a single individual, not directly from God, ideas, nature, etc. The creative energy of the imagination that is in motion can, paradoxically and ironically, only be exchanged through never abstract, concrete human beings. Because, of course, it is only in and through his humanity that man can be a creator. And Ralegh, as testified to by the existence of *Death of the Fox*, is as well as Garrett's imagination a creator.

But whereas Ralegh lived during the dawning of the imagination as a moral power and accordingly was a sometimes poet in the course of a political career, Garrett creates his form at a time when the imagination has established its moral hegemony over reason. His man is a full-time artist surrounded by political life. As a consequence, none of Ralegh's dualisms or certitudes is or can be his. No stars burn in the abstract heavens beyond his form. All he has left, amid the infinite complexity and indeterminateness of his life, is to be himself. He is a living form, his existence encompassed not by an order but by consciousness. That difference comes down finally to the difference between a man of reason whose imagination lives for death, as Ralegh's did, and a man of imagination who lives for life. One sees that his existence suffers from a metaphysical dualism and that suffering is what lasts, while the other proves the contrary, that actually it is the sufferer's joy which lasts because it is that from which those coming after him can draw their life and create new unities.

As Ralegh's existence fell between two poles of power, and man's always will, so Garrett's man inhabits the treacherous narrow strips where fact and fiction seek a marriage in living form. The proof of Garrett's imaginative power lies, however, in his astute perception of the advantage the imagination now has over reason. He sees quite clearly that the imagination is the human frontier today. That perception allows his imagination not only to see Ralegh emerging out of a morass of fact, using his world to attain his autonomy beyond it, but more importantly to imagine man's emergence out of the morass of the past into his autonomy beyond history. Thereby he is able to create a "mind of the South" subtler and more viable than that of W.J. Cash's ideal intellectual Southerner and to give life to the form that John Crowe Ransom, in *The World's Body*, could allow to have only a deadening restraint upon the man. But, above all, that perception endows Garrett's imagination with the power to strike for the difficult, delicate wedding of each and every man with his sacred, inviolable life source. That is what ultimately his creating is and affirms, not just the historical man and his form, but the power within the form of man. The man he recreates is most honored, indeed, in being put to such a purpose. Ralegh lends himself as self-effacingly as Garrett does in telling his story to the purposes of life, with the consequence that he lives anew in a truly and wholly alive present in *Death of the Fox* and in his recreated individuality celebrates the creation.

Having earlier introduced the Romantics, I must conclude by adding that the imagination that acts to incarnate what it values in recreating Ralegh in the form of *Death of the Fox* is not the Romantic imagination, which for some is the final, authoritative definition of this faculty. An imaginative apprehension of the form of Garrett's narrative will reveal above all else that it is not given over to the "trip out" to cosmic self-transcendence. It will be seen, instead, to be dedicated to the 20th-century story, the "trip back" from Romantic self-oblivion to a voluntary assumption of the finitude and the complicated responsibility of being a human individual. And it will also be seen that while *Death of the Fox* significantly contributes to the growth and clarification of the human imagination beyond where, if you will, the Romantics were able to imagine it, its greatest virtue lies in its unequaled demonstration among contemporary narratives of what each of us in our individuality derives from and owes to the individuality of others. In demonstrating that, Garrett's exact and exacting art of life challenges our imaginations to match its joy and celebration with our own. Any book which can do that is of no little consequence and promises great pleasure. Indeed, *Death of the Fox*, certainly Garrett's best novel, just could be a new standard by which we measure the vitality and humanity of not only contemporary novels but of our own lives as well.

Monroe K. Spears

George Garrett and the Historical Novel

I

George Garrett's *Death of the Fox* (1971) and *The Succession* (1983) are such remarkable historical novels that they may be considered either fulfillments of the genre or repudiations of it. The term "historical novel" will not stand up under much examination. All narratives are historical in the sense that they must be placed in time and—even experiments in using the stream of consciousness and the historical past—must be retrospective. But a narrative concerned primarily with historical fact—with what actually happened—is not a novel, and poetry is closer to philosophy than to history, as Aristotle said. So what useful meaning can the term have? The question would seem to be one of degree or emphasis: historical fiction is fiction in which history is important, in which the author lays claim to historical as well as poetic truth and the reader is kept aware of the historical aspect, conscious that the time of the action is distant from his own.

Of historical fiction thus simply defined we may distinguish two kinds. The first is that extremely popular form of entertainment in which the historical aspect is superficial, mainly picturesque and amusing or titillating. The costume romance places fictional characters against a backdrop of historical events and historical personages; but the central characters, insofar as they are real, are modern, and their doings bear at most a peripheral relation to the important events of the time. While this kind of fiction can be very attractive and sometimes informative, it rises no higher because the historical aspect has no meaning other than to provide the reader with escape (and perhaps the illusion that he is educating himself) and often to conceal the author's poverty of imagination in character and plot.

The other kind, which is much less common and much less popular, makes a serious attempt to interpret the historical aspect, to relate it to the characters and plot, and to render the "otherness" of the characters in their different time while also rendering their common humanity. *War and Peace*, by common consent, is the greatest such novel; but *War and Peace* interprets a time only a couple of generations earlier than that of the author, and one known to him not only (and not primarily) through written sources but through legend, oral tradition, and memory. Allen Tate's *The Fathers* is a similar case, and so is Andrew Lytle's *The Long Night*. (Even *The Scarlet Letter*, *Henry Esmond*, and Sir Walter Scott's best novels, though remote in time, are set in the author's own country and draw on local associations and on oral as well as written sources.) Garrett's two novels are different: their settings are more distant in time and in a different country, and they are based on written sources exclusively.

Garrett thus meets the full challenge head-on, more completely and uncompromisingly than any other "historical" novelist I can think of. If all novels are historical, but some are more historical than others, Garrett's *Death of the Fox* and *The Succession* are historical in every sense compatible with remaining novels. His central characters are major actors of the stage of history and are so remote in time that there is little or no shared bond of genealogy, legend, or other common heritage between characters and readers. His fiction is based primarily on historical documents, not on memory and shared associations (though the places still survive, to be transformed by imagination; and Garrett has lovingly assimilated the topography of England and Scotland for this purpose).

The Succession, Garrett observes in his prefatory note, began as a study of the letters of Elizabeth and James. The impression made by his novels is, in solidity, authenticity, and immediacy, more like that produced by such great letter-collections as *The Lisle Letters* or *Children of Pride* than like that of other historical novels. But letters, except for a few fortunate collections enhanced by imaginative editing, are like literal translations; they are no substitute for reimagining and re-creating the whole.

Garrett, then, doesn't take any of the easy outs: his central characters are historical and are involved in centrally important historical events, which are followed meticulously in the novels. No liberties are taken with the facts: Garrett invents narrative detail but changes nothing and adds only what is plainly justified by analogy. Since the main characters are historical and the reader knows in advance what happened to them, there can be no narrative suspense. Garrett's position is the polar opposite of Scott or Alexander

Dumas—no cloak and sword, rapid action, romance and suspense, quaintness and local color. The characters are always presented in depth from inside. Though there is a great variety of perspectives, points of view, and kinds of interest in the different sections, the unifying attitude and tone are contemplative and meditative. Garrett's attitude toward the past is neither romantic nor debunking: he has a marvelous sense of ceremony, ritual and pageantry, and of the immense significance of these things—and, of course, of religion—to the characters (in implicit contrast to moderns). The trials and executions are the most fully developed examples, though the conclusion of *The Succession* is perhaps the most impressive of all, with its picture of Christmas and of the whole cycle of the year in Elizabeth's court.

In Garrett's novels, we escape only in the sense that we do inhabit another world, fully imagined and realized. There is no explicit comparison to our own "real" world (though much implicit); Garrett never intrudes in his own person, but always speaks through the imagined mind of a "historical" personage or "ghost."

One mystery that the serious historical novel always points to is that of the relation between the individual and his times, or the individual and society. It is only in this sense that Robert Penn Warren will call his fiction historical: "Writing a story about an actual person and using him as a kind of model are really not the same. I don't pretend that Willie Stark is Huey Long. I know Stark, but I have no idea what Long was really like." What interests him, he goes on to say, is how "individual personalities become mirrors of their times, or the times become a mirror of the personalities .... The individual is an embodiment of external circumstances, so that a personal story is a social story." His novels, he says, are not historical because what he looks for is "an image, a sort of simplified and distant framed image, of an immediate and contemporary issue, a sort of interplay between that image and the contemporary world." (Floyd C. Watkins and John T. Hirs, eds., *Robert Penn Warren Talking: Interviews, 1950-1978* [New York, 1980], 71, 128-129.)

These quotations define nicely the difference between Warren's fiction, which often appears to be historical (and is certainly concerned with history), and Garrett's two novels, which are centrally historical. Garrett does undertake to tell what Ralegh and James were really like (or how they may most plausibly be imagined, in accord with the facts). And, while obviously there are connections to the contemporary world, there are no contemporary issues that the reader feels are the central theme, and the connections are not explicit. On the other hand, Garrett is also concerned, like Warren or any other novelist, with his characters as unique individuals and not merely as mirrors of the times.

II

It is a curious coincidence that Garrett needed 12 years—close to the length of time Ralegh was in the Tower (1603-1618)—to finish *The Succession* (1983) after *Death of the Fox* (1971); but no coincidence that they are in reverse chronological order, focusing on 1603 and 1618, respectively. *The Succession,* as we shall see, would seem to be motivated partly by the determination to be fair to James (who was, of course, responsible for the death of the Fox) and to the Jacobean era, thus complementing *Fox* and giving a balanced picture. In many ways, the two novels do certainly complement each other—the basic techniques and approaches are the same—and they are companion works, each dealing with characters and aspects of the age that the other does not. But each is also self-sufficient, and in many ways they are different.

To put it briefly, *Fox* is a tragedy, covering a short period of time—Ralegh's execution and the few days preceding it—with Ralegh's earlier life brought in through retrospection. In spite of the novel's length, there is a growing intensity, tension, and suspense as it proceeds to its foreknown conclusion; the focus narrows and sharpens. *Succession*, in contrast, is elegiac and sometimes nostalgic in tone; it has 16 sections as against *Fox*'s nine, and multiple narrators (though usually not in first person) instead of *Fox*'s central intelligence dominating the other narrators. The time covered in *Succession* ranges from 1566 to 1626; though the primary action is the succession of James in 1603, we see throughout the novel the messenger traveling from Edinburgh to London in 1566 with the news of James' birth and the courtier who profited nothing from bringing the news of Elizabeth's death to James (from London to Edinburgh) but came into favor on the succession of Charles. The focus, so to speak, broadens and mellows into the concluding picture of the last Christmastide at Elizabeth's court.

Both novels are profoundly "historical," showing an easy

mastery of an incredible amount of detail; but both are primarily works of imagination, to be judged by their success as novels, not by their historical accuracy. Yet Garrett's is a historically disciplined imagination: that of a modern man putting himself in the place of a historical character, as he must be; but doing so in terms of the historical background of that character, what his childhood was or must have been like, not with free-floating imagination unleashed. Garrett goes inside the minds of major historical characters (James I and Ralegh, most notably and extensively, but also Queen Elizabeth, Bacon, Robert Cecil, and many others) as they confront major historical decisions. His is not only backstage, backstairs, or behind the scenes history, but main stage too. He doesn't come up with startling revelations or solutions to historical mysteries but with plausible and sensible interpretations of larger meanings.

Throughout both these novels there is the same unusual attitude toward religion that was apparent in *Do, Lord, Remember Me* (1965), Garrett's novel about a redneck revivalist and surrounding grotesques in a small Southern town. Garrett presents Big Red's healing powers as real and Big Red as sincere, though also comic and corrupted; and he manages to sustain both attitudes at once. The mixture of the earthy and religious in these "low" characters is presented with nothing but sympathy. The complement of this attitude is the presentation of the priest in *The Succession* as he moves toward martyrdom; and Garrett manages to make his "high" religious character come to life just as fully as he did the low ones. (He does the same for Ralegh awaiting execution in *Fox*.) *Do, Lord* also anticipates *Fox* and *Succession* in using the technique of multiple narrators, with a corresponding wide array of styles ranging from Big Red's brilliant and tormented rich allusiveness to the more limited minds of the others. But all are presented with a large compassionate acceptance and without a touch of condescension, while the novel is also continuously funny. (In this, it is at the opposite pole from *Fox*, which is not comic, though it is in some sense beyond tragedy.)

In *Fox*, Ralegh is a tough old soldier (among other things), no angel but decent, with many fine qualities (but enigmatic), a victim of circumstances but no whiner. In this, he is like the equivocal hero of *Which Ones Are the Enemy?* and Garrett's other stories of the postwar Army: tough, competent, skeptical but not wholly cynical; finally overreaching himself and suffering a downfall. It is much harder to like James, the central character of *The Succession*; he is a winner, but a villain insofar as history has villains. But Garrett is at the opposite pole from making history a simple morality play; both books constitute a profound and continuing meditation on the meaning of time, memory, and history.

By presenting each segment as meditation or reverie by a specific character, as he remembers or dreams, Garrett can use neutral language, not noticeably modern or antique either. Thus he avoids the problem of archaic language—*gadzooks, egad, zounds*— one of the biggest stumbling blocks in the historical novel. But it is a real challenge to write like Ralegh or Bacon or Queen Elizabeth so that the reader is not shocked by the transition from their own prose to yours, and Garrett manages this with great success. It works partly because they were such good writers, and when pruned of minor surface anachronisms, do not seem at all dated or antiquated, but the "naked bone and sinew" of the language, and this is what Garrett seems to pattern his own prose on. The style, then, is not based on pastiche or fake antiquarianism, but on the solid middle ground of English. But having established this as basis, Garrett goes on to produce a great variety of individual voices and to write in very different styles according to the occasion.

As we have seen, Garrett employs multiple narrators, each of whom tells his story. Unlike the great exemplars of this technique, *Ulysses* and *The Sound and the Fury*, however, his novels do not attempt to reveal the stream of consciousness. Instead, they exhibit a great variety of levels of consciousness, from dozing reverie to full alertness and decision. Wisely, he avoids too much use of the first person, preferring to use the third person (sometimes even second) and varying degrees of distance. The device of having ghosts appear who are "characters" in the manner of Overbury—a soldier, a courtier, a sailor, to describe authoritatively these aspects of Ralegh— is very effective. But Garrett is perhaps best on the characters the reader loves to hate: Bacon, James and his favorites (in *Fox*; James is seen differently in *Succession*), and Stukely, Ralegh's kinsman and betrayer.

Shakespeare is handled effectively and with restraint. It is plausible that Ralegh would not be overly impressed by his plays, preferring Marlowe and Jonson, and of course he would not have known him personally, nor wanted to. *Troilus* is certainly the right play to have performed to represent the Jacobean mood, and

Pandarus the right character for the Player to act. *Fox* is wonderful on sailors, voyages, sea battles, and the like, and *Succession* on reivers of the Scottish border, players, messengers, and other lowlife characters.

Ralegh was the perfect hero for *Fox* because he was enigmatic, skeptical, and tough-minded, and because he was many-sided, more man of action than poet. (No character in *Fox* is primarily a poet or artist of any sort.) But he was also appropriate because, in his writings, his central theme was the triumph of time and the meaning of time and history. Nothing could be more in keeping with this character, then, than to present him meditating over the meaning of time and history.

III

The Succession, as we have said, while the same kind of "venture into the imaginary past," as Garrett calls them, and while obviously so closely related to *Fox* that in many ways they are companion volumes, presenting complementary views of the same period, is in other ways quite different. For one thing, it covers a longer time: while *Fox* was dominated by the image of Ralegh on the eve of his execution in 1618, *Succession* ranges from the birth of James in 1566 to the succession of Charles in 1626, though of course it is focused on the succession in 1603. (Both novels are focused on highly dramatic events which were, at the time, highly suspenseful; for it was by no means a foregone conclusion at the time either that James would succeed or that Ralegh would be executed. Though we know the historical outcome and therefore feel no suspense about what happened, we do feel suspense about just how and why it happened. And this suspense both novels satisfy through the exercise of the informed or historical imagination.) More importantly, the novels differ in that *Succession* has no hero, as we have said; insofar as it does, the hero has to be James, the villain of *Fox*. *The Succession* shows us the sense in which we must say, however much we continue to dislike him, that his succession was a Good Thing.

Against all our impulses to write history nearer to the heart's desire, this prig, pedant, and spoiled boy is here understood and appreciated. Secretary Robert Cecil and others who were pro-

James and appeared as villains in *Fox* are also seen in a different light here. Certainly one motive must have been to explore aspects of the age not covered in *Fox*: e.g., the sovereign as concerned with larger problems than the fate of Ralegh, the Player (wonderful scenes here of playhouses, actors, taverns), the reivers of the Scottish border, the Catholic priest, messengers, and spies of 1566 and 1603, the courtier of 1626 and 1575, and many others. (The Succession of the novel's title is not only that of 1603, but those of 1566, 1587, and 1626.) The book ends with a last glimpse of Elizabeth at Christmas, 1602-3—the last season of the flourishing Elizabethan age and court—so that the final retrospective vision is that of Elizabeth's court, not James'.

The Succession is less obviously appealing than *Fox*: there is no fascinating and "romantic" central figure like Ralegh. The challenge, then, is greater: to make the reader, and the author, accept James and see the other side. The wisdom of acceptance is always rare and difficult, and it is perhaps especially unpopular and implausible now. It is much easier to say that any fool can plainly see that everything is absurd than to say that, in some deep sense beyond complacency, whatever is, is right. We will return to this point at the end; but before leaving *The Succession*, let us look at a few of its other remarkable qualities.

The novel begins with the dying queen in March 1603 and ends with Christmas 1602-3, the last time the queen and court flourished. Garrett's account of this season includes the list of Christmas presents to the queen; with its description of the festivals, customs, ceremonies, and liturgies, it evokes the timeless cycles of the Church and of the land as against the ceaseless passage of time and what the Elizabethans called Mutability.

"Reivers" is wonderful: this world of the Scottish border is that of the ballads specifically, but that of feudal, anarchist societies in many times, in places everywhere from Sicily to the American West.

"Courtier 1626 (1575)" is Robert Carey, now Earl of Monmouth, writing Sir Ferdinando Gorges about his young protege. He describes Elizabeth's visit to Kenilworth in 1575, when Leicester was her favorite (preceding Essex and Ralegh). (The Essex rebellion is covered in "Player: 1602," and the Essex trial and execution [1601] contrasted with Ralegh's.) Carey was the first to bring the news of Elizabeth's death to James; he got nothing from this, but profited from the favor of Charles when he was crowned in 1625.

Thus the whirligig of time brings in his revenges.

Part of the appeal of bad historical novels is to the perennial yearning of the audience to be assured that the rich and powerful and historically famous are no better than they are, and to know the secrets of skulduggery in high places. In contrast, Garrett affirms the reality of heroism, courage, unselfish love in his characters, while also affirming their common humanity. Both novels are acts of faith in the possibility of heroism, affirmations of the reality and validity of love and courage, honor and patriotism, of significance in history— all this while confronting the full reality of evil and apparent chaos. This is clearer in *Fox* than in *Succession*, which is essentially a Novel without a Hero, except to the limited extent that James can be called one. But however good a case the intellect may make for James, the heart's heroine remains Elizabeth, as in the long, nostalgic concluding scene of her last Christmastide.

Perhaps this is the real surprise of the books considered as interpretation of history: instead of coming up with some new and startling thesis about Ralegh, some answer to the innumerable rumors and enigmas that surround him (concerning the School of Night, for instance), Garrett makes him at heart a thoroughly orthodox and, in his way, devout Christian. This is beautifully rendered in Ralegh's letter to his son:

> "Yet even without thinking of mysteries beyond understanding we see how those whom we love are transformed. And being loved by another, we find that we ourselves have been somehow remade and restored . . . . If human love is a weak reflection, a wavering image of the light of infinite and eternal Love (to the extent that it is *caritas* and not the fevered fancy of our lust), then it may be that in the transformation of lovers, each one to the other, we are given a sign of hidden truth . . . . If so, then love has within it the power to transform all of creation, though none of us will ever see it until Judgment Day brings us to life again." (*Fox*, 527)

This faith informs the whole extremely moving last section, in which Ralegh awaits execution, as it does the poems Ralegh wrote about his own death: especially the final couplets, "But from this earth, this grave, this dust,/ My God shall raise me up I trust" and "Just at the stroke when my veins start and spread/ Set on my soul an everlasting head." Similarly, in the letter Ralegh writes to his son, Ralegh concluded that the yeoman farmer is much better off than his father or grandfather—in other words, that the accomplishments of Elizabeth's reign were real, not illusory; that progress is possible and does sometimes occur and that history can be meaningful. (The whole long letter to his son meets the challenge successfully of writing in a style suggesting Ralegh's without producing a travesty of that style.) The scene of the last visit to Ralegh in the Tower by his wife on the night before his execution is beautifully handled; it is not sentimentalized or made to fit any cliches, but shows the reality of unselfish love and courage, as enacted by both Ralegh and Bess.

On the other hand, it is obviously impossible to know precisely how people in the past felt and thought; even when they are quoted exactly, the words don't mean the same thing now as then. So pedantic sticking to the "facts" of history won't work. Thus the only method is Garrett's: to "make a work of fiction, of the imagination, planted and rooted in fact," as he said in the prefatory note to *Death of the Fox*. After mastering all the facts, soaking in all the details, he must imagine the novel, create it from scratch, but staying within the limits of what is not only possible but most probable historically. This will be the "imaginary past," as Garrett calls it in his note to *The Succession*, but faithful to the facts, and hence the past as conceived by a rigorously disciplined imagination.

As Garrett says, this is the "imaginary past" in the sense that it has to be imagined—there is no way of automatically reconstructing it (or them, for the past is not one but many, of course) from facts—but it is solidly based on a thorough knowledge of what historical facts and documents are available and, more importantly, of the writings (both literal and personal—e.g., letters) of the period. So this kind of historical novel is a kind of communal product, in a sense: not based on the limited scope of one man's imagination, but on the productions, fictional and real, of many people's minds—a kind of collective reality created by all of them together. (I am not suggesting that it is a Jungian collective unconsciousness; this communal product is conscious, too, and includes art.) It is at the opposite pole from fantasy, where the writer simply unleashes his imagination with no regard for reality or possibility and no constraints. But it is finally dependent on the unifying imagination of a single author.

IV

Though Garrett scorns the meretricious attractions of the conventional "historical" novel, this kind of deeper historical grounding has its own legitimate delights and satisfactions. Perhaps the chief is the deep sense of difference from the characters. Of course one feels primarily the sense of shared human nature, of common humanity, and this is never lost; but the characters are very different from transplanted moderns, and revealing this difference is one of Garrett's most difficult and most rewarding feats. They have a different sense of time, based on the seasons and the church year; ceremonies and rituals are immensely more important to them than to us; they feel themselves to be far more intimately related to the past than we do. (It is difficult to express these matters abstractly, as Garrett never does: Garrett never mentions them and never calls attention to them; the reader gradually becomes conscious of them as the novel proceeds). Thus without explicit comment, the reader enjoys what is in a sense escape, but meaningful escape—another world that is the same yet different, a comparison and contrast (but always implicit rather than explicit).

But the final wisdom is that of acceptance because the imagined world of the past is not simplified or distorted; neither prettied up nostalgically nor shown as inferior to the present (as in Eco's _Name of the Rose_) but revealed as essentially the same, yet different. (I am, of course, only repeating a Renaissance cliche, as in the title of Joseph Hall's _Mundus Alter et Idem_.) "Wisdom of acceptance" is a dangerous phrase, calling up visions of cosmic Toryism and Margaret Fuller accepting the universe. A better parallel is the reconciliation beyond tragedy, in Shakespeare's romances or in the tragedies at the very end, when the bodies must be carried offstage and life must go on. _Fox_ is, so to speak, the tragedy itself; _Succession_ the moment beyond. Though in history nobody wins permanently (as Carey's story in _Succession_ shows most explicitly), history does have meaning; there is something to say for winners as well as losers, and _Succession_ says it. The attitude is ultimately a religious one, I suppose, and at the risk of pious platitude I have to say that the suggestion is that what thou lovest well remains (thinking of Pound rather than the Bible): this surely is the implication of the

end of *The Succession* with its last long loving look at the last
Christmas season of Elizabeth and her court. The theme is parallel
to that of *Do, Lord*, which ends with the beatific vision of Howie
Loomis, a most unheroic drunk old man, who sees his dead wife
transfigured because he loves and accepts her wholly, choosing her
over any heavenly vision:

> But I had to choose, you see. So instead I looked at her. The
> light of that place and the shade too was on her. She didn't
> change and yet she was changed. What I mean is the light
> wasn't magic and it didn't wipe away any lines of scars. They
> remained. Yet they were beautiful. Even the scars were beau-
> tiful . . . . She looked at the place and smiled at it, and I looked
> at her and wept like a child, not for loss, but because the world
> was so large and so wonderful and we were both in it now and
> forever.
> Then the old dream was gone and I was back in myself
> again, a drunk old man asleep on the floor. A drunk old man
> who had slept like a baby all night long. (253)

The Succession ends with a somewhat similar, though more
communal and more inclusive vision of a Plowman (the fine tissue of
allusions recalling, of course, the Piers Plowman of Langland's great
satire, as well as the archetypal plowman. (His plow will be blessed
on Plow Sunday, which marks the end of Christmastide, for the
plowing race on Plow Monday, with which the cycle of the year
begins again.)

> Now still reeling a little and staring up into sky lit with cold star-
> light. Fearful of nothing, not past or the future. Except for the
> certain knowledge that your head will be heavy and aching by
> daylight. And your laughter will have turned into such groaning
> as will arouse the laughter of others. But for now you are full of
> food and drink and gratitude.
> You believe you are full of love and charity also. And you
> can wish all the world, your friends and your enemies, nothing
> but well. Nothing but good fortune. Wishing the dead, from
> Adam and Eve until now, their rest in peace. And wishing the
> living, one and all, from the beggar in his hedge to the Queen in
> her soft bed . . . .

And what is it she can be dreaming of now, as he, half dreaming, imagines her, that lady minted on his hard-earned coins, lady of ballads and of prayers in the parish church? Is there a place in her dream for this happy drunken plowman, mud of good English earth thick on his boots, out under the stars, who is wishing for her and the rest of the world, for the sake of our own sweet Jesus, a good night? (538)

Garrett's two novels belong in the exalted company of *Ulysses* and a very few other works that carry the novel form as far as it can go, exploiting all its resources and revealing new possibilities. They exhibit the novel operating at so high a level, with such verity of styles and perspectives, with such an easy mastery of the "historical" aspects—of all details of time and place—and so deeply mediated in their study of the relation between the individual life and the history, that they are really something new. (In depth of learning and historical imagination, they belong in the company of Yourcenar's *Memoirs of Hadrian* and Broch's *Death of Virgil*.) They are the finest historical novels I have ever read because they are not, in the conventional sense, historical novels at all.

The paradox is seen most clearly in the styles, which are not imitation Elizabethan or pastiche, but seem authentically modern. The discipline is somewhat like that of translation: as a poetic translation must be, to exist at all, modern poetry, and then be faithful to its original, so the historical novel must work first of all as a modern novel, and then maintain its fidelity to the historical past. These are nearly impossible demands, yet Garrett's novels are as fully historical as they are modern. They are, however, much more than acrobatic feats or displays of virtuosity: they are beautiful, profound, and deeply moving works of art.

Richard Tillinghast

The Fox, Gloriana, Kit Marlow, and Sundry

> Not to forget, now or ever, the long-lost brightness and shine, the hope and glory of those times. But likewise to remember, keeping in mind, the other side of it. Stony discontent, cold despair, end-of-the-world indifference.
>
> Bear with me, ghosts.
> And bless us, one and all, your newfound, long-lost friends.
> Speak to me.
> Speak through me.
> Speak to us.
> —from Arthur's greeting, *Entered from the Sun*

Life in the age of Sir Walter Ralegh, Queen Elizabeth I, Christopher Marlowe, King James I, is familiar to scholars—at least on a professional level—but no one has brought the age to life so encyclopedically and with such animation as George Garrett has done. He has given breath to the ghosts of late sixteenth- and early seventeenth-century England, made the place and the people real and more than real, just as Joyce did for early twentieth-century Dublin, as Tolstoy did for nineteenth-century Russia, as Faulkner did for nineteenth- and early twentieth-century north Mississippi. Garrett appears to have all available knowledge of the material at his fingertips, and he handles it with maximum torque. The flow, the comprehensiveness of his chronicle, might be likened to the figure he gives for the Thames in *The Death of the Fox*: "Longest and largest of English rivers, swallowing other rivers, freshets, streams, rills, and these are fed by the waters of wells and springs beyond counting." In the first chapter of *Entered from the Sun*, the actor Joseph Hunnyman goes "[s]tumbling and staggering through darkness, foot-dragging in mud, in a web of lanes and byways already lost beyond all possibility of finding where he might be or ever again remembering how he might have managed to come this way"—an apt metaphor for the pleasures of becoming absorbed in Garrett's story. Opening one of these books (*Death of the Fox* in 1971, *The Succession* in 1983, and finally, in 1990, *Entered from the Sun*), you gladly give yourself up to the seduction of being led through the city by a master guide whose purpose is to get you good and lost before revealing the secrets he will choose to reveal. London is for Garrett not so much a city as a presence, not delimited by spatial boundaries or even by time:

City of sturdy walls, of stout gates, narrow streets, and long memories. Ever changing and rearranging, repairing and razing, ripping and tearing down, with license and abandon, to build out of your ruins and rubble anew. Spading up the skulls and old coins and broken shards to make room for more.

When we follow Garrett—and I mention the author rather than a deliberately created narrator or character because the authorial narrative voice is always a character coequal with the actors in his stories—down the muddy lanes of London, there is a sense that this is a habitation with no beginning and no end: a matrix.

Garrett's approach to narration is perhaps the most radical development in these novels. *Death of the Fox* starts with a tried and true narrative approach—what we were taught in college to call "central intelligence" third person: "Sir Henry Yelverton lies warm in a great curtained bed, half awake, hearing the sound of breathing, the rustling of his servant . . . . He has heard the sound of chimes and bells, near and far." Much of the book proceeds through similar third-person ruminations by Ralegh. But when we find ourselves about one-third of the way in, characters start confronting us, start getting "in our face." First a soldier. The narrator cautions us: "Best let him speak before he spits on the ground, turns heel, and vanishes." The man squares away and begins, "Well, now, I'll talk to you the same as I would to any man."

We might naturally speak of this soldier, the sailor who follows him in these books, the messenger, priests, border outlaws, and other Elizabethans of high and low estate, as characters in a work of fiction—owing something perhaps to Thomas Overbury's *Elizabethan Characters*. And so they may be thought of. But let us not be in too much of a hurry to take conventional approaches to these books, which have a way of deceptively employing conventions to subvert conventional understandings. Listen to the author's note to

The Succession: "These people, real and imaginary alike and equally, were generous guests and good company, but altogether unhurried. For what does expense of time mean to a ghost?" Ghosts again. I would suggest that the reader take the word very literally. Through the mediation of our author, we feel we commune not with "characters" but with the spirits of the departed. I am convinced this is what is going on. Write me off as a mystic if you like—but not before reading the books.

The Royal Progress is a feature of Queen Elizabeth's reign well known to students of the period. To achieve or to retain royal favor, noblemen and other prominent citizens were expected to invite the Queen for a visit to their country homes. Though the Queen was rich in prerogative and power, she was not necessarily rich in money; so, like the Duke and Duchess of Windsor in our own century, she was an avid house guest. She and her entire entourage. The Section dramatizing one season's Royal Progress, seen in *Death of the Fox* through the eyes of a minor courtier, contains riches enough for ten ordinary novels. The abundance of Garrett's prose makes it impossible to summarize adequately. These royal visits provided diversions and entertainments, with "[h]unting and bearbaiting, tilts and chivalric tournaments. Dancing and music and masques for the garden and in the Hall. Plays performed by Mr. Burbage and the newly licensed Earl of Leicester's men. A very old play done by yokels from Coventry, for laughter."

These junkets gave her subjects a chance to see her, and perhaps more importantly they allowed the Queen to live off other people for weeks at a time, removing the necessity of feeding and housing the Court out of the royal exchequer, and shrewdly, regulating the power of her nobles by reducing their substance. One can imagine the mixed feelings a host must have experienced when the Queen and her army of courtiers and hangers-on descended, as Garrett's courtier puts it, to "drink you dry, cellar and wells, gobble your fodder in stable, pick your meat to slick bones at table. Break glasses and filch a silver salt."

Like the soldier and sailor I have alluded to, this courtier is a type which Elizabethans would have been familiar with from the pages of contemporaries such as Overbury. True enough. But being "real and imaginary alike and equally," they *live*—not merely in the sense of being rounded, vividly created and all the rest of it, though I would not minimize that accomplishment. We are allowed to witness what happens to this courtier once he leaves the court, slipping away "by dark of the moon on account of a misunderstanding with a certain greedy money-lender." How plausible and satisfying it is that the man escapes back to his village, arriving with "his wet ruff and cuffs limp and sad, his hat shapeless as an oyster; muddy as a pig farmer; all soaked to the bone—one last lost sole survivor of the Armada," to marry a prosperous widow and live out his days gratefully, in comfortable retirement!

In these books the world glows with a wholesome materiality (that materiality itself being implicit in our sense of the spirit of life in Elizabethan times), with stones Dr. Johnson could kick with satisfaction. The over-the-hill courtier, having exited London a step ahead of the moneylender, "eating bread and cheese and drinking the widow's cider from a stout wooden cup," shares with many of the characters we encounter in these pages an existential insecurity, a scapegrace gratitude for the sheer fact of having survived. This attitude is deeply Elizabethan: the soul is immortal, damnation or salvation the true contest; but as in the original literature of the period, an awareness of the precariousness of life is never far from people's minds. In this dangerous, hard-to-read world, only clever improvisers will be around to deal with tomorrow's promises and threats.

Perhaps this awareness contributes to Garrett's impulse to improvise, to fly by the seat of his pants. It's not as if he is trying a variety of riffs, to see which one best captures the reader's attention—but rather that his method is to bombard the reader with a number of different approaches. Narrators take shifts as drivers do on a long trip. "You will have noticed," interposes a voice twenty-five pages into *Entered from the Sun*, "how I have suddenly said *we*, as if claiming a place for myself. For though I play no part in this tale, I am nevertheless ever present, a witness to it all, first to last." Then the voice adds: "The others must speak for themselves." It's a game of cat-and-mouse where the narrator is always present stylistically, but where voices running counter to his carry authority too.

Garrett's portrait of Queen Elizabeth and her age is a triumph of research, of imagination, and of that less easy-to-define area where research and the imagination fuse. The novelist has in his imagination entered so deeply into his material that his intuitions allow him to make guesses that turn up facts. I had remembered the passage in

Death of the Fox stating that the Queen's

inmost bathing chambers, where she was alone with herself as naked as God made her, were made of mirrors—walls, floors, and ceiling. To see herself. And not in delusion or vanity or self-love. But naked from all sides, as no one sees himself so that she would know and never forget the truth of herself.

I owe to Fred Chappell, however, with whom I discussed this question one rainy evening last March in a Georgetown bar called The Tombs, the information that only after reading Garrett's book had the curator of royal properties at Windsor Castle divined what the huge rectangular frames stored in an attic there had held—the mirrors having long since been broken. Thus the imagination marries the fact.

Historical novels tend to be popular because they dress up twentieth-century assumptions in period dress. Here, by contrast, readers with a feeling for the period will appreciate that Garrett thinks like an Elizabethan, employs Elizabethan tropes, is obsessed with the obsessions of the period. Take, for example, clothing. We know from Shakespeare's plays the fascination dress holds for everyone from cross-gartered Malvolio to Polonius, with his conventional wisdom: "Costly thy habit as thy purse can buy, / But not express'd in fancy; rich, not gaudy: / For the apparel oft proclaims the man." Count on the author of *Entered from the Sun* to show us not only the splendor of the courtiers, but also the labor of their servants:

And long before first light, all over London and Westminster and the suburbs around them, gentlemen and ladies (false and true) are busy preparing to dress themselves for the pageants and shows at the Tiltyard . . . . And unlucky is that man or woman who has the benefit of the services of nobody else but an ancient, weak-eyed, stiff-jointed servant who has forgotten where all the parts come together and how.

In the account of the Queen's Day at the Tiltyard in London, one of the set pieces one learns to look forward to in these pages, the widow Alysoun—third leg of a triangle with Captain Barfoot and the player Joseph Hunnyman in the final book of the series—gives her companion Hunnyman a lesson on that subtle nexus where fashion and psychology meet (supposing there exists any place where these two do not coincide). Hunnyman questions why, since her hair is blond and beautiful, she insists on wearing a costly red wig, with a pin, "a little sailing ship of fine gold, with brightly enameled sails and flags, to wear in her wig." Why, Alysoun counters, flaunt her golden hair in front of the Queen and her ladies, "young or old indifferently, who have struggled to turn their hair to gold for this occasion. A wig can offend no one or arouse any envy—except for the cost of it." Likewise she makes up her face, which needs no help being any more beautiful than it is. And sure enough, as it turns out, the Queen will notice her, "will poke with the point of her jewelled fan to gain the wandering attention of one of her young maids of honor" and point out the woman who without the red wig and makeup "would be more handsome to behold than any of you."

Entered from the Sun, the last book in the series, concerns itself less with background or atmosphere than its predecessors do. No catalogues of Elizabethan and Jacobean fashions appear here. The pace is faster. This is in some sense a detective story, in which two fictional characters, Captain Barfoot and the player Joseph Hunnyman, investigate the death of Christopher Marlowe. Having created his period atmosphere in the first two books, Garrett seems to have enjoyed the headlong sprint to the finish. England under Elizabeth and James was a viper's nest of spies and counter spies, as Protestant and Catholic, Established Churchman and Dissenter, schemed to position themselves to advantage, while Catholic Spain sought to undermine the kingdom itself. It's fitting, then, that in the last volume of the trilogy we find ourselves plunged into one of the many sub-plots of political intrigue that made the times so hazardous.

The murder of Kit Marlowe, the execution of Sir Walter Ralegh, the struggle for the Succession: these perilous and weighty matters provide Garrett's trilogy with its bedrock of "subject matter," and yet it's rather the great gusto for life's sensual pleasures, the bawdiness, the sense of personal style and courage that we take away from these books. Given the insecurities of the times, the risks both to the self and to the state, why do Garrett's characters laugh, why do they give us so much to admire, why do they enlarge our sense of life's possibilities? It seems to me that this largeness, or "glory" as it is sometimes called in these pages, offering the maximum possible contrast to our own culture, is Garrett's greatest gift to us, living in an age where our personal safety and the stability of our state provide us with a security that the Elizabethans could only dream of. While the Elizabethans lived their fabled lives between peril and joy, · our culture seems to live between comfort and "fun." The difference is immense.

Will late twentieth-century America be remembered as the time when the melting pot deconstituted itself—when each constituent part of our ethnic stew became aware of itself once again as separate and distinct? And not only each ethnic group, but each gender and "lifestyle," confidently telling the rest of the world to butt out? All of this is supported by literary theorists who, having caught the French flu, make an orthodoxy out of fragmentation. The English language at least is still our common tongue, though the culture from which the language—with its vocabulary of 600,000 words and counting, with its claim to be spoken by one quarter of the world's population— has sprung, has come to seem distinctly marginalized in the field of literary studies. Reviewing a new book by Toni Morrison in the April 5, 1992, *New York Times Book Review*, Wendy Steiner writes: "The fact that she speaks as a woman and a black only enhances her ability to speak as an American, for the path to a common voice nowadays runs through the partisan."

In this literary/cultural climate, one way to look at George Garrett's Elizabethan trilogy is as the efflorescence of one of America's several ethnic traditions: the Anglo-American. Those of us who belong to the embattled group can take justifiable pride in the achievements of one of our own. Alternatively, if the tree of the English language, that "great-rooted blossomer," in some sense *belongs to*, is most consanguineous with, the cultural seed from which it sprang, then what subject could be more fitting than the Elizabethan Age, when—largely, we are told by historians, through the efforts of the great poets and playwrights, stimulated by the Age of Discovery and England's self-assertion as a nation—the language defined itself? With brilliant strategy—or is it purely instinctive tropism (or do the great strategists work, as Stonewall Jackson and Mao Tse-tung seemed to do, largely from intuition)?—George Garrett has gravitated back to the English language's cultural home, both in space and time.

If you asked me to point to what I consider the essence of these books, I think I should say: the marvel of vanished glory. Here is the Fox himself, Ralegh getting up out of the boat in which he has been brought down the river to be tried for treason: "'May I ask what you were thinking of?' Apsley still touches his arm as if to direct him, to keep him from falling when he stands. 'I was thinking of the light in our late Queen's eyes . . . .'"

Vanished glory, then. A sense of life lived on a heroic scale. Laughter and courage. Shrewdness and belief. A common voice that transcends the fragmentation of our age. If our great storytellers can discover in themselves the largeness to imagine that glory, and to transmit it to us, then perhaps the rumors of our demise have been greatly exaggerated.

The Succession

Brendan Galvin

Your Messenger of 1566

(For George Garrett, after *The Succession*)

All royals and their conspiracies
be damned, then and now: I wanted
to be Jack Scarecrow, Jonathan
Beanstalk, a name changing with
the weave of the day, Tweed, Cheviot,
birdsong in their saying,
my hoofbeats knocking on bridges
across the Eske, Wiske, Swale, Ouse,

to seem to have risen from earth
and grass four-hundred-thirty
summers ago, galloping past
ruined Lindisfarne—its cormorants
and eiders already migrated
into calligraphy in the Book of Kells—

to pass through Grassmarket, Wansbeck,
Morpeth, Peltry, Tuxford, as through
textures of heather, bracken, and broom
wild with wefts of marigold and cherry,
rose and oakwood strawberry, Sir,
riding down the England of a man
who knows the strength of a named thing.

Richard A. Betts

"To Dream of Kings": *George Garrett's* The Succession

The same year, 1983, that saw Umberto Eco's *Name of the Rose* published in English also saw another significant contribution to historical fiction, George Garrett's second novel of the Renaissance, *The Succession: A Novel of Elizabeth and James.* While the former received, and continues to receive, much deserved critical attention, as well as a surprising popular success, the latter has been relatively neglected by both critic and reader. Why this disparity in their cultural reception should exist lies outside the purpose of this study and, no doubt, beyond the scope of strictly literary considerations in general. But their fundamental similarities as novels remain striking: both engage unfamiliar materials rooted deep in the past; both are erudite, complex and stylistically sophisticated works of art; indeed, both exhibit a postmodern sensibility and the innovative techniques of metafiction; and, finally, while both belong to the genre of the historical novel (a notoriously baggy monster, ill-defined and shape-shifting), they each uniquely expand and reinvigorate what is meant by that term. Although Garrett's novel has been highly praised, it has received little of the critical attention it merits and rewards.[1] In his monograph on Garrett, however, R.H.W. Dillard does invoke Eco's distinction between "closed" and "open" texts in order to claim for *The Succession* what he sees Eco envisioning in his own novel, "a reader capable of active participation in the openness of the text" (150). One of the things that "openness" entails for the reader of *The Succession* is the necessity of adapting to radical change, for the novel is an elaborate meditation on the nature of history, here revealed as a mysterious yet intensely human fabrication, the essence of which is change. Change in all its guises and ramifications—as succession, alteration, alternation, conversion, transmutation, metamorphosis, turn and counterturn—constitutes the theme, the overwhelming preoccupation, of this work. In Garrett's detailed exploration of this phenomenon, however, he will insist that the more things change, the more they stay the same. Garrett's "world" may be described as "the Christian fallen world:

a world of unrelenting change, inevitable decay, unavoidable death; a world of sin in which vice and folly, lust and betrayal, sins deadly or merely degrading do not just afflict human beings but are of their very nature; a world in continual decline toward perpetual failure" (Dillard 10). But within the clamor and commotion of historical life, beneath (or above) the chaos of folly, failure, and sin, Garrett is able to find a measure of stillness, stability, and order.

An equally important preoccupation of the novel, animating Garrett's protean conception of history, is the power of the creative imagination to encompass, shape, and recover the elusive and mutable past. The imagination, acting on and through memory in a variety of ways and from many different motives, allows access to the past and finally conveys to consciousness in mind or art our private and collective histories. If change in human history is the irreducible substance of this novel, then acts of the imagination are the method, the means, of its recovery. Furthermore, as Dillard suggests, *The Succession* engages not only the author but the characters and the reader as well in these crucial acts of imagination. Garrett, himself, has brought to our attention the special importance of the imagination to his historical fictions, where there is deployed "the human imagination in action, itself dramatized as it struggles with surfaces, builds structures with facts, deals out and plays a hand of ideas, and most of all, by conceiving the imagination of others, wrestles with the angel . . . of the imagination" ("Dreaming" 420).

All of the historical material of this novel, the substance of the story and the stories within the story, may be subsumed under the heading of change. The world here represented asks, what is history but change? It is the obscure but inexorable metamorphosis by which the future becomes the present and the present instantly becomes the past, which, thereafter, exists only in the fallible memory of man. The novel is "an aesthetic meditation on the creation and revelation of meaning in the succession of moments (real, remembered, dreamed, and imagined) that make up the living nexus of time" (Dillard 140-41). The diurnal present is the center, the eternal moment when one thing becomes another and all change takes place. The chaos of the quotidian is epitomized by the aged, dying Queen Elizabeth as she shuts herself up in her chambers in order "to banish the clamor of the present" (Garrett, *Succession* 533). Daily existence for everyone from the Queen to her lowliest subject is confused, uncertain, and often mortally treacherous.

The most obvious change is that which gives the novel its title, the succession to the throne of Elizabeth by James. This alteration, deriving from the ultimate transformation one can undergo, will bring momentous changes to the country and its people, but these events are not really the main concern of the novel, and, of course, we know what they are, just as we know all along that James will succeed, despite the Queen's silence and Secretary Cecil's doubts. What the novel concerns are successions of all kinds, alternations and transformations experienced by a wide variety of historical man. In Garrett's imagination these experiences also become questions of perception, an exploration of the ways the characters perceive, in their various imaginative recollections, the changes which constitute their histories.

Appropriately enough, midway through the novel there stands the section called "Reivers 1602," which clearly shows the author developing variations on the theme of change. The reivers are Scottish outcasts and thieves engaged in a seemingly endless series of raids and escapes back and forth across the border between Scotland and England. This literal border stands figuratively for many "borders" between one state or condition or another, between which everyone must inevitably shuttle. Just as the succession depends upon Elizabeth's finally crossing the bounds of mortality, so that change will entail a similarly profound change in James as he crosses the border to take possession of the English crown. James, himself, sees that "in changing from one place to another, from one throne to the other, he, too, will be changed . . . a complete reformation of himself, a new birth (as it were)" (259). Ironically, the border skirmishing which seems such a way of life to these reivers, gathered for an evening of storytelling in their round tower stronghold, is destined for extinction with the coming unification of the two kingdoms. As old Blind Jock tells the young firebrand, "the bells of Scotland ringing to announce it . . . will mark the end of us" (228).

The stories within the story that is the "Reivers" section, itself a story within the whole, especially underscore the notion of history as story, historiography as storytelling, a narrative with a beginning and an end encompassing change. The stories range from the fantastic, through the apocryphal and legendary, to the eye-witness account supposedly "shoveling up plain truth" (240). But the theme is invariably change in one or more of its manifestations, especially those occasioned by the interplay of appearance and reality and the occurrence of unexpected reversals. A King pretends to be a commoner and transforms a poor deserving farmer into a rich man (228-36); the imaginative daring of the Bold Buccleuch brings about the miraculous rescue of Kinmont Willy from his English captors (237-46). The theme is sounded first by the reiver Sly's tale of love and betrayal, which concerns a young man whose gypsy wife imparts to him the secret of transforming himself into a bird and back again. In the course of the story, which, having been interrupted, has had to be modified by the teller in the act of telling, there are several metamorphoses. These culminate with the gypsy wife, now changed into a hunting hawk, perched on the arm of the Earl of Bothwell (195-212), an actual but incredible historical figure, whose escapades make up the following story. Thus, ends turn into beginnings, and fiction modulates into history and back again.

Not only is change constant and pervasive on the border, but it suffuses every facet of Elizabethan life and times as depicted in other scenes, widely displaced in space and time. One need only recall the radically various experiences of the Priest, revealed in the poignant documents that constitute his history. For him, as for many, the most significant changes are grounded in the religious turmoil resulting from the break with Rome, the dissolution of the monasteries, and the rise of militant protestantism. The conflict between his faith and an accommodation to these cultural realities has transformed his relationship with his persecuted fellow priests, with his conformist family, and, most importantly, with himself: "So much has passed, so much is greatly changed for all of us. So much is changed that I cannot easily recognize myself in my own story" (86). Or one might recall the Queen at the outset lamenting the fact that "there is no one for her to listen to. No one left for her to hear." Most all who now surround her are "frivolous children," and those of her own generation "have gone to darkness" (3). Or recall the Queen later musing on the vigorous, profit-minded, forward-looking London merchants, who are gradually gaining control of government and supplanting the nobility in leadership: "Change is the music these merchants sing and dance to. Change is the fire where they warm their hands and hearts" (535). Or one remembers the Courtier, thinking, "It is strange how things turn and change. Strange the distance between beginnings and endings" (164). From his perspective in 1626, he is especially qualified to remark on the mutability of men's fortunes. He recalls the Earl of Leicester first in all his shining glory at the

Progress of '75 and then later grown old and fat, barely able to sit his horse, during the crisis of '88 (156-65). Equally to the point are his own changes in fortune, which, befitting the gambler that he (and every courtier) is and must be, have left him, for the moment, in the good graces of the new king.

Perhaps the most important aspect of change in the novel involves the succession of time, the continuous alteration of the present as the unrealized future is transformed into the recollected past. Thus, the characters live in an ever-changing present which has a problematical relationship to both the future and the past, and this greatly affects the perception of their history. Garrett shows them, at any particular moment, experiencing the existential now, imagining what might be, and recalling what they believe to have been. In the minds of his characters past, present, and future all have equal importance, and any of the temporal dimensions may, at times, be privileged. The Queen, for example, gives precedence to the past; the Messenger has a talent (and a need) for imagining the future; and the Priest most intensely feels the weight of the present. Visions of the times (past, present, future) as good or bad, disastrous or fruitful, succeed and alternate, one after another, even in the same consciousness. *The Succession* seems to present a history more like a daydream than a chronicle. Without inherent logic or chronological continuity, this version of history is characterized, at least on the surface, by chaos and discontinuity and dominated by change.

Although at first disconcerting to the reader, it is entirely appropriate that the disorientation which marks the thematic texture should be reflected in the formal structure and prose style of the novel. Garrett's complex manipulation of the time scheme, for example, reinforces the perception of public and private histories as subjectively relative, fragmented, and riddled with change. If one must assign a present time, a "now" in the foreground of this novel, which abruptly shifts back and forth from moment to moment within the half-century encompassing the reign of Elizabeth I, it would be the winter months of 1602-03 directly preceding her death. More specifically, present time consists of those few moments of reflection and recollection which constitute the opening and closing sections, devoted to the Queen, the two sections where Cecil is the locus of consciousness, and the short section at the center focusing on James. An apparent aim of these sections, together less than a fourth of the book, is to dramatize the "suspense" of the succession,[2] but ironically and in keeping with Garrett's purpose of maintaining a sense of cosmic uncertainty, the Queen's death and the naming and notifying of her successor are not revealed here but rather in a casual, near throwaway turn by the fatuous Courtier. Nor are these present-time sections, in their historical representation, at all free of "the snarls and skeins of memory" which pervade the entire novel (3). Elizabeth recalls a whole gallery of ghosts from the past, prompted by a taking of the roll of bygone New Year's Gifts, which are conjured up item by item without reference to their historical chronology but according to their personal, emotional weight and significance (516-33). Similarly, for Cecil, it is his personal ambition which arbitrarily sends him back in time to fragments of his childhood or the mosaic of motives behind the long dead royal letters.

The reader may also be disconcerted to encounter a novel, set in the remote, unfamiliar past, that is made up of sixteen separate sections focusing on, or using as a central consciousness, seven different major characters, both historical and imaginary. Furthermore, each character speaks primarily from a different period in time. The Queen, for example, ruminating on her life in 1603, is abruptly followed by the Messenger, riding south from Edinburgh to London in 1566, the earliest narrative point in time. The Priest, writing out his fears and frustrations in 1587, is followed by the Courtier, happily dictating his memoirs in 1626, the latest narrative point in time, but he is looking back to a historical moment in 1575. This series of narratives, without apparent order, is partially repeated several times, with some characters, the Messenger, the Courtier, the Secretary, making several appearances, others only one. In addition, within every section, because the theme and purpose is the recovery of history, albeit a scattered, elusive, fragmentary one, there are numerous flashbacks and flashforwards, which disrupt and complicate the evocation of the past as it is individually and collectively perceived. There is a moment in one of the Messenger's sections when the flux of time and change, in all its complication, is strikingly rendered by the narrative structure. From the outset the Messenger is seen primarily from without by an omniscient narrator, who elaborately imagines him, but also, in part, through his own narrative voice, speaking in quotation in the first person. At a particular moment, as he rides south to London with the news of James's birth, he undertakes to imagine (unbeknownst to the reader) not only what he will see and hear and do on this trip but also what he will think about in this present of 1566. In his reverie he imagines a future in which he has retired from the craft of secret-agentry and will be sitting at a friendly tavern playing cards with a few drinking companions (169-71). In this future he imagines telling the fascinating story of his past as a schoolboy, student at Cambridge, man-about-town, and exile spying on other exiled Protestants for the elder Cecil. Past, present, and future are juxtaposed on the same page, held in precarious suspension by the author's manipulations. To further complicate matters, the narrator engages the Messenger in a dialogue about his future, using both the third and second person (171). In this way Garrett achieves a sense of the simultaneity of temporal perception and evokes a complex matrix of historical change.

Finally, Garrett employs a number of linguistic and stylistic devices to reinforce thematic concerns about the changeable, ambiguous, elusive nature of historical experience and our recollection of it. Garrett's use of language reflects an Elizabethan sense of the possibilities of a new, vigorous English. Exuberant, at times verbose, it is uninhibited by rules of usage calcified by time. It deliberately defies static conventions in order to reinvigorate expression and involve the reader in a dynamic esthetic interchange. Abrupt shifts in point of view, tense, and person are typical, and sentence fragments are commonplace, especially in the Messenger sections, where sentence subjects are routinely left off to emphasize the verb and its tense: "Will be riding southward along the North Road first from Beal to Belford" (169). Such shifts and fragmentation, as well as the often elliptical syntax, effectively suggest the incompleteness and discontinuity encountered in the historical subject matter. Furthermore, the range of expression is considerable, nearly all-inclusive, from the lyrical to the prosaic, from the highly formal to the immediately colloquial, from the intensely metaphorical to the necessarily discursive, collectively reflecting the various, protean nature of experience.

Even though *The Succession,* in form and content, teems with change of every conceivable kind, especially that occasioned by the passage of time and our perception of that process, one can also discern stability within the chaos, quiet amid the clamor, and inevitable mortality at the culmination of life. In this sense the novel's representation of change recalls that "living literature" Faulkner spoke of which derives from the fact that "'living' is motion and 'motion' is change and alteration and therefore the only alternative to motion is unmotion, stasis, death . . . ." George Garrett elsewhere has argued that "the period of the Tudors witnessed more radical changes than any in our time." He further contends that although the Elizabethans welcomed and delighted in constant change, accepting it without undue concern, there existed below the surface a deep-seated conservatism: "while England burned with change, turn and counterturn for half a century, it was, we can see now, a time of relative sameness and stability" ("Dreaming" 418). This paradoxical situation is mirrored in the very narrative structure which seems so disconcertingly complicated and disjunctive when first encountered.

Underlying or coexistent with the narrative flux, there is a redeeming stability and symmetry. Indeed, it is surprising, as Dillard has noted, that "out of all this apparent disorder and disconnection such a coherent and orderly and meaningful whole takes shape" (144). For example, the five sections devoted to the Messenger, which seem to be scattered among the total sixteen (which are deliberately not numbered or listed in a table of contents), are actually systematically placed, with one exception, at intervals of three: in the 2nd, 6th, 12th, and 15th positions. Significantly, the Messenger occupies the next-to-first and next-to-last positions, for it is his journey from Edinburgh to London, from James to Elizabeth, which is the main thread binding together this novel that spans so many polarities. Similarly, the passages belonging to the Courtier appear at the (nearly) symmetrical positions of 5th, 10th, and 14th. In addition to providing comic relief and offering a perspective removed in time and social status, the Courtier directly corresponds to the Messenger in their two last appearances, where the one rides north with the news of Elizabeth's death, as (structurally) the other concludes his ride south with the news of James's birth, which precipitates the issue of succession.

The placement of each of the other sections of the novel is also carefully calculated to provide an orderly and stable base in the narrative structure to support the complex superstructure of change and variation. The aged, past-obsessed Queen is introduced first; impatient, middle-aged, and anxiously looking to his future, the King enters at the midway point. Robert Cecil, the Secretary, vitally concerned with the succession, appears in the 3rd and 11th sections soon after and comments upon the rulers he must serve. In the latter section Cecil brings together Elizabeth and James in the only sense in which the two protagonists meet in the novel, that is, in their correspondence, which Cecil thoroughly mines for every nuance of character and motive. As we have seen, the "Reivers" occupies a kind of border position, taking the reader into Scotland at the half-way point just before he meets James. Finally, the two major sections focusing on the Priest and on the Player, the one dramatizing the religious upheaval of the first part of Elizabeth's reign, the other concerning a political crisis in the later part, are placed strategically in the middle of the two halves of the novel.

The "sweet truth at the heart of changing" (393) is further evident in the fact that the novel begins and ends, as it appropriately should, with Elizabeth. Significantly, the brief opening section, set in March 1603 just before her death, is the latest chronological portrait we have of her. In the final section, "Christmastide 1602-1603," the novel ends where it began with the Queen as the center of consciousness at the end of a long life and reign. The course of public, collective history is paralleled by private, individual (even royal) histories. Just as Garrett has, in large, effectively obliterated time as a chronological sequence progressing along a linear continuum, so he, in small, reveals a Queen trapped in and pondering the ephemeral nature of human existence—from dust to dust—"How dust will begin to dance and then be gone again with the coming or going of a shadow" (518). Elizabeth's great burden now is the knowledge of her impending death, a death which here stands metaphorically for all mortality, all "dust dancing," and it lies at the thematic center of the novel even as it is elaborated in the framing sections. Ironically, however, in Garrett's narrative her death takes place off-stage, remaining at last the immutable, ineffable, indescribable mystery that it is.

Death is the ultimate moment, the final continuity in the midst of constant variation, the reconciliation of the opposites that generate change. There and in other significant moments in the midst of life the universal and the particular, time and eternity, stasis and change, are held briefly in suspension. The novel, in which so much happens over such a length of time, is anchored by a number of still moments set amid the maelstrom of activity. Each of these occasions is brief and transitory but carries lasting significance, like the gold which Elizabeth contemplates, forever being "melted down and new minted" (520), changing but unchanged. There is the Queen musing alone in her ghost-filled gallery at Richmond Palace; James warming his backside at the fireplace after the aborted hunt; Cecil, late into the night, reading and re-reading the royal letters; the Messenger leisurely riding south through the Lammermuir hills. The Player, the Courtier, the Reivers can similarly be linked to precise, specific moments in time, which recall T.S. Eliot's "moment in the rose-garden," each "At the still point of the turning world" (Eliot 119, 121). Such is the importance of Christmas in the final section of the novel. Despite the "sorry and dangerous days," the "Time has come round" (501). The holiday represents stability, even transcendence, in a chaotic, turbulent world.

Christmas is being kept in England as it has always been. According to the old traditions and customs, which, since they solve no riddles from the past nor answer any questions put to the future, must be wholly of the here and now. Each time recovered and renewed. Each time . . . partaking of the spirit of the first time. (536)

In the last paragraphs of *The Succession,* in a scene reminiscent of the ending of Joyce's "The Dead," the compass expands beyond the Queen's chambers to include at this Christmastide all of celebrating England, which finally becomes embodied in the image of one "happy drunken plowman" standing under the stars after the holiday festivities. Garrett has already explicitly enjoined the reader ("you") to place himself in the plowman's muddy boots as he, "half dreaming," attempts to imagine for his dying Queen, and everyone, a peaceful goodnight. Simultaneously, Garrett offers a corresponding image of the Queen perhaps "dreaming" of this same universal plowman (537-38). This reciprocal vision is simply the last, but eminently typical, of an extraordinary series of acts of imagination, which Garrett claimed of his earlier novel, *Death of the Fox,* "were the chief burden of the story." He has made it quite clear that recovering the past in a historical novel requires "a commitment of one's own imagination," as well as recognition of the centrality, in such fiction, of "the human imagination, the possibility, limits, and variety of imaginative experience" ("Dreaming" 416).

To recreate a world dauntingly unfamiliar and distanced nearly four centuries into the past calls for an imagination that is essentially innocent, unmediated by present concerns, and unencumbered by

preconceived notions. According to Garrett, much must be un-
learned if one is to reinvent accurately and honestly ("Dreaming"
416). The artist's imagination, acting on the available facts, documents, and minutiae of history, is the necessary means by which the
reader gains access to a credible but not necessarily transparent
past. Although the same could be said of other historical novelists,
Garrett differs, at least in degree, in the extent to which he insists
upon the active imaginations of his characters, actual or invented, as
indispensable to the task of creating their own histories. In addition,
the author frequently draws the reader into the imaginative enterprise, forcing him to engage his imagination along with the characters
and their creator.

The interwoven story of the Messenger is instructive in showing
how Garrett dramatizes the crucial importance of the imagination,
transforming an esthetic need into both a literary theme and a
narrative method. The Messenger, spy for Cecil, riding south with
the news of James's birth, has been described as he registers in great
sensory detail the castles, towns, and countryside along the way and
as he imagines a future time and place in which he tells of his past
adventures as a youth, student, and eventually master spy. At the
end of his last section, as he and Cecil finally approach the Queen's
palace to fulfill the mission, there occurs one of the most startling
sentences in the novel: "But none of this has happened yet" (492).
Suddenly, the reader, at the end of the Messenger's story, is taken
back more than four hundred pages to the beginning, where the
Messenger is just starting his ride from the lowlands and first enters
into the "long daydream" which is his story and a history conceived
as an act of the imagination. Garrett, imagining what might have happened in Elizabethan England, encompasses the Messenger's imagining what is happening, did happen, and will happen. Garrett and
the Messenger accomplish complementary acts of imagination; the
author's imaginative reconstruction of history derives from imagining
his character's imagination in action. The reader, also, is deeply
implicated in the process when Garrett explicitly draws attention to
it and underscores the point by concluding with an irony directed at
the reader:

"To imagine too much beforehand," [the Messenger] would tell
you, "can only double the pain of disappointments when they
come along. (As they will come.) And, so far as I can judge,

imagination can add nothing at all to life's pleasures. Therefore, let be what will be." (493)

Garrett has written, "To dream of kings you must imagine a world to contain them. Imagining that world makes it so . . ." (*Death* 42). His grand elaboration of the myriad acts of imagination, large and small, in *The Succession* is the means by which he and his characters recover and convey the broad yet detailed panorama of the Elizabethan past. It is revealed not as conventional history but as a complex fictional montage, reveling in its confusions and contingency while capturing simultaneously both its public and private historical significance. Often the activity of the imagination takes place in those still moments when the major characters recollect in tranquility the history with which they are familiar but which in their memories or daydreams has become individually ordered, invested with personal significance, distorted by hopes and fears, or even obscured by forgetfulness and illusion. An example is the author's portrayal of the Queen, who reveals much of her history of public and private relationships, not chronologically but as she muses randomly on the lists of old New Year's gifts, which conjure up a melange of memories of love, hate, ambition, loyalty, betrayal, and death. Like the other main characters, she is shown at a point where her imagination is "free to shuffle and deal the greater and lesser cards of memory. Arranging and rearranging them in different patterns" (533).

There are, moreover, acts of imagination within acts of imagination within the ultimate creative act which is the novel. Typical is the imaginary colloquy between the Messenger and Captain Norton, who meet briefly in the Messenger's prescient imagination, but in Garrett's containing imagination they are juxtaposed to contrast their cultural and political values in a changing world and to bring to the surface the Messenger's continuing anxiety about his own, probably violent, death (30-40). It is ironic yet highly plausible that it is the Messenger, secret agent in a treacherous world, who has the least chance of realizing a future and yet is so adept, indeed desperate, in imagining one. He who fears to sleep and dream must find refuge in the creative daydream, "seeking not to waste himself in regret for a lost past. Hoping never to allow himself to fear the future" (493). As previously suggested, the "Reivers" section combines several different stories of varying degrees of probability within a framing story carefully controlled by an anonymous narrator, but it should be emphasized that Garrett deliberately draws attention to the tales as creative acts, which are intimately bound to their source in the story-teller and whose imaginative truth is independent of their proximity to fact or fantasy. The crippled Sly, old Blind Jock, brave Red Tom are all as different and specific as their stories, which manifest that "what is true is always more secret and subtle than what is witnessed and that there may well be as much or as little of truth in a tale of talking ravens as in a messenger's report of victory or defeat in battle" (237).

Garrett's controlling act of imagination is replicated in every character who plays a major role. To point briefly, however, at several instances cannot do justice to the overall importance here of the imagination as the dominant actualizing principle, informing an extremely complicated interplay of character, action, point of view, and narrative structure. For example, there is the emotional intensity packed into the captured documents of the fugitive Priest, especially the "letters," which are all that remain of him, since we know by the framing device that he has been taken, tortured, and executed by Walsingham's men. In the restrictive but highly personal epistolary form the Priest vividly portrays the plight of the persecuted English Catholic and poignantly dramatizes his own fear and faith, courage and despair. Elsewhere, there are Cecil and James, both engaged in the risky endeavor of fathoming the intentions of the enigmatic Queen, whose imagination is clearly more than a match for theirs. Indeed, they both essentially fail to imagine her course of action and, thus, their own prospects. Cecil retires with the equivocation, "True or false, it's too late now to do anything more than hope and pray" (361). James, finally, can imagine the Messenger but not his message (262). Understandably, the old Courtier, acknowledging that memory is a "deceiver" (151), remembers "that time of Queen Elizabeth . . . as another country, a place on the far edge of some ragged map" (153). Even so, and despite the reductive commentary of his young clerk, he furnishes valuable historical insights. The foregoing are meant merely to suggest the hundreds of instances, major and minor, of the imagination at the task of recovering the past. Imagining, visualizing, picturing, half-dreaming, and daydreaming constitute the action of the novel and the means by which the past is rendered.

Garrett, the daydreaming artist responsible for this historical novel based necessarily on the disparate, voluminous written record, has found an analogue for himself and the reader in the figure of Robert Cecil studying one portion of the record, the exchange of letters between Elizabeth and James. He sees himself, as Garrett must also, like other men of vision, merchants and Princes, who "can, from some broken pieces, imagine and recreate the world anew" (299). Furthermore, Garrett frequently urges the reader to participate in that creative process.[3] Early on, we are asked to "imagine" ("Imagine that, would you") with the Queen (5) and be the "someone else" looking over her solitary shoulder (10). Later, of the Messenger, we are invited to "Ask him directly about this, and he'll tell you nothing much" (189). But it is in the lengthy *tour de force* which is the "Player's" section that the reader ("you") is most thoroughly integrated into the imaginative activity through the device of having the narrator/secret agent refer to himself in the second person. Throughout, as "you," we are identified with the secret agent who seeks out the Player at his theater, engages him in lively conversation and food and drink, and finally analyzes the secret letters which were the result of the Player's stint as a spy. The reader and "you" (the narrator/secret agent) clearly merge at a point when he has just finished reading part of the Player's testimony. He ("you") says, "Strange to be reading this now. Strange after so many things . . . have been resolved" (425). The reader of historical fiction must also find it strange to be reading a version of history, *The Succession,* after that history has long been "resolved." Garrett's method is to place the reader, imaginatively, in the shoes of those contemporary with the times, when one does not yet know how it all comes out. By doing so, Garrett exploits the appeal of historical fiction and engages "The thing which from one imagination kindles another . . . the unseen power which serves to set imagination free to adventure as much as any soldier, sailor, or adventurer" (300). Even though historical experience is ever-changing, chaotic, and ultimately unfathomable, this novel demonstrates that the human imagination, not only the artist's but everyman's as well, has the power to stop time, impose order, and create the world anew. Like many another historical novel, *The Succession* provides in full mea-sure the people, events, and circumstances of the past, the raw materials of history, but it is unique in the extent to which it allows the characters and the reader to participate along with the author in the vital act of imagining a world to contain them.

NOTES

[1] In a front-page review Maureen Quilligan called *The Succession* "a major achievement in fiction." Monroe Spears considered the novel worthy of "the exalted company of *Ulysses* and a very few other works that carry the novel form as far as it can go, exploiting all its resources and revealing new possibilities" (276).

[2] For a useful discussion of Garrett's *Death of the Fox* and the unique rhetorical situation in the historical novel, where the materials "exist prior to and independent of [the novelist's] rendering of them," see Turner (44-45).

[3] Tom Whalen focuses exclusively on the numerous formal devices by which Garrett attempts to implicate the reader in his novel (14-21).

Works Cited

Dillard, R.H.W. *Understanding George Garrett.* Columbia: U of South Carolina P, 1988.

Eliot, T. S. *The Complete Poems and Plays 1909-1950.* New York: Harcourt, 1952.

Faulkner, William. *The Mansion.* New York: Vintage-Random, 1955.

Garrett, George. *Death of the Fox.* Garden City: Doubleday, 1971.

_____. "Dreaming with Adam: Notes on Imaginary History," *New Literary History*, 1 (1970): 407-21.

_____. *The Succession.* Garden City: Doubleday, 1983.

Quilligan, Maureen. "A Time for Spies." *New York Times Book Review* 25 Dec. 1983: 6.

Spears, Monroe. "George Garrett and the Historical Novel." *Virginia Quarterly Review* 61 (1985): 262-76.

Turner, Joseph W. "History and Imagination in George Garrett's *Death of the Fox.*" *Critique* 23 (1982): 31-46.

Whalen, Tom. "The Reader Becomes Text: Methods of Experimentation in George Garrett's *The Succession: A Novel of Elizabeth and James.*" *The Texas Review* 4 (1983): 14-21.

Reginald Gibbons

George Garrett's Whole New World: The Succession

Near the end of George Garrett's great novel, someone thinks, "world is upside down and inside out these days. All things changing for the worse and no help for it." It's curious that an apocalyptic sentiment should appear in this novel too, but perhaps it is only a measure of the sweep of any large novel, that must come inevitably to such considerations. What is certain is that Garrett's long-awaited sequel to his novel of Sir Walter Ralegh, *The Death of the Fox*, has a whole world in it, begins with a birth and ends with a death, and compasses an astonishing range of experience between them, all of it convincing and masterfully orchestrated to touch on many serious and weighty subjects.

Garrett experimented with novelistic form in *The Death of the Fox*, which proceeds in no straightforward way, but by moving back and forth in time and place, draws all of Ralegh's experience, and the mood and complexities of England and the Elizabethan court, toward the hours before Ralegh's execution. His imprisonment in the Tower has turned, under King James, from a political expediency into an appointment with the headsman. His recollections of youth, of the death of his young son, of every precious memory he retains whether of happiness or pain, adventure or court intrigue, gradually build such a convincing intimacy that his death horrifies the reader as much as any fictional death can. The triumph of Garrett's formal experiment was a triumph of feeling, and it is very powerful.

In *The Succession*, the experiment continues, and has taken a further step. This novel also weaves back and forth in time and place, but with a principal difference: there is no single central character through whose life this world may be gauged; there is no single narrator; there is no plot, but only plots, in both senses of the word. The element common in all of Garrett's plots is the language. While this is not truly Elizabethan (it would be a great obstacle if it were), it is nonetheless greatly enriched by echoes of an earlier usage, full of the lively freshness of diction and syntax that have not yet yielded to the written word, but still have the unraveling delights of spoken cadences full of qualifications, reminders, place-names of great individuality and historical weight, and curious, vivid vocabulary. The novel is a kind of stage—no surprise—on which actors in related, but separate, dramas appear, briefly or at length, and from which they then exit, some to return for another scene, others not, even though their stories have not been played out to the end, and we must guess what those ends might be.

Two minor characters appear repeatedly, linking top and bottom of the social order, a courtier whose fortunes have undergone typically Elizabethan and Jacobean reversals, and a messenger, who picks his way by horse through the length of England southward in 1566 to take word to Sir Robert Cecil, Elizabeth's closest advisor, of the birth in Scotland of James, a male cousin to the unmarried Queen, and the likeliest candidate for the crown, if at her death he is still alive and no one has interceded. Elizabeth did not indicate her successor until she lay on her deathbed many years later, and even that equivocal nod of the head was open to varying interpretations. Claimants to the throne were various and contentious; the long stewing war with Spain would be affected by the identity of her successor; bitter cruel suppression of the Catholics in England had taken many lives and was not yet over. Elizabeth's strategy was to refuse to name her successor. She made everyone play a game of loyalties that were nothing more than guesses and bets—on which life and property were ultimately staked. Out of this period of great political anxiety for the future, and of widespread suffering among the poor, Garrett has made the unlikeliest sort of historical novel, in which the very situation of the nation is the subject, and no one life rehearses its history fully to provide the reader with the customary satisfactions of plot.

The novel does not even proceed far enough in time to settle the effect of the succession; after Elizabeth has nodded her head to James's name, the book returns to Christmas, 1603, favoring the keen uncertainty still in the air then, to a dead resolution of tensions. Thus Garrett has chosen a fictional method that is the very embodiment of his subject: an artful refusal to settle the narrative on a single course. His three main themes are large. One of them is change: our perception of the Elizabethan and Jacobean world as being much of a piece is false, for the actors on this stage see such great decline from earlier times that one of them can say in 1626 that in 1603, just before Elizabeth's death, "the world was powerfully simple then."

Garrett portrays an age of shifting ground, and this too matches his own shifts from scene to scene, and from one year to another one far off, as his method gradually offers the perspective of many figures in a series of tableaux.

Another manifestation of this is the way in which Garrett's purely technical resources often convey one man's thinking or talking dissolving into another's, at another moment, as if to suggest a crowded simultaneity of diverse historical moments and experiences, especially in the brilliant section "Player." A second theme is all manner of duplicity, deceit, dissembling, disguise, treason, treachery, tricks, spying, acting, and so on. The instances of this are so numerous they seem finally to be the fabric of life, from the intricate ploys of Elizabeth's letters to James, to the ruse by which a wounded small Scot beats a great emboldened English lord and steals his horse. A third theme is the richness of intense consciousness: of the moment, of place, of pleasure, of conviction and cause, of peril and fear. These three themes are braided in a single cord, which is the struggle for knowledge that will give one man, or woman, dominion over another, or, in a few cases, over himself and his soul.

Perhaps "braid" is the wrong figure. The novel is more like an enormous web or network, each knot of which will tremble when any other in touched. Cross-references, echoes, abrupt truncations and later continuations, a marvelously complicated interplay between past and future, known and unknown, one moment's certainty versus the next instant's doubt—such virtuoso manipulation of the stuff of the novel makes it seem even larger than it is, for its capaciousness stands in great contrast to the mere encyclopedic variety of the usual sort of historical novel, or the voluminous exhaustive campaigns of writers like Gaddis or Barth, or for that matter the catchalls of popular writers like Michener. *The Succession* is actually a work of great compressed intensity, cleverly disguised by the complicated leisure that must be taken by the characters in it in order for them to recover as fully as they can their memories of what has happened to them. (In the case of the messenger, it is time taken to look ahead and foretell what the journey will be like—yet another surprising twist.) There are so many tricks of fiction in the novel that it can be read as a kind of demonstration of the powers of language to erect the most splendid mansion of possibilities and actions. And no element of this world, or of the possibilities of the novel, has so fascinated Garrett as contradiction. To take a simple instance: the novella-length section, "Reivers," presents the crippled, blind and late-comers who have been left behind in a thieving raid across the Scottish border into England. Awaiting the triumphant return of their abler companions in arms, they sit around a fire and tell stories of heroes and escapes. But the raid they regret having missed is turning into a disastrous failure as they sit talking, and men are dying for less than nothing, up the road.

Garrett never plays such ironies as heavily as they must seem in summary, and he makes use of the greatest delicacy in proposing much of the action as something that *may* or *will* happen, or might have happened, when in fact it is already accomplished. This further confounds and enriches the novel's perspective, till another theme emerges, I suppose inevitably, the one that lies behind many of the most substantial novels of the tradition: the nature of reality. Garrett has the good taste and respect not to embark with drawn sword on *that* expedition, but in section after section the quest for the truth of a matter raises this question. The dazzling section in which Sir Robert Cecil analyzes the whole history of the correspondence between Elizabeth and James comes to mind in this regard. Again the peculiarly convincing verisimilitude of a manifestly artificial manipulation of narrative time reproves all conventional dependence on plot and unfolding action in fiction.

But to enumerate themes will not serve to suggest what a pleasure the novel is. Nor will themes manage to suggest how effectively the novel, which seems to have turned its back on our own world, very much restores our own daily actions and troubles to us, in illustrating the powers of consciousness, the pleasures of keen perception, and the persistence of our desires for contradicting human realities: both peace and dominion, both love and power. Hidden in these many narratives, Garrett is offering comment, as well, on the vanity of some desires. But that is for the experience of reading the book, not for any reviewer's comments.

The critical opinion that the postmodern American novel has been understandably dominated by abstraction and an abandonment of subjects that do not bring with them ruminations on the creative act, rests on the vaunted impossibility of saying anything meaningful after the Holocaust, the atom bomb, all the facets of an increasingly absurd and inhuman world. But the bloodshed, deprivations and injustices of the seventeenth and eighteenth centuries in England are as cruel as any; the Middle Passage killed millions of men and women and children, as cold-bloodedly as the Holocaust, if not with mechanical efficiency; and the sexual debasement of men and women is not trivial: to take only a few countervailing instances. The responsibilities of the novelist have never excluded consciousness of such horrors as these. If the pursuit of abstraction seems to some to have set the course, out of the sixties, for all the rest of this century, then I think that's a mistaken perception of contemporary writing, emboldened and self-authorized by the hegemony of academic criticism over the reactions of readers outside the academy (and I do not mean the contrast between highbrow novels and mass culture confections—which is interesting for other reasons).

Experiments with the novel have not been confined to the postmodern writers and in many cases have opened new ground for the novel that postmodern fiction has entirely abandoned. Writers like Garrett and William Goyen, each in his own way, have accomplished their own experiments, and they are of lasting value to the course of fiction. Neither Goyen nor Garrett has written a novel that can be dismissed as conventional; how can one proceed by convention when the purpose is ultimately to address the nature and consequences of human action, the responsibilities of consciousness, conscience, and spirit, and the identity of man? There should be more novels like *Arcadio* and *The Succession*, but it will take great honest artists, unswayed by fashion, and always hungry for this world's horrors and splendors, to write them.

Thomas Fleming

The Historical Consciousness of George Garrett

"Well then, let us hear the tale of Kinmont Willie." With that voice, heard near the center of George Garrett's *The Succession: A Novel of Elizabeth and James*, we are introduced to a group of old and disabled Scottish reivers gathered around a peat fire in a tower, drinking malt whiskey and telling tales, as they watch through the night for the return of a raiding party. The tale of Willie Armstrong comes only at the end of the chapter, where Red Tom—who claims to have been "there in the midst of it"—offers a version somewhat less romantic than what is handed down in the great Scottish ballad. Garrett, however, does not let the reiver have the whole of the telling, and the narrator takes over, merging his own voice with that of Red Tom. In the end, he asks, "Did it happen that way?" and answers, "No man in this tower knows. It is how they have heard it, how they prefer to believe it. It gladdens their hearts, for a while, to think so."

If religion, as Walter Burkert argued in *Homo Necans,* is the creation of neolithic hunters, then narrative literature was at least the second invention of men out in the bush, seated around their campfires, drinking and telling stories of the past. Even today, someone wanting to hear a good story would be well advised to take a leave of absence from his creative writing program and head out to the nearest deer camp. In his historical novels George Garrett has blurred the line that divides fiction from history and restored story-telling to its primitive vigor.

For the Scots, the ballad of Kinmont Willie was history, their history, and at the beginning of European literature, Greeks sat drinking wine as they listened to some son of Homer singing them the tales of Achilles and Hector and of the homecoming of Odysseus. German scholars of the 19th century were convinced that there never was a Troy, much less a Mycenae; that if there had been any historical basis for the *Iliad*, it lay in petty skirmishes of Greek chieftains in the far North. Heinrich Schliemann, an uneducated merchant who put his faith in literature rather than in the professors, found the sites of both Troy and Mycenae because he believed the lines of Homeric Greek he had first heard recited in a barroom. How could he not? If the Torah served to remind the ancient Jews of who they were, the Homeric epics had the same function for the Greeks. Noble families traced their ancestry back to the fighters who sacked Troy, and territorial wars could be settled by reference to the Catalogue of Ships.

In times closer to our own, the Serbs, after the Turkish conquest, preserved their national identity by singing and resinging their great songs of the last battle on the Plain of the Blackbirds and of the exploits of Prince Marko Kraljevic, who is invariably drinking wine to show his contempt for Muslim prohibition. When they began to throw off the Turkish yoke in the early 19th century, new songs were composed to honor Karageordge, and in the recent Bosnian Civil War, I heard these old songs being sung, with additional lyrics commemorating the heroism of a new generation of Serb guerillas.

History begins, not in the accumulation of data or in the examination of evidence, but in a narrative recreation of the heroic past. The Greeks had been singing songs of Troy for over three centuries before they were written down, and even after there were written texts they continued to perform the old songs and compose new ones. As time went on, the stream of historical epic divided into channels: one led in the direction of heroic lyric and tragedy, whose plots were always rooted in the past; the other toward the more prosaic investigations into geography, ethnology, and political events made by Ionian Greeks who called their work *historie*, that is, inquiry or fact-finding. If tragedy, as Aristotle observes, is more philosophical than history, because it aims at the essence of things, history, nonetheless, never gave up its claim to be a kind of narrative literature, and Herodotus is almost as great a narrative artist as his Athenian contemporaries who were writing tragedies.

As much as professional historians like Polybius might try to make history accurate and boring, ancient history rarely strayed too far from poetry, and *vice versa*. In the reign of Augustus, Livy took Polybius' account of the Punic Wars and turned it into something better, not just a more entertaining narrative but more significant history, if history means making sense of the past. His theme was the Roman people, and his book was a character study of that people from the mythical founding of the city down to his own times. At almost the same time, Virgil composed his *Aeneid*, which is superficially the tale of defeated and exiled Trojans, but is really (as the poet tells us at the beginning) the story of "the Latian realm . . . and the long glories of majestic Rome."

Historical fiction then, in prose or verse, whether it bears the name history or romance, is as ancient as the human race; it is, perhaps, the fundamental form of our literature, which, although it celebrates the deeds of individual men (which is what Achilles is doing, when the ambassadors come to his tent), is really telling the tale of a people, refreshing the memory of the old and forming the character of the young. Historical fiction, so far from disappearing with the fall of Rome, lived on in the Greek east, where Digenes Akritas is a border-hero like the Scots reivers, and in the Latin West, where tales of Beowulf, Sigurd, and Roland embodied the tribal memories of Franks, Goths, and Anglo-Saxons: at Hastings, the Normans went into battle with the *Chanson de Roland* in their ears.

The Renaissance is nothing if it is not an attempt to recreate historical epic: Petrarch's *Africa* (in Latin), Tasso's *Gierusalemme liberata*, Shakespeare's English Histories (as much as most Englishmen have ever known of the Wars of the Roses), and Milton's *Paradise Lost*, whose subject is nothing less than the history of the human race and its quarrel with God.

By the end of the 17th century, when Europeans aspired to something like the same level of civilization as the ancients had enjoyed, the historical stream divided again, one branch flowing into the novel of domestic manners and personal narrative, the other toward more scientific history. But, just as in the earlier Augustan Age, critically minded historians did not lose sight of the narrative origins (and purpose) of history; Gibbon and Hume were masters of the narrative art, perhaps greater masters than their novel-writing contemporaries. For the English, a nation already forged in the civil wars of the 15th and 17th centuries, critical history may have sufficed, but for nations still aborning, like poor Scotland that is always aborning but never born, the old ballads and folktales remained necessary fixtures of historical furniture. Many of Burns's poems are new versions of old songs, some of them political and historical, but it was Sir Walter Scott, first in his short epics and later in his novels, who showed how national history could, once again, be written in fictional forms. His Waverly novels, which took Europe by storm, have set the pattern for historical fiction ever since, even for those (like Mark Twain) who professed to hate him. George Garrett, who has done more than anyone since Scott to advance the historical novel, also shows himself Scott's heir in many ways.

Scott's relevance for *The Succession* goes well beyond a general indebtedness to the creator of a genre. The tale of Kinmont Willie, so beloved by the collector of *The Border Minstrelsy*, serves Garrett's narrative purposes as a connection between Elizabeth and James (although there are dozens of other connections that could have performed the same service as well or better). The climax of the story, in Garrett's telling, is the triumphant meeting of "Bold Buccleuch" with the Queen. The Dukes of Buccleuch were, it needs not be said, the chiefs of Scott's family (which branched off, apparently, in the 14th century), and in the course of the chapter we are told of another of Sir Walter's ancestors, his namesake Auld Wat of Harden, "that ancient chieftain, whose name I have made to ring in many a ditty" (Lockhart 3). In retelling the ancient ballad, in bringing on a cast of Scottish reivers whom Scott would gladly have drunk with (he once said he could not find it in his heart to condemn his thieving ancestors), and in connecting his tale with Sir Walter's ancestors, George Garrett invites (perhaps unconsciously) comparison with the greatest of historical novelists, whom he has, in some sense, challenged on his own ground.

As narrator, Scott is inferior to many of his contemporaries (including the historians) and is once said to have exclaimed that a plot was only a device from which to hang his characters. In variety of characters, however, Scott is excelled only by Shakespeare. As a shirttail connection with the Scotts of Buccleugh, Scott was keenly aware of class distinctions, but he despised snobbery and pretension (he once exploded at his daughter for deprecating something as "common"). As memorable as some of his noble and gentle heroes are, it is the simpler characters such as Meg Merrilies and Jeanie Deans, Dandie Dinmont and the blacksmith suitor of the Fair Maid of Perth, who became household names and archetypal figures. The very same qualities can be found in Garrett, a writer who has more than once acknowledged that he comes from old American stock but whose characters run the gamut from Anglican ministers to fundamentalist Bible-thumpers to Elizabethan bravos to circus performers.

What is astonishing in Garrett's narrative technique is his generosity. While most novelists write from a point of view, whether their own or that of a fictional character or of liberal philosophy's impartial spectator, Garrett allows his people to speak for themselves and to justify their (often miserable and sometimes worthless) lives. In this impartiality, he brings us back to the dawn of historical writing, to Herodotus who would repeat conflicting versions of a story and allow the readers to make up their own minds.

The multiplicity of voices in *The Succession* has the effect not so much of a mosaic—lifeless fragments forced into a single pattern and reflecting, however diverse they are in hue and tone, a single light— as an Elizabethan play filled with characters who go their own way, sometimes in contempt of either the hero's destiny or the author's apparent intention (e.g. Pistol in *Henry V*). As we are reading their tales, hearing them in their own voice, we inevitably take the sides, successively, of the Machiavellian secretary, the committed but fearful papist priest, the hedonistic and irresponsible actor, the reckless courtier. If, as Dr. Johnson once suggested, every man's life is worthy of a biography, then Garrett has given us a varied cast of Everymen, each one of them with something to say in his own defense.

As a novelist of character—there is no more plot to *The Succession* than there is in *Poison Pen*—Garrett is able to write a kind of social history of Elizabethan and Jacobean Britain. He is not, let us be careful to note, making up his material as he goes along. His original ambition was to write a more formal kind of history, for which he read everything and took volumes, boxes, roomfuls of notes, much as Scott spent his free time roaming the border country, getting drunk every night with the farmers and shepherds, collecting the materials for his *Border Minstrelsy*. (All that time, said one of his companions, he was making himself.) But, as Garrett explained to Madison Bell in an interview, when the time came to write *Death of the Fox*, the task of digesting his information turned out to be insurmountable:

As fast as I would think I was reading everything I should know, 50 more books would come out. Trying to know enough to do it, handling truckloads of notes got in my way . . . . So I changed the model of my book from term paper to test . . . and then I just closed the trunk and wrote it off the top of my head. (22)

As historian, then (and not just historical novelist), Garrett is more like Livy or Herodotus than he is like an academic historian; indeed, his work is more historical in the classical sense than any living American historian except Shelby Foote, whose *Narrative History of the Civil War* is a Proustian novel of reminiscence. If Foote has written history using the techniques of the novel, Garrett has composed a novel that serves the original purposes of history. As Clyde Wilson, himself an American historian, has pointed out, Garrett has revivified the historical novel and "brought to life Elizabethan England" as well as demonstrated "that it was still possible for a modern American writer to make contact with the pristine English language, the authentic religious belief, and the terrible immediacy of both glory and disaster that marked Shakespeare's England" (408).

In his profound examination into the uses and possibilities of history, *Historical Consciousness*, John Lukacs distinguishes the aims of fiction from those of history and sees the borders of the novel being invaded, on the one flank by poetry, and on the other by history. For Lukacs, the truest history should be not so much an account of facts as a rendering of the consciousness of different times. Deprecating the current state of the historical novel and skeptical of the fictional documentary, Lukacs sees history as the successor to the place of the novel. In fact, however, George Garrett's *The Succession* comes closer than any recent works of fiction to realizing Lukac's criteria for historical consciousness.

Ancient (by which I mean pre-academic) historians wrote with a purpose in mind, a general theme to be illustrated as events unfolded. It may be too much to say that Garrett writes with such a purpose or formula; he does, however, have a distinct view of Elizabethan and Jacobean England, a period which he finds both stranger and yet more relevant than is sometimes supposed. Asked about the political behavior exhibited in his historical works, he told Madison Bell that the earlier age

had more integrity in a certain way—you died for your positions. You don't die for them now, you just deny everything and run on the other ticket. I think you would shake a lot of guys out of American politics like rotten apples off a tree if they thought their lives were on the line. (23)

The most extreme case in *The Succession* is the priest, whose life we have come to see through his own eyes: his drunken, fox-hunting father, the timid old parish priest who, though still Catholic in his heart, has switched sides to save his skin, his fellow renegades who are making a last-ditch effort to save England from the most cynical of reformations. The last words of the chapter (as in the ending of Aiken's "Mr. Arcularis") belong to the government agent expressing his dismay that the priest died before revealing anything worthwhile. Only at that point is it brought home to the reader that all he has heard and experienced is from documents confiscated from a man who has been tortured to death. His public epitaph is the official lie handed out by Elizabeth's scrvants: "It has been agreed by the physicians and the jailer that it shall be given out (to the shame of the Papists) that the priest, in fear of torture or death by execution, has hanged himself in his prison cell."

But the other actors play equally dangerous games: Buccleuch in rescuing Kinmont Willie, the actor in joining Essex's household (and conspiracy) and, even while serving as double-agent, maintaining a sentimental loyalty. Even the Cecils, both Machiavellians who knew how to play all parts, stayed loyal to their royal mistress and to their country (at least to their own view of their country). The later days of Elizabeth were not, however, by any stretch of the neck or the imagination, Merry Old England. The religious and political wars had infected the English character with a self-serving cynicism that is poison to simplicity. The messenger, whose periodic appearances serve the function of tragic chorus, spends an evening drinking in the North with an old captain, who has received some favors from Cecil, but who has never been asked "to do anything that might be misconstrued as disloyal to the Percys." The captain might be corruptible, but—who knows?—his loyalty "might turn out to be true and deep."

The reign of Elizabeth is interesting, precisely because it is the threshold between the old world of violent honor and the newer world of treacherous statecraft. The messenger permits himself a nostalgic longing for an old England, before the time when he realized that "there is no one—no servant, no ally, kith or kin—who cannot sooner or later be sold off like a sheep." However, Garrett's 16th-century sellers and fleecers all know what they are doing and display more than a little courage, even in their policy and their treachery.

More than one reader of *The Succession* has told me they found the messenger the most sympathetic character, the nearest thing to a hero in the book: a man too weak to be anything other than what he is—a spy for Cecil—and too honest and courageous to lie about anyone including himself. Old enough to remember a better England (or at least to think he does) but unflinching in his determination to make the best of his admittedly disappointing life.

If history can be useful, it is not as a mirror in which we see ourselves reflected in a different time, and it is not as a set of universal archetypes that reduces all ages and all men down to a few simple principles (as in the philosophical criticisms of Leo Strauss and his followers); history is more like a love poem written by a stranger, in which we can hear our own experiences, true, but in different accents, with different names, and even with suprisingly different attitudes. Garrett's company of Elizabethan players are men and women with most of our own desires and frailties, but they play their games with conviction and courage, and it has been some time since those qualities could be attributed to Americans.

In his satiric works (most recently in *The King of Babylon*), George Garrett reveals himself as one of the sharpest social critics writing fiction. What is not always so well understood is that his historical works, in their depiction of an England that belongs as much to modern Americans as to the English, offer a social criticism of American life that is no less savage for its implicitness.

Works Cited

Bell, Madison Smartt. "George Garrett Talks to Madison Smartt Bell." *Chronicles* June 1988: Z2-7.

Burkert, Walter. *Homo Necans: The Anthropology of Ancient Greek Sacrificial Ritual and Myth.* Tr. Peter Bing. Berkeley: U of California P, 1983.

Garrett, George. *The Succession: A Novel of Elizabeth and James.* San Diego: Harvest-Harcourt, 1991.

Lockhart, John Gibson. *Memoirs of the Life of Sir Walter Scott.* Boston: Houghton Mifflin, 1901.

Lukacs, John. *Historical Consciousness: The Remembered Past.* 3rd ed. New Brunswick: Transaction, 1994.

Wilson, Clyde. "Review of George Garrett's *Poison Pen.*" *The World and I* 12 (1986): 406-11.

Nicholas Delbanco

The Succession: A Novel of Elizabeth and James

"The big bad abstractions are back in town again." So begins
a poem by George Garrett, and a copy of that poem—"Little Movie
without a Middle"—hangs on my study wall. Soon enough we
should move to specifics and the self-refuting opening of *The
Succession*, where voice after voice still resounds in the ear: "Now
there is no one for her to listen to. No one left for her to hear . . ."
But let me start with generalities, those "big bad abstractions . . .
again."

The field of "historical fiction" has been often traversed and well-
mined. The telling of stories is, almost without exception, a rehearsal
of what went before; those who pretend to originality are, likely as
not, suppressing their sources—and most of us delight in "twice-told
tales." We have history as fiction, and fictive history; to the widely
accepted notion that "history is written by the victors" we might
append the corrolary that it is rewritten by bards. Or, as Samuel
Butler averred, "The history of art is the history of revivals."
Charlotte Brontë and Jane Austen hold their own at the box-office
nowadays with *Robocop* and *Terminator II*; the recent discovery of
Jamestown's site will no doubt fuel a spate of romantic or corrective
Pocahontas fables. George Washington and Thomas Jefferson and
Chief Joseph and Lewis and Clark and the rest retain—indeed,
increase—their hold on our national attention. Though we look
forward as a readership we turn, Janus-faced, equally back.

(It might be worth mentioning, parenthetically, that much of what
we construe to be the world's great literature—the *Iliad, The Tale
of Genji, Henry V*, etc.—replicates a history long past. One need
not have been eyewitness to an era or event in order to imagine it
persuasively in language. Stephen Crane's vivid war-book is based
on battles that antedate his birth, and Fabrizio in *The Charterhouse
of Parma* watches the Battle of Waterloo from all-engulfing mud.
Every present action will be some future someone's history, and
distance may prove useful in the space-time continuum; we have no
way of knowing—and may reasonably question—if the poet who

sang Beowulf was present at the table when Grendel came to dine.) In this present age, however, there are three subsets of historical fiction that seem to me germane.

The first, and the least interesting as well as the most popular, is that form of history that borrows names and costumes and clothes itself in the regalia of a collective memory. This is the sort of book that recreates the Death of Christ or the birth of Abraham Lincoln or the love affair of Empress Catherine's lady-in-waiting with Rasputin, and does so with no attempt at verisimilitude in language or period style. The details may be accurate; in fact, they're quite likely to be. Anachrony is to be avoided, yet though the research may be scrupulous the psychological enterprise is, for all practical purposes, sham. It's a kind of bodice-ripper, in which the heroine is always fetchingly in *deshabille* and the hero always handsome and the toilets always flush. The villain may not have horns or claws for hands or fins for feet, but he's a constant double-dyed villain who must repent or fail to at tale's end. These are books about King Arthur or Piltdown Man and his pet bear or forward-facing history: sci-fi. At times the writer conjoins the two, as in *Jurassic Park* or *Neanderthal,* where the stuff of prehistory vaults to the future, so that what's past is prologue. If you think of science fiction as a kind of historical novel you'll see, perhaps, what I mean: the details of the enterprise are ingenious often, and usually inventive, but the fancy dress of it cannot disguise the recognizable forked animal beneath— the robot with the heart of gold or extra-terrestial thug . . . .

Second, and more artistically ambitious, is a present reconsideration of the past. I have in mind those books that recreate a history but tell you that they're doing so—that focus, as it were, through microscope or telescope then proudly display the machine. In this subset of the historical novel the writer may seem to embrace Joyce's notion of a dramatist—"outside, indifferent, paring his fingernails"—but sooner or later he'll step stage center and take a curtain call; she'll tell you that the whole of it was fond illusion, sleight-of-hand, and show you what she carries up her sleeve. Consider Charles Johnson's *The Middle Passage,* in which the enslaved nineteenth-century narrator, Rutherford, spouts Aristotle persuasively and conjures Disneyworld. Or think of John Fowles's *The French Lieutenant's Woman,* with its alternative endings, or John Barth's *Sot-Weed Factor* or Julian Barnes's *Flaubert's Parrot* or A.S. Byatt's *Possession*—the list is engagingly long.

These are ruminations, as it were, engendered by a bygone time and profiting therefrom for drama—but nonetheless and ostentatiously contemporary texts. They use the past as a kind of vanishing point in order to triangulate the present moment and to establish perspective. It helps if it's a darn good yarn, a rollicking entertainment, and often these stories are at least in part comedic, as if we're all invited in to share the joke.

And then there's that strange hybrid, the marriage of convenience between style and substance, what the French call *forme et fond*. It's a kind of inflection from context, a viral transmission, infection by data: a way of being so wholly absorbed by matter that manner follows suit. I think here of Mary Lee Settle's Beulah Quintet, of Ford Madox Ford's *The Fifth Queen* trilogy, of Thomas Flanagan's *Year of the French* and *The Tenants of Time*, of Patrick O'Brien's series of Aubrey and Maturin novels. Or—just to list recent recipients of the Booker Prize—Barry Unsworth's *Sacred Hunger*, Michael Ondaatje's *The English Patient*, and Pat Barker's *The Ghost Road*. It's a popular strategy now. These books are not so much recreations of as inventions of a language. They might not persuade historians of perfect authenticity in detail and of discourse, but they enter imaginatively into and thereby make—remake—a world.

In this last category and version of the singing school, George Garrett's trilogy remains, I believe, nonpareil. It sets and solves the puzzle of how in historical fiction the writer still must strive to "Make it New." To use familiar history as a source for stories is to remember in advance the resolution of the conflict and conclusion of the retrospect. We readers are likely to know how Walter Ralegh and Christopher Marlowe died their respective and celebrated deaths; we know beyond question or narrative tension that, in 1603, King James VI of Scotland became England's King James I. So what the novelist must do is reconstitute that tension; what was strange becomes familiar while what was familiar grows strange.

For several years George Garrett and I were colleagues at the Bennington Writing Workshops, which I co-founded (with the late John Gardner) in 1978. I revered *Death of the Fox* this side idolatry, though I had not met its author, and wrote to ask if he might be willing to join us the third summer; to my delight he agreed. What arrived with him on campus—as those who know George can attest—was a carnival: to name only some of his titles, we were made *Welcome to the Medicine Show, An Evening Performance, The Magic Striptease*; we shared *Enchanted Ground.* He was *King of the Mountain, Luck's Shining Child, The Finished Man,* and if I contradict myself, well then I contradict myself. Indispensable from the instant of arrival, Garrett taught us—all of us—about the glad contrarieties of focus: how you labor while not appearing to, how you set yourself a problem and then solve it by seeming-avoidance. No one worked harder at the trade or made less fuss about it; no one was more ambitious and at the same time self-deprecatory. Those were the years he wrestled with the shape of his novel-in-progress, *The Succession*, and the verb "wrestled" is apposite; it sometimes did seem like a physical contest, an attempt to bring that great fierce shape-shifting book to ground. Or perhaps, like a bout of jiu-jitsu, in which you seek to transfer your opponent's force and motion to your own advantage, breaking balance by a side-step or bent knee . . . .

George would arrive with cartons of material and spread it across desk and floor. His apartment would be cluttered with ordinance maps of England, with books on heraldry and costume and Elizabethan manners, the rent-rolls of villages and the genealogical tables of tertiary characters, with photographs of manor houses and the London docks. Over vodka at day's end he would smile that rueful smile of his and shake his head and complain that he was working on a problem that had no possible solution, no protagonist or resolution, no way of getting around the issue: he was writing a book about an era and an island and many of its people, not—as had been the case with Ralegh—one man in one place on one day.

A majority of "historical fictions"—I make this claim anecdotally and not statistically—have to do with previous periods in an author's own national story. Thus Americans will tend to write about the Revolution or the Civil War, Italians about the Renaissance or Imperial Rome, the Japanese about the Samurai, and so on and so forth. But Garrett's work is exceptional here too: he conjoins to the data of the Elizabethan and Jacobean periods a style and sensibility from the American South. There are those who argue that the language of Elizabethan England is most nearly preserved in Appalachia, that Shakespeare's rhetoric has been best replicated in our reverberant air. But whatever transatlantic criss-crossing these novels perform, they somehow manage to be situated both *here* and *there*, both *then* and *now*. It's not as if a twentieth-century American author impersonates a seventeenth-century Englishman, but rather as though the gap between them were a dimple of a ditch. With a compression that approaches simultaneity as to place and period, Garrett's language and the language of those documents (the letters, the testaments, the edicts) he incorporates have been, by the narrative, fused.

Bits and pieces kept appearing; shards of the whole were displayed. Or, to shift the metaphor, threads of the tapestry began to appear recognizable, yet the pattern in the carpet stayed unclear. Acknowledgement, when the book appeared in 1983, was made to the following publications: *The Agni Review, The Bellingham Review, The Bennington Review, Black Warrior Review, Carolina Lifestyle, Chelsea, Crescent Review, The Georgia Review, Hard Scuffle, Jeopardy, Lowlands Review, New Mexico Humanities Review, New Virginia Review, The Sewanee Review, Sounding Brass, South Carolina Review, The Texas Review, The Virginia Quarterly Review* and *Willow Springs Magazine*. I read, if not all, most of these and, as Editor of *The Bennington Review*, solicited one; it came to seem improbable that a single book might incorporate each of these disparate parts.

But George had discovered his method, his narrative through-line and the connective tissue of the Messenger's long ride. (I remember when he went to England, following the hoofprints of his own invented horse. There must have been a remarkable fusion and confusion of periods as well as sequence: the writer in a motorcar or on a railway train, using public and private conveyance beyond the reach of sixteenth century augury and scouting out a landscape at one and the same time constant and altered.) Making his way south from Scotland, tracking stables and shelter and coach-houses, he fashions an itinerary "West on Fleet Street to Temple Bar and . . . Then only short way along Strand (not far as St. Martin's Lane or Charing Cross) to gate of Cecil House close by & across from Ivy Lane & Russell House and . . ." (486). The ellipses are his. The book weaves forth and back from 1566 to 1626, narrated by Courtier and Player as well as the omniscient author who reports upon the messenger. ("Here comes the man, slope-shouldered and loose-limbed, rocking easy to the rhythm of his shaggy-haired Scots horse . . ." [13].) It advanced by indirection from the opening beat of the dying Queen in 1603 to—more than five-hundred pages later—the precedent and yet concluding Christmastide, 1602-03. For, as Garrett wrote in his introductory Note, when describing this procedure:

> I was forced to summon up many others to help me, ghosts from that time, some of them "real" (Sir Robert Cecil, Sir Robert Carey, the Earl of Essex) and some of them "imaginary"—a messenger, a priest, a player, some Scots reivers, etc. And very soon it was clear that if they were to bear witness, they must be allowed to tell their own tales also. They jostled each other for places in the story. And so, finally, here they are in a story which has changed its shape and form many times before it settled into this one, a story which surely took its own sweet time to become a book . . . . (vii-iii)

I think these several voices and "their own tales also" are the defining innovation of the trilogy, and in particular of *The Succession*. Garrett does not pretend to omniscience; the parenthesis and query are his characteristic rhetorical form; he writes from no Olympian vantage nor temporal remove. On a sample page such interjections as "Ah no," "But more," "Why not?" (228) or, overleaf, *(Amen to that!)*, "Or did they?" and "So then" (230) punctuate the discourse, lending it a kind of fits-and-starts verisimilitude. The mode, appropriately enough, is verbal: we should *listen* to this book. As readers we enter the room of the story and are muddled by its muddle, caught up again as though in fact participants by the truths and whispered secrets and hidden messages of conversation; we half hear what we overhear and puzzle out what we've been told. Most historical fiction invites a passive readership; *The Succession* requires an inquiring and even a deciphering intelligence, an audience that's actively engaged.

Indeed, we have a sort of Shandy-like digressiveness; the anecdote and the twice-told tale and sub-plot structure the trilogy, so that the reader-listener follows story after story through a kind of verbal maze. What may be summarized as history is brief, but it requires elaborate telling. The narrative entails digression, and the narrator delights in "pauses in the consequence" or the confidential "aside." As with a maze (whose perimeter is limited but internal intricacies can sometimes feel near-limitless), getting there is half the fun . . . .

Here's the Earl of Essex after a failed assault, and when his troops have retreated to the trenches:

"Jesus, Jesus, oh sweet Jesus!" He was calling out even as he laughed. "Sweet wounds of Jesus, we have done it again. The damned ladders are short by two yards or more!"

How, all of a sudden, after that bloody charge, the stupidity and failure of it, this seemed the greatest jest in all the world. And all of us in those muddy trenches began to laugh, too; and the French Papists on the wall began to laugh, unable to contain themselves against the noise of several hundred men laughing as if to empty themselves of laughter forever. (289)

I pick this passage at near-random, but it seems to me representative. We should situate the paragraphs; they come in a letter from Robert Carey, Earl of Monmouth, to Sir Ferdinando Gorges. It's difficult—an unrewarding task—to separate out the speaker from the author; this is Garrett in the guise of courtier, an old man rehearsing his past. He has a young man newly arrived to his employ who helps him shape his memories; he's writing to report on how he likes his auditor, and what the boy has, by listening, learned. There's an anecdote with which the excerpt ends about bawdry and gambling and drink. There's military action reported on as retrospect; there are historical figures brought engagingly to life. There's colloquial usage ("Sweet wounds of Jesus") that's period-limned and precise. There's dialogue rehearsed in monologue; there's humor and laughter and horror and blasphemy and active faith; there's "the greatest jest in all the world" that empties the speaker-writer of laughter. The Earl of Essex is long dead, as are most of those who joined him in the attempt "against the walls of St. Catherine's Castle." ' Yet the Courtier (Robert Carey, whose remembrance we now read, as of 1626) cannot help but reconstruct what he might have preferred to forget. There's accurate research and much information, purveyed for the sake of the youth: "I sought to explain to him the sense of it. How time and again, in the reign of the Queen, the English scaling ladders had somehow proved to be made too short for walls to be taken". There's a knowingness about the way old age regales itself, a wry nostalgia for lost innocence, a voice near-indistinguishable from the actual quoted voice of the *Memoirs of the Life of Robert Carey* which provides the epigraph to the brief chapter itself. There's more in these eight lines than eighty could begin to scan, yet it's an unimportant passage, a narrative by-blow and pause.

And if that be true of a pair of casual paragraphs on page two hundred eighty-nine, how daunting to parse out the whole! *Death of the Fox*, *The Succession*, and *Entered From the Sun*, taken alone or together, are both representative of and exemplary solutions to the problem posed; they yoke "matter" to "manner" inventively throughout. Neither an act of willed ventriloquy nor mere costume drama, this contemporary foray into Elizabethan England constitutes, or so it seems to me, an enduring achievement and one that will doubly trick time.

So we end where we began: with praise. Or, as Garrett's poem would have it, ". . . the simple and specific common nouns come forth again / to clean up the mess . . . ." *The Succession: A Novel of Elizabeth and James*. This book is an excellent book. Read it. Then read it again.

R.H.W. Dillard

The Elizabethan Novels: The Succession

In her first major breakthrough into radical form, *Tender Buttons*, Gertrude Stein uttered the imperative: "Act so that there is no use in a centre" (63). In his second Elizabethan historical novel, *The Succession*, George Garrett breaks through himself, developing a form much more radical than that of *Death of the Fox*, denying himself the unifying element of a dominant central character, moving beyond events to the creation of meaning in events, opening the novel to the study of meaning itself: acting, in other words, as Stein demanded, so that there is no use in a center.

The Succession is, as its subtitle claims, "A Novel of Elizabeth and James," a re-creation of the complex events surrounding the succession of James I to the throne of Queen Elizabeth. It is a historical novel; it does cover much of the same historical ground as its predecessor with many of the same characters, Ralegh among them; it does have the same sort of dense, rich texture of detail, an almost palpable re-creation of things and thoughts, the manners and ways of Elizabethan and Jacobean England. It is another imaginative dreaming of the dream of Adam, the dream of history; but it is also an aesthetic meditation on the creation and revelation of meaning in the succession of moments (real, remembered, dreamed, and imagined) that make up the living nexus of time.

Garrett's original intent, as he explains in the prefatory note to the novel, was to follow the success of *Death of the Fox* with another novel, "a tidy and limited task, if not an easy one," to be based on the letters of Elizabeth and James:

It began with the letters—first with the actual letters of Queen Elizabeth (weighty in syntax, knotty in thought, generally obscure in their gnarled tangle of motives) to James IV of Scotland, her godson and cousin and, as it might come to pass, perhaps her heir. His letters, almost always answers and reactions, tend to be more open and obvious to us even though (it seems) he aimed to be sly, canny, clever, forceful, and persuasive. The gist of that story was to be, purely and simply, a narrative accounting of the two of them, Queen and King, exchanging letters over the years, each seeking to come to know and understand the other with a kind of urgent and thorough intimacy that even lovers seldom achieve. (vii)

That original plan became lost as Garrett's imagination, engaged in the task of "trying to contemplate two splendid characters," found it needed the help of

> ghosts from that time, some of them "real" (Sir Robert Cecil, Sir Robert Carey, the Earl of Essex) and some of them "imaginary"—a messenger, a priest, a player, some Scots reivers, etc. And very soon it was clear that if they were to bear witness, they must be allowed to tell their own tales also. (vii-iii).

He moved away from an account of the relationship of two people—of necessity, since those two people were a queen and a king—to an account of an entire world, an experiential field in which the realities of the rulers took on substance and meaning and into which their individual identities were subsumed. As Garrett's epigraph (from Arthur Golding's 1567 translation of Ovid's *Metamorphosis*) indicates, the novel itself metamorphosed from the narrative of the interrelationship of two lives into an account of the nature of life itself:

> The high, the lowe: the riche, the poore: the mayster, and the
> slave:
> The mayd, the wife: the man, the chyld: the simple
> and the brave:
> The young, the old: the good, the bad: the warriour
> strong and stout:
> The wyse, the foole: the countrie cloyne: the lerned
> and the lout: ﹅
> And every other living wight shall in this mirrour see
> His whole estate, thoughtes, woordes and deedes
> expresly shewed to bee.

Having decided to move beyond the concerns of *Death of the Fox*, Garrett had no choice but to move beyond its form, to develop a radical form of sufficient complexity to allow him to deal directly with the larger imagination of life itself. When asked by an interviewer about his comment that he had hoped to demonstrate "something about how history happens," Garrett pointed to his method in constructing the book, to his concern with time itself rather than just with remembered time:

> I think what I really meant to say there was something about time—something which is more evident in the second novel than in the first, although the first one is involved with memory. The second one has less organized memory than it does [a] kind of simultaneity. In both of them I was trying to deal in different ways with a variety of characters, some of whom don't really cause large things to happen in history but are a part of the whole picture. ("Interview" 158)

The novel has no central character, although Queen Elizabeth and King James are at the center of its events. The succession of its title is certainly that of James to Elizabeth's throne in 1603, but, as Monroe Spears has pointed out, it "is not only that of 1603, but those of 1566, 1587, and 1626" (270). Instead of a central character the novel has many almost unrelated characters—a messenger bearing the news of James's birth to William Cecil, a Catholic priest disguised and on the run, a band of reivers on the Scottish border, an old courtier looking back on the days of his youth, Robert Cecil brooding over and explicating his collection of the letters of Elizabeth and James, a player who was caught up in the rebellion of Essex, a worried King James awaiting word of the old Queen's death, a brooding Queen Elizabeth celebrating her last Christmas, and even a happy drunken plowman walking off his Christmas dinner under the reeling stars.

The novel also has no central time; it shifts in an apparently unordered succession back and forth from 1566 to 1626, not according to the memory of any one character, but according to the experiences and memories and imaginings of all these characters. The brilliance of the novel is not so much that it has so many characters and covers so much time, but that out of all this apparent disorder and disconnection such a coherent and orderly and meaningful whole takes shape. It does not have a modernist preoccupation with fragmentation, but rather a thoroughly postmodernist awareness of interrelatedness and interdependence. By acting so that there is no use in a center, in a completely post-Einsteinian way, Garrett has developed a form in which, even though there is no apparent center, the center holds.

Spears noted the complexity of Garrett's compositional method and his sense of the interdependent nature of what he calls the "imaginary past":

> As Garrett says, this is the "imaginary past" in the sense that it has to be imagined—there is no way of automatically reconstructing it (or them, for the past is not one but many, of course) from facts—but it is solidly based on a thorough knowledge of what historical facts and documents are available and, more importantly, of the writings (both literary and personal—e.g., letters) of the period. So this kind of historical novel is a kind of communal product, in a sense: not based on the limited scope of one man's imagination, but on the productions, fictional and real, of many people's minds—a kind of collective reality created by all of them together. . . . It is at the opposite pole from fantasy, where the writer simply unleashes his imagination with no regard for reality or possibility and no constraints. But it is finally dependent on the unifying imagination of a single author. (273)

The philosophical position that gives rise to the complex form of the novel is that things and events, experienced directly or experienced solely imaginatively, are real. An alder leaf falls between two men standing "almost in the shadow of squat old St. Cuthbert's Church in Norham village. Sun beginning its summer glide toward twilight, bleeding a faint and wavering reflection of Norham Castle onto the steely-smooth flowing of the Tweed" (34). One of them is the messenger bearing the news of James's birth south to William Cecil; the other is Captain Norton, an old soldier retired in Norham.

> A single leaf—waxy green on one side, dusty gray on the bottom, ribbed and shaped like the fat bowl of a lute, floating in motley shade, lighting on the chipped gravel of the footpath, resting briefly between the toes of the four boots of the two of them, then, touched by the merest sigh of a breeze, lifting all at once like a book page to tumble away. (35)

Captain Norton studies the leaf. The reader later discovers that the other man, the messenger, is imagining the entire scene in which Norton studies the leaf. The reader knows that George Garrett has imagined the two men, the scene, and the leaf. And yet, there is the leaf, more real to the reader of the novel than any leaf that falls unnoticed in the forest, as real as any leaf that falls noticed or unnoticed in any wood or on any patio or onto and into any fish pond. As real as any page of this book, of any book.

That Essex, for example, does not understand this truth of the imagination—"it was his folly to believe that the Queen had no more substance than the crown and robes she wore. That without his eyes to give her life she was diminished to the edge of nothingness" (443-44)—leads him into a solipsistic self-regard that is the source of his failure, morally and politically. Quantum mechanics suggests that the observer affects the thing observed, but it also notes that, despite the blurring of distinctions, the observer is *not* the thing observed and that the reality in which the observer participates has its own integrity and acts on the observer as well. The nature of real experience is much too complex and dynamic for any individual entirely to comprehend, much less to generate singly and sustain in existence.

The key to the formal method of *The Succession*, then, is that meaning is not inherent in any event. Rather, meaning accrues to experience from its relationships in time (past and future and present) and in consciousness, individual and shared. To a Christian, the Old Testament became fully meaningful only after it was given meaning by the coming of Christ, but any action that a Christian may now take is fully meaningful only because of Christ's having lived two thousand years ago. The leaf falls; the man notices it; the other man imagines both the leaf and its observer, although the first man is a real man who does live in Norham village. The leaf and the event take on meaning as they are imagined by the character; the leaf and the event and the character take on meaning by their being part of the political events surrounding the birth of Prince James to Mary, Queen of Scots; the leaf, the event, the character, and the birth of Prince James take on meaning thirty-seven years later upon the succession of James to the throne of England; the leaf, the event, the character, the birth of James, and the succession of James take on meaning when imagined and shaped into a novel, *The Succession*, by George Garrett some four hundred years later. And, of course, this actual leaf, the ground reality of this lengthy complex of events, did not even exist until the novel was written, although king and queen and Captain Norton of Norham village and the imagining messenger all did exist centuries before.

The Succession is a novel, a work of the imagination, and as such does not discuss the nature of meaning and its development in the manner of a philosophical text; but its very texture and form allow its readers that rare opportunity, the chance to consider the very nature of experience, to witness and participate in the actual creation of meaning and coherence and order in an apparently meaningless and incoherent and orderless world. Of course, human beings engage in the creation of meaning all the time, but the activity of the committed imagination, the simultaneity of experience that it offers, makes them aware of what they are doing, of "how history happens," and gives them the opportunity to understand what they are doing even as they are doing it.

The actual structure of this novel that behaves as though there is no use in a center is still, in one sense, familiarly linear. The reader is expected to read steadily from the beginning of the novel successively to the end, unlike other radically constructed modern novels such as Vladimir Nabokov's *Pale Fire*, Julio Cortázar's *Hopscotch*, or B.S. Johnson's *The Unfortunates*, books that demand of a reader active participation in decisions determining the very order in which pages are to be read. But any reader who expects the 538 pages of *The Succession* to corroborate a "common sense" view of historical process along the steady flight of the arrow of time will be quickly and sorely disappointed. The reader's progress through the sixteen unnumbered sections of the novel may be steady and progressive enough, but the movement of the events in the novel, the imaginative movement through the years between 1566 and 1626, is far from linear, is as radical in conception and execution as any of those more overtly radical novels. "I was hoping I wouldn't be abandoning too many readers," Garrett said. "On the other hand, I couldn't think of any other way to tell this particular story. If I could have, I'd have been delighted to tell it in a straightforward way" ("Interview" 158). Like Umberto Eco, Garrett is counting on the integrity of what he believes to be a necessarily radical form to "produce a new reader" (48), a reader capable of active participation in the openness of the text.

The novel moves from a first section set in March of 1603 back and forth through the succeeding fifteen sections in the following order: 1566, 1603, 1587, 1626 (1575), 1566, 1602, March 1602-1603, 1566, 1626, 1603, 1566, 1602, 1626 (1603), 1566, and finally Christmastide 1602-1603. The story line shifts back forth, too, among a set of characters, most of whom have never met and have no direct connection with each other. Even the two most historically important characters, Queen Elizabeth and King James, never meet but only write letters to each other. And yet all of these characters—the Queen and King, the anonymous messenger, the desperate priest, the band of Scottish reivers, the courtier (Robert Carey, Earl of Monmouth), the actor who has gotten himself tangled up in political intrigue, and Sir Robert Cecil pouring over the letters between Elizabeth and James—function in a vital field of space and time and affect each other directly and indirectly, back and forth, in a dynamic nexus of action, speech, memory, dream, and imagination, of transforming and transformative meaning.

Queen Elizabeth, in the first and last sections of the novel, offers the reader both ingress into the book's complexity and egress from it—an Elizabeth near death, looking back over her life, attempting to understand it, to determine its meaning. Her mind wanders, mingling present and past: "And in truth she, too, has lived to become a kind of ghost. Her heart and mind are elsewhere. As if she were exiled to a strange place, a far country she cannot yet name or imagine" (9). She finds herself in her last days, in March of 1603, "moving amid a moving crowd of ghosts. Some of whom are known and named. Named and more or less remembered. Other are like figures from a dream. They are perfect strangers" (10). Like the reader of the novel, she is living in a timeless simultaneity, surrounded by a cloud of ghosts, a web of memory, imagination, and meaning, moving back and forth among known and named figures and perfect strangers. "*Is that how God creates the future?*" Garrett asks in the last section of the novel, a meditative description of the Queen's last (and, therefore, the last Elizabethan) Christmas. "*In the same way that we, who can create nothing out of nothing on our own, constantly seek to recover, repair, and redesign our past?*" (533). The answer to that question may not be answered in any strictly rational manner, and yet the very shape of the book does offer an answer, one of belief and blessing, but one that must be earned by an active involvement in that cloud of ghosts, that web of consciousness which determines all meaning.

The reader, like the old Queen, must listen and remember, note the details of the text, and "recover, repair, and redesign" its varied narratives, forming them (with the complicity of the author) into a meaningful whole. Sir Robert Cecil, in the third section of the novel, "by a wild inspiration" (65) succeeds in hiding from the Queen the dangerous fact that he is receiving letters from James, but the reader knows (and must recover) that the Queen does know of his allegiance all along:

> She will hear him out on any subject whatsoever. But without truly listening to him. Certainly without truly believing him. For she knows that his heart and mind are chiefly elsewhere. Are uneasy in attendance in Scotland. For a fact. Heart and mind secretly in service of that man he takes to be most likely to be the King when she is gone. (9)

The reader must put those two pieces of information together with other information about Cecil—that he is a partner of Ralegh, a man who knows that he must support the right successor in order to survive. It is through Cecil's eyes that the reader gains the opportunity to read the actual letters of Elizabeth and James, and whose interpretations of those letters the reader must trust or disbelieve (in any case, judge) along with his or her own interpretations of them. The meaning of the letters, the thoughts of the character reading the letters, the reader's thoughts about the letters and the character—all of these form the web of meaning which develops in the reading, the experiencing, of the book.

That experience is as richly varied and entertaining as it is complex and intellectually rewarding. The tone is dominated by the old Queen's reveries and is meditative and cloudy with ghosts, but it is no monotone, for the chapters abound with vividly rendered scenes and great liveliness. In the midst of the fourth section, "'Priest: 1587," which is composed of the letters and papers of a doomed Catholic priest in hiding and on the run, the single most comic sequence in the novel occurs: an account of the priest and his companion being caught in their disguise as dentists and forced to pull teeth for their very lives. They pull, by accident, the one good tooth in their chief tormentor's mouth, and their only escape is to convince the townsmen that the good tooth is the cause of all the bad teeth in the man's mouth:

—It has been proved beyond any question or doubt that the cause of much trouble among teeth is the power and dominion of one great, fat, solid tooth over the others. This tooth—though sometimes there may be more than one, depending on the age, general constitution, and good or ill fortune of the patient—this fat and lordly tooth does set himself up like a hardhearted, arrogant, rack-rent landlord. He does take away the health of the mouth at the expense of the others, his poor tenants, leaving those scranny, shabby fellows nothing but decay and discoloration and grief. He, this great, rich, fat and lordly tooth does grow huge and white like a spoiled ram grazing on common land that has been enclosed and taken away from the people! (84-85)

When, later, this comic priest and teller of the tale is captured and "subjected to considerable rigor" by his captors, only to die "in his sleep sometime during the night after our first session of interrogation" (146), the comedy of his story dissolves in horror, and yet the comedy remains, is as true as his death and is as much a part of the meaning of his life and of its place in the meaning of the larger context of life around him.

Garrett's confidence in his method and his imaginative re-creation of the Elizabethan world have advanced to the point that, in this novel, he even dares match himself directly with the primary originator of the historical novel, Sir Walter Scott. In the fifth section, "Courtier: 1626 (1575)," Robert Carey tells of the Queen's famous visit to Kenilworth, the subject (or at least the historical backdrop) of Scott's *Kenilworth*, and in ten pages Garrett summons up "the ghosts of Kenilworth" (166) with sharpness and clarity in a novel that requires none of Scott's romantic interludes and complicated subplots for its excitement. The Kenilworth section does function in the novel beyond its wry tip of the hat to Scott, of course, for it allows Garrett to place Leicester in the nexus of Elizabeth's recollections, along with Ralegh and Essex, whose rebellion appears in the thirteenth section, "Player: 1602."

The reader, then, shares the Queen's memories and thoughts and those of the people around her, reads her and their letters, leaps back and forth in time like an excited researcher, a detective of the historical imagination seeking clues and echoes and nuances that will ultimately create the sense of the whole picture to which the text of the novel gives rise. But this particular "open text" also enforces upon the reader an involvement in the crimes and duplicities of the time beyond that of a detached, even if excited, observer. The moment of electrical imaginative connection in this novel—an equivalent of sorts of the shared letter from Garrett and Ralegh to their sons in *Death of the Fox*—occurs in the thirteenth section when Garrett shifts away from first or third person to a second-person narration; "'You have yourself an excellent seat'" it opens, "'most comfortable bench with a back and a soft, fat embroidered cushion you'd be happy to own" (373). The reader is forced into an identification with an agent "come to London to tie up loose ends in this business of Essex," to cover up any evidence "that your patrons had a genuine interest in the Earl's strategems" (415). It is in this guise that "you" examine the papers of an actor, looking for signs that he "may have somehow stumbled on more pieces of knowledge than he ought to" (415). "You" find nothing to indicate that he has, but "you" do find out things about "yourself," your imaginatively shared self:

> Early you discover he has not. Which is well. For if he had known too much, it might have been necessary to have him killed. Or kill him yourself. Which, either way, by hired hacker or with your own piece of steel, is always troublesome. And which would be a loss, for you took much pleasure from his performance on the stage. (415-16)

Reader and author, intruders in this cloud of ghosts, discover just how deeply an act of committed imagination involves them and unites them with their ghosts, their imagined ancestors, their secret sharers in this fallen and dangerous world, then and now. The use of the second person is a brilliant strategem and is integral to the narrative stance of the entire novel. The world of the Elizabethan succession was, according to Garrett, a world of spies and spying, of lies and lying, duplicitous and deadly and almost staggeringly complex. The reader of this novel is, then, required by the text to become a spy as well, reading over shoulders, listening in on private thoughts, assembling the data, adding them up for private reasons. And in the thirteenth section the reader becomes, by the use of the second person, a player indeed—an actor, a liar, a spy, a killer, a fully human person in a fully human world. And all this by the power of words— words and the committed imagination.

Sir Robert Cecil, reading over the letters of Elizabeth and James, marvels at that power, at the Queen's use of the power of words in her own duplicitous and terribly important game with James:

> It could be a subject fit for laughter. How a wonderfully clever Queen was able to control her young cousin (and all his neighboring northern kingdom) without the use of force of arms. And without fulfilling the usual requirements of large bribes and pensions. Indeed without spending more than the most frugal sums. And how? Chiefly by and through words. Her letters. No small victory in that mastery over a King who is poet and scholar. Defeating him, then, on his own ground and with his own favorite weapons. (330)

As the Queen knew, words have great force. They create and they re-create experience and meaning. Words invite readers into the lives of others, allow them to share their victories and fears, their beginnings and their ends. And, perhaps most importantly of all in the work of George Garrett, they allow his readers accommodation with what it is that they are, their humanity and their spiritual identity beyond and through that humanity. What enabled Garrett to write *The Succession* is what enabled Shakespeare or Tolstoy to write at the level they did: a religious belief that gives them an awareness of something larger than the passing moment, that gives them awareness of the presence of the eternal in the temporal, of the universal in the particular, the Word in words.

The time and times of *The Succession* are fully imagined and realized: a world of complexity and duplicity, a world of masks and lies and players, a world in which reality and theatricality are inextricably confused, a world of sins and sinners in which the very existence of love seems in question, a world of a virgin queen without issue, a world in which the very future seems in serious doubt. It is a dark world which, as the messenger reminds the reader, is described accurately in scripture:

> Child of his times, he finds the truth of Holy Scripture as he reads the story of the world. Who seeks to save his life shall lose it. Who is first now shall be last later. All who have power and influence here and now shall in the end possess no more of either than any beggar lying in a ditch. (20)

And yet the succession providentially occurs, the sinful world moves and lives on, and Garrett ends his novel at Christmas, not with the death of the Queen nor even with her recollecting her cloud of ghosts, but with a happy plowman, under the stars, believing himself to be as full of love and charity as he is of "food and drink and gratitude." Garrett allows the reader to share that plowman's belief (and he uses the second person again to assure that sharing), his moment of love and grace in this terrible world:

> You believe you are full of love and charity also. And you can wish all the world, your friends and your enemies, nothing but well. Nothing but good fortune. Wishing the dead, from Adam and Eve until now, their rest in peace. And wishing the living, one and all, from the beggar in his hedge to the Queen in her soft bed. . . .
> And what is it she can be dreaming of now, as he, half dreaming, imagines her, that lady minted on his hard-earned coins, lady of ballads and prayers in the parish church? Is there a place in her dream for this happy drunken plowman, mud of good English earth thick on his boots, out under the stars, who is wishing for her and the rest of the world, for the sake of our own sweet Jesus, a good night? (538)

This Christian blessing is at the heart of the novel as well as its end; its simplicity informs and gives ultimate meaning to all of the complexity of the novel's radical form. It is not sentimentalized, for the plowman is drunk and only believes himself full of love and charity, and his dream of the Queen has nothing of her dark fears of death in it. It is the other half of the dark Christian truth expressed by the messenger, that the mighty shall be brought low and that "all who have power and influence here and now shall in the end possess no more of either than any beggar lying in a ditch." The dying Queen, brought low by time, and the living plowman blessing her in his cups share in the complex Christian description of life in the fallen world of lies that informs this novel. And that blessing is what the reader earns, is the reward for the active participation in the open text of the novel. Not a statement of rational certainty, but one of belief. And that has been the point of *The Succession*: that reality is a complex and vital web (or cloud) of shared perception and consciousness and belief. It is not an account, as most historical novels suggest, of heroes and major figures shaping history for the rest of humankind, but rather of their acting in a nexus of human consciousness, shaped themselves by their human environment even as they shape it. In *The Succession* reality and meaning are one, multiform but ultimately given singular form (a "center") by an intimate relationship with eternity.

Garrett's final meaning may be as old as Christian thought itself, but his radical, postmodern novel gives that meaning new life and new expression. Together with *Death of the Fox*, *The Succession* stands as a major literary achievement, redefining the very terms of the historical novel and, at the same time, pushing the form of the novel itself into aesthetic *terra incognita*, into the realm of the larger imagination.

Works Cited

Eco, Umberto. "Postscript" to *The Name of the Rose*. Trans. William Weaver. New York: Harcourt Brace, 1983.

Garrett, George. *The Succession*. Garden City: Doubleday, 1983.

"An Interview with George Garrett." *Dictionary of Literary Biography Yearbook: 1983*. Ed. Mary Bruccoli and Jean W. Ross. Detroit: Bruccoli Clark/Gale, 1984. 157-61.

Spears, Monroe K. "George Garrett and the Historical Novel." *Virginia Quarterly Review* 61 (1985): 262-76.

Stein, Gertrude. *Tender Buttons*. New York: Claire Marie, 1914.

Entered from the Sun

Laurence Goldstein

In Praise of Entered from the Sun

I

Who wrote *The Rape of Lucrece*? And the line
"Sin of self-love possesseth all mine eye"?
And the tragedy of that gullible Moor
whose dishonored wife dies by toxins
swifter than Time's? The author was Marlowe.
I learned this amazing fact, in 1963,
from Calvin Hoffman, a Broadway spieler
guest-lecturing the vast Shakespeare class
I enrolled in, at UCLA, my sophomore year.
"The honest-to-God truth," he said, lay in his book,
The Murder of the Man Who Was 'Shakespeare':
a staged quarrel at widow Bull's, a stabbing
of some unlucky soul lost to history,
and then a perpetual hoax, "a flim-flam,"
to keep the atheist poet safe from harm.
I became a convert, savoring this lurid
scenario, this rare fume of ingenuity,
as a sign of storytelling in its purest form.

"Truth being so often shapeless and ill-fitting,"
I came to prefer the tailored seams and stylish
cut of full-dress romance: how Marlowe,
a fugitive and spy, lingered in Italy,
wrote *Coriolanus* on Walsingham's estate,
rueful, jealous of his front-man's fame,
too publicly dead to claim his immortality.
Later that year, another assassination
fomented more no-less-ingenious plots
than the First Folio inspired; I drank them in.
The more "missing pieces in the puzzle," the more
I touted the conspiracy my fancy preferred,
making authentic events serve morbid invention,

disdaining the seemingly proven while typewriting
confessional monologues by C.I.A. snipers, a Gothic
charged with paranoia, and skeptical of the real.
Life, I imagined, was all snarled and knotty . . .
full of dark puzzlement . . . a maze . . .

II

Our species can locate DNA, walk on the moon,
put the Book of Knowledge on a tiny chip,
but not all things are possible and true.
Seasoned, and humbled, in my research habit
I gave up the notion that Shakespeare was anyone else,
not even Marlowe, whose death vexed me still.
How welcome, then, this latter-day whydunit,
"The Murder of the Man Who Was Marlowe."
It may be, as its Ralegh says, "The world
is worse than any of us can imagine," yet
not so infirm that any lie will stick.
The lawful process of sifting the implausible,
rumor by rumor, keeps the commonwealth
keen on the scent of Oswalds born to spoil
the Muses' darling, Fortune's leading man.
At both centuries' end, detection saves
the mind from too much indeterminacy, too much
of the tricksy spirit that makes all plots true.

It matters why Kit Marlowe was killed. It matters
that it matters. The player Hunnyman acts
to make sense of foul murder offstage,
and the soldier Barfoot, agent of posterity,
will hear some truth before he dies.
Truth is the daughter of Time, I know,
having been slow to discover the corpus of truth,
the body of evidence that closes a post-mortem.
The mind, too, is suveilled and appraised;
see how progeny of the printer Alysoun
make their revisions public, now on Marlowe,

now on Shakespeare, now on George Garrett,
who ends his fact-gathering chronicle
not with confusion but *Henry II, part two*
and "Mr. Shakespeare himself . . .come out on the stage."
Once I would have doubted his authority.
Now I discern the veritable playwright, wiser
than all his unbelievers, incontestably "himself."

Monroe K. Spears

A Trilogy Complete, A Past Recaptured

With *Entered from the Sun*, George Garrett completes the remarkable trilogy of historical novels he began with *Death of the Fox*
(1971) and continued with *The Succession* (1983). Since he said
that it took him twenty years to finish the first, the whole trilogy must
have occupied him, off and on, for almost forty years. He has been,
he says in his Author's Farewell, a "persistent kind of tourist" to the
world of the Elizabethans, and found them, on the whole, more interesting than we are; but he adds, with characteristic humor and skepticism, that of course "I never had to live there all the time. That
might have changed my tune."

I have discussed the two earlier novels at some length in the
Virginia Quarterly Review in 1985 (reprinted in my *American
Ambitions*, 1987). I tried then to show that they

> exhibit the novel operating at so high a level, with such variety of
> styles and perspectives, with such easy mastery of the
> 'historical' aspect—of all details of time and place—and so
> deeply meditated in their study of the relation between the
> individual life and the history, that they are really something new
> .... They are beautiful, profound, and deeply moving works
> of art. (210)

Garrett's method in these novels is, he has said, to "make a work
of fiction, of the imagination, planted and rooted in fact" (*Death* 8):
after mastering all the facts, soaking in all the details, he must imagine the novel, create it from scratch, but staying within the limits of
what is not only possible but most probable historically. This will be
the "imaginary past," but the past conceived by a rigorously
disciplined imagination, and faithful to the facts. It will be based on
a thorough knowledge not only of what historical facts and
documents are available but, more important, of the writings, both
literary and personal (letters, most especially), of the period. So this
kind of historical novel is, in a sense, a kind of communal product,

not based entirely on the limited scope of one man's imagination, but on the productions, fictional and real, of many people's minds: a kind of collective reality created by all of them together. But it is finally dependent on the unifying imagination of a single author.

Perhaps the place to begin now is with the sense in which the novels constitute a trilogy. Each is entirely self-sufficient, and there are no interconnections; characters do not reappear (with a few minor exceptions) and there are no allusions or cross-references. There is absolutely no resemblance to the popular three-decker "'trilogies" that chronicle three generations of a family, house, or town. Chronologically, the time sequence is reversed: *Death of the Fox* is focused primarily on Sir Walter Ralegh's execution in 1618, *The Succession* on James I's succession in 1603, and *Entered from the Sun* on 1597 and Christopher Marlowe's death four years earlier. The three make up a trilogy only in that together they form both a portrait of an age and an image of human life.

Entered from the Sun is much shorter than the other two, and in many ways more accessible and more obviously attractive than they are. Both the others were centrally concerned with historical figures—*Fox* with Ralegh and *Succession* with James I, most obviously—but, except for a brief scene in which Ralegh appears, all the characters in *Sun* are purely fictional. (This is not to say that they are merely moderns in period costume, as in popular historical novels; they are profoundly and fascinatingly of their own time, not ours. But they belong to private life, not on the stage of history.) Finally, *Sun* is a murder mystery, and exploits all the legitimate appeals of that genre (which includes, of course, *Oedipus the King* and *Hamlet*). Since the chief characters are all investigating the murder of Christopher Marlowe, which involves dangerous political and religious issues, there is plenty of narrative suspense and violence as well as logical deduction. Even sex and a touch of the supernatural are involved, not merely as added attractions but as central to the plot.

The most important factor, however, in making *Sun* more immediately appealing than the other two novels is that its cast of characters is much smaller—only three, plus two persistent ghosts—and these characters, being private and low in social status, can be more fully developed than any in the other novels. The three main characters are both highly individual and representative of very different parts of the Elizabethan world; they interact unpredictably at the same time they complement and contrast with each other in their historical aspects. Joseph Hunnyman is a minor actor who lives by his wits, handsome and clever, but something of a plausible rogue. He lives with, and would like to marry, Alysoun, a young and beautiful widow who carries on her husband's business as stationer (printing, publishing, and bookselling). William Barfoot, a tough old soldier, monstrously ugly but a man of conviction (a Catholic) and honor, becomes involved with them because both he and Hunnyman are employed to investigate Marlowe's murder. (Marlowe had certainly been a spy, as well as an atheist and homosexual, and though the facts of his murder—killed in a tavern brawl over the reckoning—were no mystery, the question of its significance remained—and remains—open. It was a time of intrigue and power struggles between various factions, each with its own spies.)

Alysoun (the name calls up delicious memories of Chaucer's Wife of Bath and Miller's Tale) is sexy, intelligent, and independent; she is psychically sensitive and, in some sense, possessed by Marlowe's ghost, and the suggestion is that Marlowe's spirit, which had always wanted to be in a woman's body, is satisfied and appeased by her having intercourse with Barfoot and giving birth to his child.

As in the other novels, Garrett employs multiple narrators, picturing them as ghosts speaking to him in their own voices. In *Sun*, however, there is a complication: the narrator who presides, and of whose presence we are regularly reminded, is a failed minor poet who has known Marlowe, is employed to investigate his death, lusts after Alysoun, and through a misunderstanding is almost killed; he ends his life as a drunken beggar. His soliloquies provide a different point of view, that of someone contemporary with the main characters and like them but unlucky and unsuccessful. He fits in with the gloomy aspect of the book (the title comes from Emily Dickinson's "Doom is the House without the Door— / 'Tis entered from the sun, / And then the ladder's thrown away / Because escape is done") and the pervasive feeling of the Elizabethans, which we tend to forget, that the world is decaying, that theirs are the last days not only of the century but perhaps of the world.

As in the other novels, Garrett does not attempt to provide new solutions to historical mysteries or new interpretations of what historical characters were really like. There are no backstairs revelations about Ralegh, Marlowe, or the School of Night; instead, there are marvelous distillations of the life of the time, glimpses of the notables as they would have been in 1597: Shakespeare discouraged about the stage and planning to retire to Stratford (though Alysoun says he never will), Ralegh playing his dangerous games, Essex playing soldier, Marlowe's ghost reliving his violent death scene.

Hunnyman, clever and lucky and unscrupulous, looking out for himself alone, outlives the others; he marries a rich widow and lives to a ripe old age in the country. Barfoot is killed in Ireland; Alysoun and her young husband die of the plague. But her son (fathered by Barfoot in the flesh, but spiritually Marlowe's child) may have lived; the narrator's ignorance leaves hope.

Garrett's rendering of the Elizabethans' sense of time—so different from ours—is impressive here as in the other volumes—the rituals and ceremonies, the interweaving of the agricultural and the ecclesiastical year, the public and the private. For example:

It is Blood Month in England, time for the slaughtering of beasts before winter. And not far from here . . . animals are dying amid much groaning and squealing. Throats are cut and then the bleeding beast is hung up, hoisted by the heels to be gutted and cleaned. Oh, all that red and blue! All the slime and shit of it! Never mind. Come this Christmas and that boar's head will be brought in to music on a huge platter. Smiling. (241)

This is a story of spies, of whom Barfoot writes to his brother,

"All that can be said for certain about spies, in this our age of spies, is that we can never truly know where their loyalty and allegiance may lie. I conclude that the best of them must be assumed always to have played on both sides in everything. Duplicity is the essence of their craft. And I cannot imagine that they ever believe in much more than the craft they practice . . . Knowing that Christopher Marlowe was a spy has helped me, not so much to understand him as to understand that there is much about him that neither I nor any man will ever know." (314)

It is a story of doom and fear of death; as the author says in his Greeting, a dark story of clenched fists: "Here we meet with malcontents, with the disenchanted and disillusioned. Here are murderers and secret agents. Here are bitterly ambitious and lost souls." But the remarkable thing is that the other side is never forgotten: "Not to forget, now or ever, the long-lost brightness and shine, the hope and glory of those times. But likewise to remember, keeping in mind, the other side of it. Stony discontent, cold despair, end-of-the-world indifference" (x). And at the end the author returns to this image:

Christopher Marlowe's death may have been sudden and brutal and sordid and, finally, mysterious. But the greater and deeper and very joyful mystery is how, beyond all the known facts of his life and death, beyond the boundaries of the age he found himself living in, his living words, as best we can still recollect and resurrect them, thrive and flourish even here and now—*shining!* Shining in and out of darkness. (348)

When reviewers every week hail the publication of new masterpieces in language of the most extravagant hype, what is one to say when a real masterpiece comes along? Of this one, it is enough to say that it is fully as good as (though in many ways quite different from) its two predecessors. The trilogy as a whole re-creates an age—from Marlowe's death to Ralegh's, 1593-1618—with wonderful vividness, completeness, and accuracy, and also, by implication, interprets it in relation to our own. It tampers with no facts, fictionalizes no history, but creates living characters who represent both their own time and the universally human in any time.

Works Cited

Garrett, George. *Death of the Fox*. San Diego: Havest-Harcourt, 1991.
_____. *Entered from the Sun*. New York: Doubleday, 1990.
Spears, Monroe K. *American Ambitions: Selected Essays on Literary and Cultural Themes*. Baltimore: Johns Hopkins UP, 1987.
_____. *Countries of the Mind: Literary Explanations*. Columbia: U of Missouri P, 1992.

Steven G. Kellman

Who Killed Kit Marlowe? Who Wants to Know?

In 1983, after *The Succession* succeeded *Death of the Fox* (1971), George Garrett was asked whether he intended to write any additional novels set in Elizabethan England. He replied: "I'm going to do a quite short, skinny one—like one of the sections in *The Succession*—which has to do with the murder of Christopher Marlowe, and then that's it—I'm done with historical fiction" ("An Interview," 161). That Christopher Marlowe novel, *Entered from the Sun*, appeared in 1990, and, though it is slimmer than either *Death of the Fox* (739 pages) or *The Succession* (538 pages), the concluding volume in Garrett's Elizabethan trilogy cannot, at 349 pages, be accurately termed "a quite short, skinny one." *The Succession* had been conceived in relatively modest terms, as the epistolary exchange between Queen Elizabeth of England and her cousin King James VI of Scotland—"it should have been a tidy and limited task," explains Garrett in his author's Note (*The Succession* vii). However, as E. M. Forster observed, relations never end, and in the process of connecting two characters, Garrett found himself obliged to accommodate many more:

> But what happened to that story and to me was that in trying to contemplate two splendid characters, I was forced to summon up many others to help me, ghosts from that time, some of them "real" (Sir Robert Cecil, Sir Robert Carey, the Earl of Essex) and some of them "imaginary"—a messenger, a priest, a player, some Scots reivers, etc. And very soon it was clear that if they were to bear witness, they must be allowed to tell their own tales also. They jostled each other for places in the story. And so, finally, here they are in a story which has changed its shape and form many times before it settled into this one, a story which surely took its own sweet time to become a book. (vii-viii)

Constructing a fiction around two characters each in quest of truth about the killing of Christopher Marlowe, in a Deptford inn on

May 30, 1593, might also have seemed a modest task. Yet plumbing a death that was "sudden and brutal and sordid and, finally, mysterious" (*Entered from the Sun* 348) took its own dour time. The rich resulting text begins with an epigraph from Emily Dickinson—"Doom is the House without the Door—/ 'Tis entered from the sun, / And then the ladder's thrown away/ Because escape is done"—that suggests seduction through radiance into gloom. *Entered from the Sun* conjures up a murky universe that is, according to the elegant young man who commissions actor Joseph Hunnyman to solve the Marlowe enigma, "all snarled and knotty. Full of dark puzzlement. A maze without any true entrance or an escape" (262).

Entering Garrett's brilliant novel in quest of simple truth, the reader is soon trapped within an umbral web of mingled motives and contradictory hypotheses. Two competing sleuths, Hunnyman and Captain William Barfoot, are dispatched, under duress, by separate, unidentified patrons, to determine precisely how and why an extraordinary young playwright met a squalid, violent end. Marlowe himself remains the absent referent, four years dead and, but for an interlude of epigraphs near the end of the book (304-08), silent. An inquest undertaken by amateurs conscripted on behalf of unknown interests, long after an official panel closed the case, *Entered from the Sun* is a metamystery whose object—the Marlowe murder—and subject—the men intent on reopening the affair—remain a riddle. (It is true that eventually, reluctantly, Sir Walter Ralegh reveals himself to be Barfoot's sponsor, but neither Hunnyman nor the reader ever learns who is paying the former to look into the Marlowe matter).

In *As You Like It*, quoted in Garrett's penultimate chapter, Shakespeare alludes to the killing of his fellow playwright as "a great reckoning in a little room." Was the scandalous author of *Tamburlaine*, twenty-nine-year-old Marlowe, stabbed through the brain by Ingram Frizer, in self-defense, during a drunken brawl over the dinner bill? Or did agents of Sir Robert Cecil, the Earl of Essex, or Sir Walter Ralegh conspire to eliminate an atheist whose covert activities—political or sexual—were an embarrassment and threat to his associates? A year before Oliver Stone released his revisionist assassination film *JFK*, Garrett's novel was suggesting that the official verdict on another famous troubling murder was also a coverup, but what it covered up was as clear as the unlit London night into which Hunnyman steps in the second paragraph of the book.

The bloodshed does not quite outHerod Herod, but we are told that Hunnyman once worked for a theatrical troupe whose leader died while playing the part of Herod and that Barfoot, a gruff and wary combat veteran, defies fashion by refusing to wear a ruff—"For a ruff makes his head look like John the Baptist's on a platter" (240). Yet both Barfoot and Hunnyman—as well as a poetaster who calls himself Paul Cartwright—lose their heads at least figuratively over wanton Alysoun, a ravishing printer's widow. An earlier Garrett poem titled "Salome," which deals explicitly with the New Testament tale of perilous profane passion, anticipates both the vision and design of *Entered from the Sun*. To the question: How do we arrive at truth?, Garrett's Salome answers:

> All the world knows
> truth is best revealed
> by gradual deception. (*For a Bitter Season* 15)

If *ars artem celare est*, art is in concealing art, what Garrett artfully reveals, through a floating narrative perspective, is the ultimate obscurity of truth.

Few words recur as frequently throughout *Entered from the Sun* as *truth*. "Truth is" is the formula, on page after page, for conveying information to the reader. "Truth is," we are told about Barfoot, "he has spent more time in Venice than in his own village" (19), and "Truth is, Alysoun has never allowed her quick mind to be burdened with weighty and ponderous questions of religion" (58). But the novel's most important truths are too elusive to fit this facile phrase. The truth, warns our narrator, "is likely to be somewhat tainted and confused" (25). And, noting that honor has become indistinguishable from reputation, he asks: "In such a world how can anyone tell and separate the true from the false?" (73). How at least can he? *Entered from the Sun* offers a reader the spectacle of epistemological drama, staged in a lampless theater. As if to justify the book's own formal convolutions, the narrator likens truth to a cumbersome garment—"Truth being so often shapeless and ill fitting. More a matter of rags and ragged edges than tailored seams" (158). Weary of the drivel of the preening poets whose verses she prints, Alysoun demands: "Let men begin to say what they mean! Let us have a keyhole glimpse of the truth!" (204). Garrett's metafiction offers a keyhole glimpse of the truth, though the reader's glimpse is obstructed by the key itself, implanted in the hole.

"Would it not be ever so much better for all of us if the books of the world were easy reading," muses Captain Barfoot to Eleanor Bull, the portly widow who operates the inn at Deptford where Marlowe died. "If things were no more and no less than they seem to be" (138). Barfoot's wish for easy reading is an ironic gloss on the tangled tale in which it is quoted. A book that, interrogating appearances, is bursting at the seems, *Entered from the Sun* is the work of a first-rate intelligence, defined by F. Scott Fitzgerald's famous quip: "The test of a first-rate intelligence is the ability to hold two opposed ideas in the mind at the same time, and still retain the ability to function" (Fitzgerald 69). Beginning with parallel recruitments into the plot of its two principal characters, Hunnyman and Barfoot, an ebullient actor burning with ambition and a sullen soldier who calls himself "a burnt-out candle" (92), the novel confronts both the 1590s and the 1990s in a strenuous feat of equilibrium. A chapter titled "The Tugging and Wrestling of Contrarieties" contends that " . . . the true, unfeigned character of every man and woman is formed, therefore to be found, in the tugging and wrestling of contrarieties. The opposites he or she embraces" (95). As with every man and woman, so with every book, and Garrett's contains multitudes.

Alysoun, likened to "the wondrous chameleon, she is whatever color light and air allow" (59), physically embraces both Hunnyman—as a steady, if stealthy, lover—and Barfoot—in a single erotic encounter, as sire for a child to exorcise the ghost of Marlowe that haunts her troubled dreams. As an actor, Hunnyman is adept at assuming a variety of contrasting roles. And, though a devout but clandestine Catholic, Barfoot is fiercely loyal to Protestant England, risking his life against its Papist enemies. An uncommonly unbecoming fellow who somehow exudes powerful sexual attraction, this wary warrior is the very paragon of Fitzgerald's first-rate intelligence: "Skeptical in his considerations of all things under the sun and moon, and especially of the actions and motives of men (himself included), he is usually able, like a juggler at a market fair, to hold and to keep a number of contrarieties in mind simultaneously" (158-59). In that, Barfoot is a microcosm of the ambiguous universe in which he functions. Duplicity and equivocation are not only the professional stratagems of the many spies and counter-spies who populate a society ruled by an aging, heirless queen; they are universal mechanisms for riven minds that seek to retain the ability to function. To probe beyond appearances in the murder of Christopher Marlowe, Garrett's book must accommodate all the contradictory currents that made life in London during the reign of Elizabeth I so exuberant and precarious.

Irony is the recognition of disparity, and, torn among political and religious factions and between the medieval and modern, England on the eve of the seventeenth century, "when all the world is on fire with change" (37), seems to Garrett's sardonic narrator governed by "a just (and justly ironic) Providence" (157). William Barfoot relishes the "bright and resplendent irony" (43) of his being both a devout and active Catholic who covertly assists persecuted priests, and a loyal soldier of the heretical Tudor monarch. And in our final glimpse of Joseph Hunnyman, many years after the death of Elizabeth, many more after that of Marlowe, he has become the aging master of a grand manor, savoring the contradictory twists of fortune with a "gentle and ironic smile" (346). An ironic smile is iconic for Garrett's entire novel, entered from the sun into starless gloom.

In an essay published the same year as *Entered from the Sun*, Garrett observes that during his research what struck him most about the Elizabethan era was "a sustained duplicity, a characteristic involving feelings and perceptions as much as any ideas, a capacity to entertain, simultaneously, paradoxical, indeed contradictory feelings and perceptions" ("Living with Elizabethans" 101). Irony, ambiguity, and paradox are qualities for which the twentieth century has most prized the poetry of the English Renaissance, finding anxious kinship between modern sensibilities and the strenuous minds of those who wrote between the Reformation and the Restoration. Garrett has stressed the importance of acknowledging our attachments to an earlier era but also of recognizing "the strangeness and difference of the past" ("An Interview" 282). In a study of daily life in Elizabethan England written in the wake of his research for *The Succession*, Garrett insists on a divided relationship to the period:

> Our Elizabethan and Jacobean ancestors are so distant from us in time that we must exercise an active imagination if we are to summon them up out of the long dream of history. Yet they

are near enough, in contrast with, for example, the pre-Christian world, so that we must likewise resist an easy temptation to consider them as close kin to ourselves. ("Daily Life" 215)

Elizabeth I's contemporaries were, in fundamental ways, both very like Elizabeth II's and very different, and among the many dualities of Garrett's American novel of Elizabethan England is its dialectic between contracting historical distances and expanding them. *Pace* Jan Kott, Shakespeare is both our contemporary and an alien creature from a remote universe. *Entered from the Sun* both denies and affirms a chasm between the 1590s and the 1990s.

The novel self-consciously situates itself in two eras, each self-conscious of being the end of an age, if not merely *fin de siècle*. The air of cosmic tardiness in Barfoot's reference to "these late restless days" (114) suggests not only the apprehensive sense of an ending, with Elizabeth's death, to a stabilizing English dynasty but also the millennarian, post-Cold War angst of those confronting what, in 1993, exactly four hundred years after Marlowe's fatal reckoning, Francis Fukuyama was to dub *The End of History*. When the narrator observes that "there are many thoughtful persons who in their wisdom profess to believe that this world will end with this selfsame century" (15), he could just as well be describing apocalyptic auguries in the 1990s. And his reference to "this lost, late age of the century" (15), like Hunnyman's to "this late and degenerate age of the world" (49), does double service as diagnosis of the *mal de siècle* from which our anxious, terminating decade also suffers. When the narrator describes "this late age" as "a duplicitous time" (172), he engages in narrative duplicity—pointing at once to two ages separated by four centuries but joined by a shared quality of fissure.

Deliberate anachronism is irony of the clock, a reminder of disparity through the disjointures of time. *Entered from the Sun* derives its mystery from the insuperable gap between 1597, when it is set, forever too late, and 1593, when something irretrievable happened in a chamber in Deptford. The novel derives its urgency from conscious oscillation between the end of the sixteenth century and the end of the twentieth. When the narrator refers to "our litigious age" (186), it is not immediately evident whether he has in mind the profusion of Inns of Chancery in Elizabethan London or a future New World paradise of pettifoggery in which no one cries over spilled coffee but sues. Simon Forman, the shady figure whom Alysoun consults about her ghastly visions, seems a distillation of Paracelsus and William Harvey, but he also implicitly anticipates the psychotherapists, abortionists, and herbalists who ease a later age. When Hunnyman maintains to Alysoun that, after the death of Marlowe, "[t]here is no one alive writing good new plays" (252), the sentiment is historically plausible but, in retrospect, monumentally mistaken. Conceding that William Shakespeare has been productive, if unoriginal, Hunnyman in 1597 concludes: "Yet I think he has shot his bolt and knows it too" (254). Thus does Garrett wink at the twentieth century while gazing at the sixteenth.

Hidden behind the emissaries who compel Hunnyman and Barfoot to undertake their individual investigations of the Marlowe case are powerful figures in Elizabethan society. And behind those figures is a narrative voice that, like the reader, is even more inquisitive about the circumstances of the playwright's death. It is a voice attentive to contradiction and to the spaces between the 1590s and the 1990s. Though he insists from early in the proceedings on his own insignificance, the more that the narrator attempts to deflect attention from himself, the more he attracts it. "I am here present as a voice only, a voice from the dark," he tells the reader, demanding: "Otherwise think nothing of me. For this is in no way my story" (29). Yet it is his first-rate intelligence that generates and balances the contrarieties of the drama, and he is more than a little disingenuous when he declares that "Barfoot, not I or anyone else, is the true subject here" (283). The true subject here is the elusiveness of a true subject.

We gradually accumulate details that endow this evasive voice with a local habitation and a name. The narrator is a redbearded alcoholic who retains a limp as a souvenir of the military campaign in Ireland—in which Captain Barfoot also fought—from which he returned to civilian life at the age of twenty. Though he never had a chance to attend university, he is eager to pursue a literary career. Yet he recognizes that his poetry is so lackluster that he himself will need to pay Alysoun, who excites his erotic fantasy but evades his embrace, to have it published. Though it might be merely an alias, the narrator goes by the name of Paul Cartwright. A paragon of paradox, he unequivocally confesses duplicity: "You can see for yourself at once how the alloy made from both my weakness and my ambition could render me a somewhat less than reliable and trustworthy witness" (283). "Cartwright" is a Cretan liar at large in Elizabethan London—as well as the modern world.

For all his pretense of marginality and his efforts at self-effacement, Cartwright enters into the story even more dramatically than does John Fowles when the author of *The French Lieutenant's Woman* steps into the train compartment already occupied by his character Charles Smithson. Cartwright is brutally attacked —throat slit and skull cracked—by the two burly thugs who helped persuade Hunnyman to turn detective. Perhaps not since the fictional characters within *At Swim-Two-Birds* rebelled against their fictional creator, tied him up, and tortured him has there been as forceful a literary demonstration of the perils of authorship. Cartwright works as an intermediary for the rival sleuthing operation, sponsored by Sir Walter Ralegh, and he ostensibly occupies the same dimension of reality as do Hunnyman, Barfoot, and Ralegh. However, Cartwright manages to transcend an individual's limited perspective on events in order to become a kind of hovering omniscience. "We float on the surface of time," he claims, "as you might float on a lazy stream on a soft, summer afternoon" (24). He is able to report on actions and thoughts, in secret letters that Barfoot sends his older brother in the North Country and Hunnyman's interior monologues, to which he could not possibly have access. Cartwright's knowing allusions to two centuries imply a consciousness that is trapped in neither. His direct addresses to the reader raze the fourth wall of a fictional prison. When he cannot verify what becomes of the other characters, he affirms his and the reader's freedom to imagine: "I like to pretend I know what became of each and every one of them. You are free to invent your own versions" (326).

Poised not only between the sixteenth century and the twentieth and between reality and make-believe, the voice that calls itself "Cartwright" also apparently straddles life and death. Like the narrator of Joachim Machado de Assis' *Memòrias pòstumas de Bràs Cubas*, he speaks to the reader from beyond the grave, after "death arrived and surprised me like a thief in the night" (29). Floating free of 1597, through the ether of four centuries, the voice of Cartwright ultimately merges with that of the author, who, in a metatheatrical Shakespearean flourish, steps forward in the final pages to announce an end to our revels. A valedictory "Author's Farewell" exults in the experience of having resided in two centuries, though Garrett contends that the Elizabethans "were more interesting than we are" (347). Garrett further foregrounds the machinery of his fiction by linking *Entered from the Sun* with the other two volumes in his Elizabethan trilogy. And the parting words of this final installment constitute an emphatic rejection of linear resolution. *Entered from the Sun* concludes by recycling a paragraph from the first book of the trilogy, *Death of the Fox.* The effect is of a limitless structure that, like a Möbius strip, the double helix, or the Ouroboros, circles back into itself. There is, then, no closure to the mystery of Christopher Marlowe, except that the author reminds his reader:

> But the greater and deeper and very joyful mystery is how, beyond all the known facts of his life and death, beyond the boundaries of the age he found himself living in, his living words, as best we can still recollect and resurrect them, thrive and flourish even here and now—*shining*! (348).

Entered from the Sun leaves us with a characteristically Renaissance conceit: that radiant art confers immortality. Garrett's Elizabethan trilogy is itself a luminous perpetual motion machine, one that promises escape from Dickinson's sealed house of doom, forever back into the sun.

Works Cited

Fitzgerald, F. Scott. *The Crack-Up.* Ed. Edmund Wilson. New York: New Directions, 1956.

Garrett, George. "Daily Life in City, Town, and Country." *William Shakespeare: His World His Work His Influence.* Ed. John F. Andrews. Vol. I. New York: Charles Scribner's Sons, 1985. 215-32.

_____. *Death of the Fox.* San Diego: Harcourt Brace, 1971.

_____. *Entered from the Sun: The Murder of Marlowe.* San Diego: Harcourt Brace, 1990.

_____. *For a Bitter Season.* Columbia: U of Missouri P, 1967.

_____. "Living with Elizabethans; or, There Goes the Neighborhood." *Traditions and Innovations: Essays on British Literature of the Middle Ages and the Renaissance.* Ed. David G. Allen and Robert A. White. Newark: U of Delaware P, 1990. 97-101.

_____. *The Succession: A Novel of Elizabeth and James.* San Diego: Harcourt Brace, 1983.

"An Interview with George Garrett." *Dictionary of Literary Biography Yearbook: 1983.* Ed. Mary Bruccoli and Jean W. Ross. Detroit: Gale, 1984. 157-61.

Allen Wier

The Scars of Flesh and Spirit or How He Pictures It:
George Garrett's Entered from the Sun

Several years ago I was at Johnston State College in Vermont
to hear George Garrett read from and discuss his fiction. Garrett
was introduced by the novelist Carolyn Chute, who walked onto a
small stage carrying a white, carpet-sized roll of paper on her
shoulder. Without a word, she taped one end of the wide roll along
the front of the table—say six feet long—which held the podium.
She let go of the paper which unrolled onto the stage, then to the
floor of the auditorium and down a center aisle.

"Here," she said, "is a complete list of George Garrett's publications."

That long list now includes nine novels, seven books of poems,
seven books of short fiction, two books of criticism, two book-
length literary studies, three collections of personal essays, twenty-
one books edited, scores of poems, stories, and critical articles in
magazines, plays for children, plays for grownups and several screen-
plays (including the Golden Turkey Award-winning *Frankenstein
Meets the Space Monster*, considered, by many highfalutin' critics,
the worst screenplay ever written). On *one* day, in 1961, Garrett
published a novel, *Which Ones Are the Enemy?*, a book of poems,
Abraham's Knife, and a collection of stories, *In the Briar Patch*.
Garrett has published formal verse as well as short poems in forms
he calls postcards/flashcards/snapshots. *My Silk Purse and Yours*
collects essays on the publishing scene and American literary art.
Whistling in the Dark gathers fables and literary anecdotes. The
short fictions in *An Evening Performance* and in *The Magic
Striptease* extend from traditional tales to a comic strip fable to a
movie soundtrack in various tongues and voices. His range is
limitless. Of the amazing number and the incredible variety of
Garrett's publications, Louis Rubin says, "Garrett does so many
things so well that the sheer profusion and exuberance of his work
may tend to blind us to its uncommon excellence."

For all this uncommon excellence Garrett has been widely

recognized. His many awards include: the Rome Prize of the American Academy of Arts and Letters, a Ford Foundation Grant, National Endowment and Guggenheim Fellowships, the Award in Literature from the American Academy of Arts and Letters, the Ingersoll Foundation's T.S. Eliot Award, the PEN/Malamud Award for Short Fiction, and the Hollins College Medal.

While Garrett has been writing all these novels, poems, stories, plays, essays, articles and reviews and winning all these prizes, he's also been teaching full-time at over a dozen universities and colleges, including Wesleyan, Rice, Princeton, Hollins, South Carolina, Florida International, Columbia, Michigan, Bennignton, VMI, Alabama, and Virginia, where he holds the Hoyns Professorship in creative writing. He's had residencies, participated in conferences, and given readings at some 300 other institutions. He evaluates manuscripts for publishers, judges contests, offers blurbs for deserving books. With Verlin Cassill, Garrett is largely responsible for the formation of the Associated Writing Programs, which represents the interests of creative writers in the academy. Garrett is a founding member of the Fellowship of Southern Writers.

All of the above is probably not enough said about a writer who has covered more literary ground in the past thirty years than most writers cover in a lifetime. Garrett's is a remarkable career, a career that is not nearly over. Even more remarkable than all that Garrett has done is all that he has done for others. As a writer, as a teacher, and as a friend to writers, Garrett's kindnesses are legendary. He has shared his talent and given his advice; he has also shared his home and given his money, and he continues to share—most precious—his time and his energy with writers and students a list of whom would be longer than Carolyn Chute's computer list of Garrett's publications. The volume you hold in your hand is the third (that I know of) book-length collection of assessments, testimonials, and public thanks which Garrett's contemporaries have published. George Garrett has managed to accrue all this love and good will in spite of the fact that he never shies away from a literary argument and in spite of the fact that—in a business in which many movers and shakers take themselves more seriously than they take literature—Garrett has always refused to jump on the circus bandwagon of any literary movement or school because, as he has said, "the main aim of these is to make the poet, whether as prophet or charmer, into a respected and respectable citizen." George Garrett has a sense of humor as wide-ranging as his art. He's as good a storyteller as there is—not necessarily the facts but always the truth from the mouth of someone who has been wherever and done whatever he's describing.

George Garrett's rebellious, darkly comic vision is powerfully revealed in his extraordinary and highly praised trilogy of Elizabethan historical novels. The first-published of the three, *The Death of the Fox* (1971), brought Garrett widespread critical acclaim and was on the *NY Times* bestseller list for months. It was followed by *The Succession* (1983) and by *Entered from the Sun* (1990). This trilogy demonstrates revolutionary formal innovations. Monroe Spears places these books "in the exalted company of *Ulysses* and a very few other works that carry the novel form as far as it can go, exploiting all its resources and revealing new possibilities."

Garrett's first two Elizabethan novels so uniquely redefined the possibilities for historical fiction that R.H.W. Dillard said (after the publication of *The Succession*) that they "break away completely from what has gone before them and constitute something utterly new in the history of the novel." Garrett's third Elizabethan novel, *Entered from the Sun*, is equally, though differently, bright-shining new. There's nothing in historical fiction, nothing in any recent fiction, with which to compare *Entered from the Sun* except Garrett's other Elizabethan novels.

As in the earlier books, though more overtly, the methods employed in the telling of the tale are as much a part of the pleasure of *Entered from the Sun* as the tale itself. Indeed, the various voices here gathered constitute the tale. But *Entered from the Sun* doesn't just present cool metafictional complications; rather, ghosts who "float on the surface of time" are brought vividly to life.

Historical figures appear—Christopher Marlowe, Queen Elizabeth, Sir Francis Walsingham, The Earl of Essex, Sir Walter Ralegh, Robert Cecil, Ben Jonson, Robert Greene, William Shakespeare, and others—but (with the exception of Marlowe's presence) the major characters of *Entered from the Sun* are fictional—Captain Barfoot, Joseph Hunnyman, the Widow Alysoun. The ghost narrator bore, when he was flesh, a suspiciously strong resemblance to the poet Robert Greene, and bears in his ghostly guise a strong figurative resemblance to all artful tellers of tales (George Garrett, to name just one).

In the earlier novels Garrett makes implicit comparisons between the Elizabethan present and our present. In *Entered from the Sun* such comparisons are overt. Then and now a world "on fire with change," both ages of information—"of ink and paper"—both times of personal vanity and ambition—"fame seems to be desired by almost everyone"—both ages "of false witness."

In the earlier novels, though his presence is clearly felt, Garrett never directly intrudes. In *Entered from the Sun* the first voice we hear ("Author's Greeting") is Garrett's:

> A few words of my own before I leave you in the hands of others. A few words, perhaps to reassure you or myself, before I step aside, step back to listen, as you do, to the voices of others, the noise of strangers.
> A dark story we are sharing here. No doubt about it.

Garrett is not overtly present again until the concluding "Author's Farewell," though he makes a cameo appearance as the character Jack Towne, who is John Towne, the mysterious double Garrett claims as the true author of his sixth novel, the comic/satiric *Poison Pen*. As the medium through whom imagined minds meet, Garrett's sensibility, his aura, surrounds characters who speak through him as he instigates a many-sided conversation between writer, reader and a confluence of ghostly voices. His "Author's Greeting" has this coda:

> Bear with me, ghosts.
> And bless us, one and all, your newfound, long-lost friends.
> Speak to me.
> Speak through me.
> Speak to us.

The following chapter, "How it Begins for Joseph Hunnyman," introduces, in dramatic, third-person narration from his perspective, Joseph Hunnyman, ambitious actor/performer, thrust suddenly onto the boards of our play (which is also his life) as he leaves a warm firelit tavern. A heavy door shuts behind him, and he is in cold, wet darkness:

> Next, then, as he would recall and reconstitute it later, came

a shuffle or scuffle, a kind of whispering not of breath and words, more likely of soft shoes or of clothing, close by him from both sides. And he groped across his body, snatching to the left with his right hand, clutching for the hilt of his sword. Only to find there, with a flashing of pure cold and splashed across his whole body at one and the same instant, like the chills that dance hand in hand with fevers, another hand . . . .

Snatched in darkness and dragged into a bright cellar, he is "persuaded" by persons unknown to him to investigate circumstances surrounding the death by stabbing of the poet Christopher Marlowe. That stabbing, five years earlier, in 1593, was ruled self-defense, but questions remain.

The next chapter, "Enter Captain Barfoot," begins:

Seeing is believing. And if you could only see for yourself, you would be willing to believe almost anything said about him and, very likely, anything he said to you, face to face, his eyes as if lit from behind by some inner fire, his hard face a map of scars and trouble.

Second person. Who's speaking and to whom? *You* feel as if *you* (the reader) are this voice's ear; you are immediately drawn into a participatory confidence. (Who can ignore direct address?) Or is "you" some as-yet-unnamed narrator/character?

The next chapter, "Player and Soldier," begins in second person, then shifts into first person plural, then the voice acknowledges (without yet identifying) itself:

You will have noticed how I have suddenly said *we*, as if claiming a place for myself. For though I play no part in this tale, I am nevertheless ever present, a witness to it all, first to last.

Which is only partly true. A witness, yes (likely false, as most witnesses are), and one, we discover, who does play a part in this tale.

The five major players are tangled with connections to one another—not, to be sure, all *known* connections. Hunnyman and Barfoot, the male leads, are engaged in separate but intersecting searches, tracking the dead poet Christopher Marlowe, whose ghost is also a leading player. The female lead is the Widow Aly-soun, who has intercourse of one kind or another with all three—Hunnyman, Barfoot, the ghost of Marlowe—as she does with a poet who calls himself Paul Cartwright, his ghost our narrator, who, early on, declares:

> As for myself.
> Why, that's nothing to concern yourself about. I am here present as a voice only, a voice from the dark. Hoping by the power of words and words alone (though they may sometimes cast real shadows like sudden wings) to permit you to see and to judge for yourself.

Later, in "Every Bitter Thing is Sweet" (a brilliant chapter, the fulcrum on which this question of narrative stance hinges), the narrator responds to our suspicions:

> For now it is enough to confess that, for one reason and another, I have been false with you in several ways.
> For instance, I did not choose to mention, for whatever it may be worth, that I was, quite separately and, indeed, unbeknownst by one or the other, somewhat acquainted with both Hunnyman and Barfoot.

More suspicions and confessions follow. This is an age of conspiracy and deceit, a time when "half the people in England are spying on the other half." The unravelling of mysteries surrounding the narrator proceeds apace with the unravelling of mysteries surrounding Marlowe's death and of the mysteries concerning the separate, unknown parties who employ Hunnyman and Barfoot in unravelling mysteries. Much later our narrator confesses that "the alloy made from both my weakness and my ambition could render me a somewhat less than reliable and trustworthy witness."

The testimony of any witness is suspect. The best intentions still suffer from subjectivity and errors of memory. There can be no knowable true version of how Marlowe died. But what history can't confirm, fiction can meditate. The suspense we enjoy in *Entered from the Sun* is not the suspense of plot but of meditation and speculation. Garrett dramatizes versions of Marlowe's death ("How Hunnyman Pictures it Happening" and "Barfoot's Version: How He

Pictures It"), versions of Widow Alysoun's behavior ("What Alysoun Tells Hunnyman" and "What Alysoun Did Not Tell Hunnyman"), a version of the future ("Hunnyman Sees the Future") and versions of his characters' fates ("Endings"). This is not just literary play with perspective and point-of-view. The reader merges imagination with the writer/medium and with characters. Garrett imagines, then dramatizes, a character's imagination so that the reader participates in a multi-dimensional, collaborative imagining and telling of the tale. In "Endings," the narrator (now a player, with the reader, in the drama) says:

"I like to pretend I know what became of each and every one of them. You are free to invent your own versions. Here are mine . . . ."

An admitted liar, he projects his imagined endings onstage. Like jurors who've been told to ignore a witness's remarks, we experience the drama of meditation, each of us, no doubt, adding nuances of personal interpretation.

Garrett's multiform methods—points-of-view and perspectives, juxtapositions of voices, varieties of chapters—are sufficient for the metaphysical complexities of his tale. Five chapters—"Present Difficulties of this Time: Apparel," "Present Difficulties of this Time: Plays, Players, and Playhouses," "Present Difficulties of this Time: Matters of Religion," "Present Difficulties of this Time: The Court" and "Words of Marlowe and Others"—hang like legends on scrims before scenes in a stage play. They present excerpts from Elizabethan texts, reminding us of the aesthetic nature of the experience even as they draw us tonally into the period, working the text of the time into the fictional text, weaving the rich texture of a simultaneous world, the present moment: then/now.

Validated by Garrett's thorough knowledge and unerring sense of Elizabethan England, rich with sensuous detail and wonderfully textured prose, *Entered from the Sun* fuses fact and fiction to make a living world. "Interlude: Accession Day" masterfully reveals Garrett's remarkable understanding of Elizabethan pageantry, grandeur, wickedness and squalor, with a dazzling depiction of the Queen's Day, which, paradoxically, happens also to be Blood Month, the time in England when beasts are slaughtered for meat.

Garrett's characters acknowledge evil; they know "there are no limits but Nature's own to our vanity, cunning, and depravity." Yet, these are characters capable of "brightness and shine . . . hope and glory." They recognize paradox, "the opposites he or she embraces," the "tugging and wrestling of contrarieties." Paradox is exemplified in Joseph Hunnyman, player, who knows he and the stage on which he struts are "beyond all possible redemption" and, in spite of that knowledge, still loves the world and "tries to learn to love himself," and in Captain Barfoot, old soldier, who bears many bitter scars of "flesh and spirit" with grace, in spite of his hopelessness.

Almost dead of the plague, Barfoot was piled onto a cart of dead bodies, then dumped into a mass grave, buried alive, only to be "saved" by a mysterious crone who dragged him away and nursed him back to health. We sanctify him for his wounds and his losses (he's suffered original sin, he's died of the plague and been resurrected) until, late in the novel, in "Barfoot's Guilty Secret," this man whose consciousness we've shared and for whom we've felt empathy and affection reveals:

How, in the prime of hot-blooded youth he and his companions, and once or twice later all alone, more than one time sought and found a grunting, teeth-grinding, joyous, joyless satisfaction of themselves upon the helpless, terrified bodies of women.

It's too late, now, to recant our affection. The collaborative experience makes us aware of our own blindness and, at the same time, dramatizes the paradox of creatures whose nature admits such extremes of both good and evil.

. . . as he [Barfoot] views it, it is a final kind of ironic jig and jest, a laughable thought, that a monster, himself in truth as well as appearance, can be so misapprehended by his own kind. Their folly may be the beginning of his wisdom.

We must bear the scars of one with whom we have merged our imagination. But even this darkest impulse of Barfoot's cruelty is inverted in "Alysoun's Wonderful Secret," two chapters later, when Captain Barfoot brutally fulfills the prophecy of Alysoun's imagination and her dream:

. . . as they kissed and he held her head tightly, she could feel the knife at work, as he first, and more swiftly than she imagined it could be done, with a sweep cut away the long row of buttons of her dress, the buttons all at once cut loose and free and falling, like a broken string of beads or pearls, to roll on and across the floor. Then, still holding her, still kissing her, as she snorted for breath, he cut her clothing to ribbons. She could hear the sound of the cutting of cloth and feel the chill air of the fireless room playing upon patches of bare skin, but could feel no pain. He was not cutting her. And the groan she heard from herself as he placed the blade flat and cold between her bare breasts, the point beneath her chin, was as much made up of pleasure as of fear.

And in the fulfillment of Alysoun's dream Barfoot gives her a child she bears and delivers and names Richard, the only character about whose fate the narrator never speculates. Out of Captain Death, new life; out of the darkness, light.

Entered from the Sun takes us back to the Elizabethans for "delight and instruction." The lever we pull for this time-travel is language. At the end of the journey, as he returns us to our own time, Garrett reminds us that language carries us beyond all boundaries:

Christopher Marlowe's death may have been sudden and brutal and sordid and, finally, mysterious. But the greater and deeper and very joyful mystery is how, beyond all the known facts of his life and death, beyond the boundaries of the age he found himself living in, his living words, as best we can still recollect and resurrect them, thrive and flourish even here and now—*Shining!*

What more could any poet ask? And what more could any reader ask than to merge his or her imagination with an imagination imagined so fully to bright-shining life? Such is the lasting power of George Garrett's *Entered from the Sun*.

Tom Whalen

Eavesdropping in the Dark: The Opening(s) of George Garrett's Entered from the Sun

Eavesdropping, but with the reading lamp turned full on, we read:

Laughing out loud, he turned away from laughing faces and the noise of voices, all of them talking again all at once, with one or two over in the chimney corner trying to join together to sing out the familiar melody of some old round or common country song, but from the first note so out of tune as to be beyond recognition and repair; in a few quick strides left behind him, as if tossed over his shoulder, the sweet and heavy, yeasty odors of beer and ale, these good things commingled with the undeniable and inimitable stink of a close crowd of freely sweating men and, too, the small white pungent clouds created by the smokers of pipes and the acrid grease-laden scents of the rush lights and the cheap tallow candles offering as much smoke as light; left behind, then, above all, the light and shadow, sway and dance of it, of the well-stacked, highblazing fireplace. (Garrett, *Entered* 1-2)

We hear first a laugh, the act of laughing, a sound out of the Elizabethan past, a laugh isolated for us from amidst other laughter, as we learn in the second line of this first sentence which constitutes the first paragraph of George Garrett's novel *Entered from the Sun*. And then "he," i.e., Joseph Hunnyman, "turned away," turns his back on "laughing faces and the noise of voices, all of them talking again all at once . . . ." So the first act is laughter, and the second is a turning away (from his own joke, we learn in the next paragraph: "smiling at the wit of his own jest and still relishing the loud response it instantly evoked" [2]). We have begun *in medias res*, an appropriate beginning, I would suggest, for a novel whose strategy, as in the first two novels of Garrett's Elizabethan trilogy, *Death of the Fox* and *The Succession*, is designed to submerge the reader into the swirl of those times, its smells, sensations, secretions, secrets, "the sweet and heavy, yeasty odors of beer and ale . . . the undeniable and inimitable stink of a close crowd." (For how Garrett achieves, via experimental means, this fusion of reader to the text, see my "The Reader Becomes Text: Methods of Experimentation in George Garrett's *The Succession: A Novel of Elizabeth and James*" in *The Texas Review* 4. 1/2 [1983], 14-21.)

Garrett puts even more emphasis on the need for the creative participation of the reader in this novel than in the previous two. So much so that in the novel's preface, the "Author's Greetings," he suggests that the reader consider the act of reading as one of listening to voices. "A few words, perhaps to reassure you or myself, before I step aside, step back to listen, as you do, to the voices of others, the noise of strangers." And he directs us to "[t]hink, first of all, of fists. Clenched and hardknuckled," to "[l]et them have life again" (vii). It is our responsibility, in collaboration with the author, to give these fists, these characters and their time, "life again." But this vivid and substantial reconstitution that is *Entered from the Sun*, these clenched fists ("Think of this as a story of clenched fists" [vii]), is also insubstantial, for Garrett doesn't allow us to forget that the characters we observe, listen to, breathe with, are themselves no more now than recollections and ghosts, whether real or fictive.

Again we must note this act of turning away; this is what signals the novel's elegiac tone, its epistemological plot (two men—Hunnyman, an actor, and Barfoot, a soldier/spy—a few years after Christopher Marlowe's murder, are hired separately to investigate the killing) and the dispersal of this plot into sub-plots, whisperings, ghost voices, and more murder and more mystery. It is October, 1597. Elizabeth's life and reign are nearing their end. A world is about to end. A universe. Of voices we can only, now, recall, reconstitute from the air by means of our imaginations. The novel's movement (and here I do not mean linear movement) is as inevitable and cosmic as the slow slide of the stars through the night sky, as the universe's recession. Instances come to mind: echoes of the first sentence such as "[a]mid laughter, as if laughter were a puff of smoke, he will turn away and disappear" (20), or "[s]o much of your memory of Ireland, all but the weather of it (and the fear), has begun to fade away. To whatever place lost memories wander" (83). Or passages like:

But he was speaking softly to the man's broad back. He was already walking away into the foggy dark. Then abruptly turned back, reappeared like a swimmer bobbing up from deep water.

"Fine nights for vanishing," he said. (94)

This sense of separation, of erasure, permeates the novel. It is fall. The century is nearing its end. Marlowe has been murdered. Others will be as well. Barfoot's mother has gone mad. Hunnyman's family has been killed by the Plague. Everything is leaving, falling, fading away. Even the search for truth takes us as much away from it as toward it. Truth is like a ghost, something that comes in and out of focus, something you can put your hand through and never know it was there. Deception is the order of the day. Perhaps the end of the world is near.

Like so many, great and small, virtuous and wicked, young or old, in this lost, late age of the century and the world (and, believe me, there are many thoughtful persons who in their wisdom profess to believe that this world will end with this selfsame century and with the reign of the old Queen), like many others, William Barfoot is not precisely what he seems to be. (15-16)

In such "an age of false witnesses (yours as well as mine)" (283) the lie (image) takes on more "value" than the truth.

Consider that in this age of ours, this late age when the best days of the world have long since blazed and gone up in smoke and left us with the heat and glow of dying coals, consider that, here and now, as we live in a duplicitous time, appearances, all alone and all too often, have far more weight and substance, thus *value*, than any naked truth. Consider that when the truth is too shabby, too shoddy, unflattering and unpromising, nothing more or less than a heavy cross to bear, we turn away from it as if it were part of our human nature to do so. As if it were created in us, our given and proper condition, to love the intricate pleasures of our idle fantasies (which are, after all, our own creation) more than the unavoidable wounds and sorrows of the world as it truly is. (172)

Like the novel's two "investigators," Barfoot and Hunnyman, we are allowed "to weigh and sift, value or scorn, only the evidence which they, by accident or by design, have left behind" (168), and time will ravage, alter, or erase even this evidence, as it does the "living flesh" we wear around our bones. So it's no surprise that the image of the ravaged body (Barfoot's war- and Plague-scarred face and body) and the image of the death's-head skull occur:

> To turn your attention elsewhere before you saw me for what I was and would become—on my hands and knees, puking my guts empty and wishing not only that I could vomit up and out of my nose and throat the gray mess of my brains, but also that I could empty and scour my hollow skull of its whole hoard of memories and sorrows. Then you would see my skull grin! Like any other unknown anatomy shoveled up from a common grave-yard. (164)

Nor are we surprised that the theme of appearances is emphasized. The first of the "document" chapters, that is, sections composed of extracts from documents of the period, is entitled "Present Difficulties of This Time: Apparel," one of whose extracts reads:

> It is impossible to know who is noble, who is worshipful, who is a gentleman, who is not, because all persons dress indiscriminately in silks, velvets, satins, damasks, taffetas and such like notwithstanding that they be both base by birth, and servile by calling, and this I count a great confusion and general disorder, God be merciful unto us.
> —Philip Stubbes, *The Anatomy of Abuses.* (85-86)

For Garrett, the modern (or postmodern) world doesn't begin with the Uncertainty Principle of quantum physics or the assault on faith in the mid-19th century, but in the multifarious, multilinear, self-reflexive age of Cervantes and Shakespeare, the Elizabethan age, the age of Mannerism inhabited by "creature[s] of many paradoxes and contradictions" (16). In *Death of the Fox* and *The Succession* Garrett engaged this complexity with a striking use of multiple perspectives, but I consider his point of view in *Entered from the Sun* even more radically innovative.

In his essay "George Garrett and the Historical Novel," Monroe

K. Spears notes that in the first two Elizabethan novels, the author "never intrudes in his own person, but always speaks through the imagined mind of a 'historical' personage or 'ghost'" (264). Though this could also be said of this panel of the triptych, the issue of point of view and authorial intrusion is now more complicated and mixed. *Entered from the Sun* is narrated by one Paul Cartwright, once a soldier and second-rate poet, one who "though [he] play[s] no part in this tale [is] nevertheless ever present, a witness to it all, first to last" (25). And this Paul Cartwright, it turns out, is dead. Yes, the voice who has been nudging us throughout the novel with its omniscience and its shifting from third to second person, with the second person sometimes addressed to a character, sometimes to us, the readers, is a ghost, and one who, it turns out, is not entirely reliable himself. "Well, I warned you not to trust the dead. Yet even as I say so, I doubt you will find a better witness. Better or more bitter" (172). This diegetic ghost, as I think of him, is more problematic than the ghost voices of the other two novels or the George Garrett who, as R.H.W. Dillard notes, "is very much present in the text of *Death of the Fox* as a diegetic narrative voice" (119). For one thing the ghost voice dominates point of view in a way no single voice is allowed to do in *The Succession*. *He* is the character "in the know," the one on whose authority the story is told, which connects him directly to the role of the "invisible" author.

In the first chapter where the "ghost voice" of Paul Cartwright directly addresses the reader (there are several wherein he does so, and we do learn by degrees more about him, that he was once "a common scribbler" of verses and an overimbiber of wine, that he once fought in Ireland, and he does play, despite his earlier disclaimer, a role in the stories of Barfoot, Hunnyman, Marlowe, and Alysoun), he is a disembodied voice, the one the reader eavesdrops on. Certainly he is in the know about the principal characters. He gives us a detailed analysis of both the actor Hunnyman and the soldier Barfoot. But his language is interwoven with those sections of the text where his voice is, ostensibly at first, absent—for example the novel's water/light motif ("Pools of brightness" [26], "drawn out of deep and dark and into the light like the sweetest and coldest well water" [271]), or the motif already mentioned of departures, of turning away:

He has run, fleeing from the stage—though that stage may have been no more than a piece of yard, of green grass at the edges of a church fair or, maybe, the far end of a smoky hall in some draftty castle or crumbling old mansion in far country—has left the stage in a hurry and with tears in his eyes. (26)

We can assume, then, if only by the interweaving of motifs, that the first paragraph of the novel is also narrated by the ghost. As in the first paragraph, Hunnyman is surrounded once more by voices, "[a]ll of them speaking at once" (63), but this time the ghost voice is recalling Hunnyman's entry into London as a young actor. "And then another voice, his own, spoke to him as if whispering in his ear" (63).

To come to one understanding as to how our diegetic ghost and the author function together, we have to turn to the opening before the opening—the "Author's Greetings," for what the "author" says in his greetings and the way he says it—the same imperative forms, the similar imagery—resemble that of Paul Cartwright. Like an old storyteller, the "author" calls not only on his readers, but also calls on his characters, his ghosts ("Bear with me ghosts" [viii]) and identifies himself and us with them:

Speak to me.
Speak through me.
Speak to us. (viii)

Both voices, the "author's" and Cartwright, direct the reader to im-agine the fictive, ghostly world into sensual reality. Both voices see the ghosts as plural. Cartwright says: "Ghosts, no more and no less, they cannot be clearly seen by daylight. Vague and brief as frosty breath on coldest days, they float through time" (24).

The most direct identification of ghost with author occurs when the ghost says:

You will have noticed how I have suddenly said we, as if claim-ing a place for myself. For though I play no part in this tale, I am nevertheless ever present, a witness to it all, first to last. (25)

Like a writer, Cartwright has "lived out a watchful life":

As for myself.

Why, that's nothing to concern yourself about. I am here present as a voice only, a voice from the dark. Hoping by the power of words alone (though they may sometimes cast real shadows like sudden wings) to permit you to see and to judge for yourself.

Otherwise think nothing of me. For this is in no way my story. Except, perhaps, this much. To know what I profess to have known and to believe what I claim to have believed, I must have lived out a watchful life, as awake and alert and as thoughtful as I could manage. (29)

The diegetic ghost can enter into the minds of the characters, can tell us things only an author could know. Of Hunnyman, we learn the following secret:

[. . .] no one knows how in his own private chambers he still keeps a chest containing the clothing of his dead children. Keeps these things clean and folded and fresh-scented with sweet herbs. And once in a while, coming home half-drunk and weary to his very bones with the weight of the world and the flesh and the Devil, he has unlocked and opened up that chest and, one by one, unfolded the little clothes, holding them up to moonlight and starlight at the window. As if by holding these things high in the dim light he might somehow cause their emptiness to fill with life again. (99)

And when the novel picks up the motif of the fist mentioned in the "Author's Greetings" ("Will fist his face into a horrifying frown" [16]; "'Tight as a clenched fist, sir,'" Eleanor Bull, the owner of the house where Marlowe was killed, tells Barfoot [139]), it's as if the ghost had eavesdropped on the author.

Obviously connections are being drawn between the ghost narrator and the "author" and the *author*, but these connective lines are in motion, now they touch, now they don't. But why is the ghost's knowledge limited, why can't he illuminate the novel's central mystery? He floats, as he says, "on the surface of time" (24), a time that extends even to our own, but still he cannot give us the definitive answers about the death of Christopher Marlowe. Having once been of the time and now a ghost, Cartwright can address us in our time, but the "surface of time" on which he floats is still limited.

The dialectic this point of view generates and the speculations it engenders in the reader are unending. Who is responsible for the patterns of the novel, the dance imagery, say, of life and sex and death? (Hunnyman dances "round and round his little room, clutching the soft, sweet clothes" of his dead children [99]; the narrator tells us that in "the final jig of Judgment we will all dance like ants in a hot pan" [164] ; Barfoot's last words, as he confronts his assailants, are "'[a]nd the time has come for us to have our dance" [346].) Who is Paul Cartwright and how is he able relate this story from beyond the grave? Who is the "author" of the "Author's Greetings" and "Author's Farewell"? And where amongst these shifting lines is George Garrett?

Well, the honest answer would be that he is everywhere and nowhere. What Garrett has done, what he has *achieved*, is to invent a single point of view that embodies multiple points of view, one that is simultaneously disembodied narrator and character and author and able to move into other characters' points of view and yet is also limited. The effect isn't one of confusion or blurring, but more that of swirling, of rippling as in the paintings of Mannerist artists such as El Greco, Parmigianino, or Ramano.

We find, too, this interconnectedness in our two principal characters, Joseph Hunnyman and William Barfoot, who are, in more ways than not, opposites, yet are given surprising similarities. The actor Joseph Hunnyman (one of whose psuedonyms, by the way, is William Ashborne) imagines "he had just now been enabled to split himself into two beings, one of which (the soul?) being or becoming a young girl" (3). And the soldier William Barfoot's "gestures are often as graceful and delicate as a girl's" (15). Or we find the disembodiedness of the ghost in the voice of Alysoun: "[H]er voice is as disembodied as if she had been summoned up by a necromancer from the spirit world and were speaking out of the chilly darkness" (174). And often we catch, for a moment, aspects of the author, the hand or face or eye of George Garrett dissolving into and out of the faces of each of our main characters (and especially the persona of Cartwright), not unlike the dialectical dissolve of the Towne/Garrett relationship in *Poison Pen*.

In the section entitled "The Tugging and Wrestling of Contrarieties," the narrator tells us that it is in this dialectic, this "wrestling of contrarieties," that we learn about our true characters:

There are those, wise men among them, who firmly believe that, saints and devils aside (and who can claim to have seen many of either kind lately?), the true, unfeigned character of every man and woman is formed, therefore to be found, in the tugging and wrestling of contrarieties. The opposites he or she embraces. Admitted or denied, no matter, it is the contradictions in and of himself that tell us—and himself as well, if he should happen to have the courage to examine himself without excessive flattery or contempt—who he truly is. Or, anyway, to reveal as much of truth, arising from inward voyaging and exploration, as any of us reasonably can bear. (95)

George Garrett, I think, would agree. "In a way," Garrett has said, "fiction is dialectic: As soon as one force starts, you try to oppose it in some way or another" (Ruffin 31). The novel's primary elegiac tone, for example, is balanced by Alysoun's brilliantly comic monologue in the section "What Alysoun Tells Hunnyman." In an essay on Faulkner's humor, Garrett said that "if [Faulkner] always felt the tears of things, he likewise could hear, as some hear voices, the sourceless laughter which is at least half the music of this world" (Garrett, "'Fix My Hair, Jack'" 230-31). And in the comic names of Hunnyman and Barfoot their tragic lives are countered: Hunnyman equalling both the sexual Honey man and the actor/fool Funny man, and in the comic Barfoot is embedded the German *Barfüsser*, a barefooted or discalced monk, which alludes to Barfoot's deeply felt (and hidden) Catholicism.

The loss we sense immediately in the first paragraph of *Entered from the Sun*, the sense of recession, of falling away, is countered by the dynamics within the novel that pull you inward. The "Author's Farewell," the novel's last words, for example, provides us, paradoxically, with a means of entry. Here Garrett quotes from a description of an earlier ghost, one found in *Death of the Fox*, the first volume of the trilogy:

This ghost, an ageless young man, ever idle and restless, courteous and cruel, unchanging child of change, this man will say no more. He touches his lips to signal silence. He smiles and, miming the blowing out of a candle, he takes a thief's farewell, first the color fading, then the sad cold light of his eyes gone, and one last blinking of something—a jewel, a ring, a coin cupped in his palm, and darkness comes between us and is final. (350-51)

This "ending" folds the last novel of the triptych into the first, and we realize, if we haven't already, how each novel sends ripples into the others. Yes, there are the principal historical figures (Ralegh, Elizabeth, James, Marlowe) who make appearances one way or the other in each book. (Ralegh, it turns out, plays a significant and generative role in *Entered from the Sun.*) And there is the age itself, its politics, religion, drama and imagery. The echoes can be direct: in *Entered from the Sun* we are told of a pamphlet "Papist in origin" whose "text then goes even beyond [the Queen's illegitimate claim to the throne] into the forbidden topic of the Succession" (111). Or they can be buried, as in these parallel descriptions of two British soldiers *and* Catholics:

He [William Barfoot] long since learned to fix his face into a blank mask, ever the same in pain and pleasure, hope or fear. (24)

If he [Sir Edmund Sheffield] keeps a straight face and grave countenance, it will work. For a blank mask becomes the face of comedy or tragedy according to the wishes of the beholder. (Garrett, *Death of the Fox* 650)

Both men must mask their beliefs if they are to help the outlawed Catholic priests, and we recall the disguised priest on the run and in hiding in *The Succession*. And there are the three ghosts—soldier, courtier, sailor—of *Death of the Fox* and the "cloud of ghosts" of *The Succession*. The trilogy forms a tapestry interlaced with themes of truth and illusion, observer and observed, "false witnesses," indeterminacy, eschatology. Though the age, like the universe, continually recedes from us, Garrett, by interrelating the three novels, draws us again and again back into it.

What Hunnyman turns away from in the first paragraph, the reader is pulled toward by the vividness of the imagery. He has stepped out of the circle, but behind him begins "the familiar melody of some old round or common country song," even if "from the first note" it is "so out of tune as to be beyond recognition and repair." He has "left behind him, as if tossed over his shoulder, the sweet and heavy, yeasty odors of beer and ale, these good things [that] com-

mingled with the undeniable and inimitable stink of a close crowd."
And he leaves behind the ghostly "small white pungent clouds
created by the smokers of pipes and the acrid grease-laden scents
of the rush lights and the cheap tallow candle offering as much smoke
as light." And "above all" he leaves behind "the light and shadow,
sway and dance of it, of the well-stacked, high-blazing fireplace."
The senses that dominate this opening, those of sound and smell
(aspects of air), like the other dominant image (light), cannot be held.
They fade away, leaving behind, if anything, only a memory, a trace,
smoke marks on the wall—like these disembodied voices, these
words on the page.

I have written of the opening and of yet another opening, the
"Author's Greetings," and have in the farewell found a pulsation
toward a re-entering of the beginning of the trilogy. Each novel
slides into the next and the one before and the one after. Embedded
in them are the voices, the ghosts, traces of our present in our past.
Themes, imagery, the long ride through this vanished age, this vanishing landscape, clarion calls, resurrected texts, imaginary ones,
words aware of their element like leaves the wind, and all fading
away as surely and elegiacally as in a text by Beckett.

I have written of the beginning, but this is a work that doesn't
concern itself with beginnings. The epigraph from Emily Dickinson
tells us that.

> Doom is the House Without the Door—
> 'Tis entered from the sun
> And then the ladder's thrown away
> Because escape is done.

Marlowe is long since dead. Ralegh in *Death of the Fox* is two
days away from his execution. In *The Succession* James is moving
into power and Elizabeth is at the threshold of a door past which we
will never see. And in *Entered from the Sun* Alysoun will die of the
Plague and Barfoot fighting for Essex in Ireland. We don't know
who killed Marlowe, nor are we ever sure who it is that hires the
actor to investigate the murder. At the end of the novel we can't
answer its central mystery. Is this historical novel implying, then, that
"history" can teach us nothing, which would oppose Ralegh's belief
in *Death of the Fox* that, as Spears notes, "progress is possible and
does sometimes occur and that history can be meaningful"(272)? In

one sense, yes, for history is no more than a compilation of memory and conjecture about a time that we can know, as with all things, only through the senses. Our soldier and actor perform the role of the historian (and the historical novelist), and they find no final answers, only more mystery, deception and death the deeper they descend into the labyrinth.

In terms of narrative *Entered from the Sun* has no beginning. We begin, as I said, *in medias res*, already immersed within the text, within the texture of the times. We enter *Entered from the Sun* as easily as turning from a side street into a crowded bar. An actor laughs, then turns away, and we never hear his joke.

Works Cited

Dillard, R.H.W. *Understanding George Garrett*. Columbia: U of South Carolina P, 1988.

Garrett, George. *Death of the Fox*. Garden City: Doubleday, 1971.

_____. *Entered from the Sun*. San Diego: Harcourt, 1990.

_____. "'Fix My Hair, Jack': The Dark Side of Faulkner's Jokes." *Faulkner and Humor*. Ed. Doreen Fowler and Ann J. Abadie. Jackson: UP of Mississippi, 1986. 230-31.

Ruffin, Paul. "Interview with George Garrett." *The South Carolina Review* 16.2 (1984): 25-33.

Spears, Monroe K. "George Garrett and the Historical Novel." *Virginia Quarterly Review* 61 (1985): 262-76.

Joseph Dewey

A Golden Age for Fantasticks: Imagination, Faith, and Mist-ery in Entered from the Sun

"We're through the looking glass here, people. White is black, and black is white."
—*JFK* (Oliver Stone)

"Ah, circumlocution!"
—*Entered from the Sun*

It is by all accounts a most ordinary intersection. A main drag turns into another, joined at a sharp angle by a third—a most unremarkable confluence. Even the names of the streets that meet to form the triangular intersection—Elm, Houston, Main—are common enough. The urban landscape about the intersection is strikingly unstriking—an overlook formed by a rolling grassy knoll topped with a picket fence; a highway overpass; a scattering line of trees; a nondescript brick warehouse. Indeed, the sole remarkable feature is a decorative white pergola overlooking the intersection.

And yet in the shattering chaos of 5.2 seconds just past noon on a fall Friday awash in the surreal sunshine of a Texas autumn, this unremarkable confluence of streets would become a most remarkable landscape, one whose every feature would become packed with association, indeed would become part of the symbolic landscape of a culture's century. To mention Dealey Plaza now is to teach—in the same way that My Lai or Hiroshima, Auschwitz or Watergate or, more recently, Oklahoma City instructs. They are sobering places that speak to us, resonate, mark those uneasy moments when we are compelled to look not *at* events but rather *into* them, not merely to witness, but to learn. They become the places we all visit, the places we all know, the places we all share.

Given the horrific drama that unfolded there, Dealey Plaza might well have become a most powerful civics lesson on a government pitched into sudden crisis or, given the age of the slain president, a

dramatic caveat on the vanity of human aspiration or the speech-
lessly sudden intervention of mortality. But Dealey Plaza has come
to teach a far different text. It has come to speak of the depth of our
need for plot, our hunger for narrative. It teaches that despite our
apparent empowerment by centuries of Enlightenment assumptions
about the sheer power of the imagination to speculate and then
secure solution, despite a virtual industry of interpretation, our facts
have not constituted the slenderest reliable truth. In Dealey Plaza,
"truth" requires scare-quotes. We are left within conflicting readings—some outlandish, some terrifyingly probable—that involve, in
turns, the CIA, the FBI, the Syndicate, Cuban sympathizers, right-
wing extremists, Communist sympathizers, an efficient paramilitary
cabal of any of the above and even, in the more rococo exercises,
the Dallas police department and the emergency staff at Parkland
Hospital. In Dealey Plaza, despite 692 eyewitnesses, despite 22
cameras trained on the sequence of events, despite painstaking
analyses of ballistics, forensic reports, audio and visual evidence,
despite a small library worth of theories, event eludes understanding.

Indeed, Dealey Plaza cautions that despite the Faustian pre-
sumption of our pretense to understand, we live in a world where
event will always resist our capacity to package it. We are thus
rudely dropped in a vertiginous freefall into a world where understanding is demonstrably unreliable, forcing us to acknowledge that
even the simplest domestic shooting ultimately resists our persistent
need to ask "why." After all, Dealey Plaza makes for a remarkably
poor narrative. It lacks a reliable culprit, definable motivation, reassuring heroes, a clear line of action, and even a final page. That
mystery has compelled historic fictionists from Earl Warren to Oliver
Stone to engage in an energetic game of narrative, a vast exercise in
the imagination that, if divorced from the horrific execution that
actually took place at 12:30.52 PM on 22 November 1963, becomes a most bizarre parlor game. Dealey Plaza, then, shows both
the absurdity of explanation and, concomitantly, the intricate
achievement of the inexhaustible imagination engaged full throttle in
the face of the haunting, unanswerable *why*. What Dealey Plaza
teaches is that perfect facts pieced together make for perfect
fictions.

It may seem most eccentric to approach the closing volume of
George Garrett's magnificent Elizabethan trilogy via Dealey Plaza.
Surely a trilogy so widely praised for its evocation of the feel of

Elizabethan England, its ability to plunge the participatory reader into the interior and exterior life of an elegant world now centuries gone, has little to say to our century—indeed, Garrett closes the book, which investigates the death of Christopher Marlowe, regretting having to return to his own time (this "bitter, shiny century"). Critical response has lauded the trilogy's lack of contemporariety, its full-scale indulgence of one creative mind's extravagant fondness for a time decidedly not our own.[1]

Yet the murders of Kennedy and Marlowe share intriguing similarities. At the simplest level, they are both powerful lessons in cultural grief, in tragic waste. They died, to borrow from Garrett, "too young, badly and sadly" (29). Both men, despite very public lives, sustain strikingly contradictory sinner/saint readings of their character. Both deaths, so violent and so sudden, cut short not only a young man, in many ways the shining (if imperfect) expression of each one's generation, but the promise of each as well. Both deaths have dragged into glaring light, like some tentacled seacave creature, the ugly reality of conspiracies among those who ruthlessly scramble for power. Both deaths, shrouded in mystery, were carefully (and quickly) explained by official inquiries riddled with contradictions and gaps, inquiries that leave speculation irresistible. But in their shared unresolvability, both killings reveal the inaccessibility of truth, the limits of the imagination to fashion truth—that, despite our eagerness to explicate, we must content ourselves to dwell within possibilities.

History, of course, is not so easily contented. It relishes its privileged status as fact-based, a premise that, if unexamined, encourages taking its conclusions as pat truth. But historians, like narrators, are simply plotters. With casual arrogance, positioned comfortably after the action, they invent patterns, seeing in our imperfect struggle amid the crosscurrents of contingency linkages that become inevitabilities, actions that are bent into convenient waves of risings and fallings, satisfying—if only in a most superficial way—our human hunger for design. To those who tire of the deliberate openendedness of fictions, history offers a reliable clarity, the hard edge of dates and places, the calming tiller of functioning causality, the pleasing shape of handy eras that lead with remarkable inevitability one to the next like circus acrobats swinging on trapezia. The murders of Marlowe and Kennedy, however, are among those awkward moments when our compulsion to impose narrative fails.

They mark those most disconcertingly public moments when "history" reveals what we suspect in our darkest moments as we must negotiate most imperfectly through the poorly marked labyrinth of contingency—that any act of explanation is the purest legerdemain, an exertion of the fallible imagination. That these events resist, that they leave even their most fervent students in a heavy fog of supposition, raises critical questions about the sufficiency of the imagination. In the upstairs dining room of Eleanor Bull's tavern as in the sunny intersection of Dealey Plaza, history conflates with mystery; history, if you will, becomes mist-ery.

I

How can the human imagination be cut off? There is no way. Oh, you can be robbed or shed of poor reason by pain, drugs, fright, or even the fierce fist of the unconscious. But who can deliver us from the human imagination? (Garrett, *Do, Lord, Remember Me* 111)

It is surely no revelation to suggest that Garrett, who abandoned conventional historic studies to produce historic fictions on Elizabethan England, asks his participatory reader to recognize that the truer subject of his trilogy is the imagination itself, what it can do, once unleashed, to revive dull facticity, to make sensual and immediate an age turned dry as chalk by conventional historical approaches.[2] But surely the focus is far more on the invented in this closing volume. Garrett throngs us among artistes—poets, playwrights, publishers and printers, pamphleteers and sonneteers. We listen to actors, we visit the theater. More to the point, we follow figures most of whom have been drawn from the imagination, not from history. We are reminded of the import of such a narrative strategy when one of Garrett's invented characters confides that when he attends a performance of Shakespeare's "new" play, *Henry IV, Part II*, he relishes not the orchestrated (and predetermined) movement of the historic personages but rather the rollicking antics of the invented characters who gambol about the play's ample comic subplot.

Moreover, we close the trilogy investigating a poet, or rather a poet manqué (Marlowe has been dead four years when the narrative opens). We follow two characters, an actor and a soldier, employed (we are never quite sure by whom or why) to discover (or perhaps obscure) those responsible for the bloody murder of Marlowe, tricky and often dangerous investigations that close, finally, without closure, without resolution. We do not—cannot—learn anything new. By selecting an event from history that defies explanation and hence delights (even demands) the activity of the imagination, Garrett conspires to coax us to reject the rigid expectations of explanation (singular) and to indulge the wildfall of explanations (plural). Indeed, we are given a choice of explanations for Marlowe's death, and the closing chapter is an open invitation to the willing reader to imagine endings for the three main characters.

But we do so at our peril. We cannot enjoy undisturbed this ludic text. It is as if after the splendid imaginative performance of Garrett's massive first installments in the trilogy, he skews the very premise of the viability of the imagination itself by showing, in this slender volume, what the imagination cannot do. In this closing novel, characters talk at length, banter elegantly, recite extravagantly, converse wittily and colorfully, pen lengthy letters, indulge barrage after barrage of language often against the threat of being silenced by a slit throat—but such sound and fury, finally, cannot happen on even the slightest sort of truth, a frustration underscored by Garrett's repeated use of the idiomatic phrase, "Truth is." Guided solely by our own resources, we are left in a foggy (and rainy) nightworld of hopeless contradiction, where character is ultimately indecipherable, where solution is ironic, where the truth itself is a matter of a moment's limited insight, its tenure startlingly brief.

How then do we make such a world bearable? That, in large part, is the job of the imagination. It intrigues—in both senses of the word. It mesmerizes *and* it plots; it fascinates *and* it explains. Primarily, of course, it enthralls. Garrett understands the imagination as the energy that compels the artist, the poet, the actor to engage us by giving depth and color to our most ordinary moments, showing us what we might otherwise pass as banality and routine. Garrett understands the imagination's ability to stun. There are shattering moments when characters find themselves moved not by the power of memory but by the exercise of the unleashed imagination. Barfoot re-creates the day long ago when his father, an Irish rebel, departed on the run from British forces, an event that is not within his memory but one that has been, over the years of his adult life, powerfully particularized by his fueled imagination. And the high point of Hunnyman's investigation is not his discovery of Marlowe's murderers but rather his imaginative recreation of the moment of Marlowe's death. Hunnyman is moved to tears (although admitting it a "childish, weak, and womanly thing to do" [146]) as he imagines the death of the helpless poet—an event, of course, he did not witness. The graphic detailing is not for the squeamish—we are told of the knife point impaling the soft dark wet jelly of Marlowe's eyeball. It is a most powerful evocation. And the narrator, Paul Cartwright, indulges vivid recreations of his own—the ostentatious pageantry of the Accession Day festivities, for instance, and later the lively (and decidedly malodorous) theater crowd gathered at the Rose. In such descriptive setpieces—by themselves valueless indulgences that do not forward any plot line—we are pulled by the potent magic of language, the enthralling concoctions of the inspired imagination.

But if the imagination coerces unsuspected emotional depth from the worldly Barfoot and from the gently cynical Hunnyman (and perhaps even from the jaded contemporary reader), it works in far more elaborate ways to fuel our eagerness to find order, not to be intrigued but rather to intrigue. It is this sense of the imagination that compels scientists and engineers to render the universe intelligible and law-abiding; that draws historians and journalists to find movement and direction in the otherwise pure motion of event; that inspires the novelist, again and again, to shape beginnings, middles, and ends into plots. It is what fuels the political intrigue, the often odious work of Machiavellian realpolitik, all about the world of Garrett's London. Restless within contingency, terrified by the concept of random event, politicos and historians, journalists and scientists rush to plot, seek mightily to explain, to shape a reassuring line of accountability, to provide satisfying structure to what unfolds as raw event—not to secure *the* truth but rather to fashion a usable truth. Here, ruthless courtiers with imposing bodyguards, intelligencers, paid informants, spies, counterspies, professional liars with deep agendas move about the shadowed nightworld of Garrett's London, investing enormous energy into the baroque construction of a viable "truth."

Whether intriguing or unintriguing, the imagination makes the immediate world sufficient, bearable, explicable, even enthralling—and that, ultimately, is the problem. It can surely illuminate; it can offer intricate design; it can give depth and particularity to event; it can delight. But the novel collapses into a sobering subtext of frustration.

Although it can discover pattern, the imagination can offer no meaning—characters meet coincidentally, Barfoot talks to sources just after Hunnyman or, vice versa, characters know of other characters. But we are given only the cold satisfaction of such deftly crossed lines—pattern that cannot generate purpose. Further, the imagination cannot sustain reliability. We are dropped into a shadowy world where no assertion bears authority, no character is what he claims, where trust is always misplaced because everyone lies (including the narrator, who betrays without apology the norm-ative trust extended by any reader). All is pretense and role-playing as we move about through increasing levels of deception in a world without clarity—Barfoot's spectacles, he concedes, improve his appearance but not his vision. Of course, deception comes easily to Hunnyman—an inveterate actor, he not only lives by faith in conning but he freely and repeatedly costumes about London in the outfits of a gentleman (we first meet him in a tavern as he costumes about as a country gentleman). When Barfoot visits Eleanor Bull's tavern, he is momentarily shaken when he notes rust-colored smudges on the wall—when he inquires, he is told that the stains are dabs of chicken blood, put there to intrigue the curious by the cheerful woman herself (whose last name is all too appropriate).

The murder of Marlowe reveals, then, both the richness and the poverty of the imagination, inevitably invoking a running list of paradoxes. The imagination is (un)limited, (un)erring, (in)appropriate, (in)exhaustible, (in)fallible, (un)failing, (dis)honest, (un)true. It leaves us adrift amid possibility. Barfoot decides at the close of his "investigation" that a cabal of agents under the hire of Marlowe's patron, Francis Walsingham, murdered a drowsy, drunken Marlowe either to prevent him from fleeing the country or because Marlowe refused to flee the country—a curiously contradictory "explanation." Indeed, as we close the novel, Cartwright simply invents endings for each character—Hunnyman lives to a ripe old age, a harmless dirty old man in a manor house; Barfoot is slain during Essex's disastrous expedition against the Irish; Alysoun dies during a sweep of the plague. But (as with Dealey Plaza) it is not that such events compel—Cartwright offhandedly invites us to cast our own endings—but rather that we need to meld stochastic event into the pleasing shape of narrative.

It is Garrett's point, of course, that we can never understand even the simplest event nor the most accessible person in our immediate lives. The imagination here measures our vanity within a most forbidding void that we fill by our voices noisily (and nervously) intriguing, knowing the terrifying alternative to such desperate construction is the awful wash of insuperable silence. And, without clear alternative, we thus invest a Faustian pride in the works of the imagination. We testify that Marlowe, murdered in his twenties more than four centuries ago, lives on in the sheer staying power of his work. Garrett, who steps in to close the novel, points out that perhaps the subtlest mystery of all is how such scribblings find their way to immortality.

Yet surely such unalloyed heresy must make uneasy any writer such as Garrett who explicates the world according to traditional Christianity. Anyone who accesses the broad reach of Scripture sees literary immortality as rightfully puny, a trifling when set against the infinities casually handled by God. Consider the evidence Garrett himself presents—Marlowe wrote among hundreds of others in an age teeming with poets who each (mis)invested faith in language, voices now lost (indeed, we hear momentarily from one of the forgottens, Robert Greene). Even Marlowe himself enjoys a most risible sort of immortality—a minority enthusiasm of a marginalized profession here in the closing moments of the Great Age of Reading. To be generous, Marlowe (unlike Elizabeth and Ralegh, who form the cores of Garrett's earlier trilogy installments) is a marginal figure, significant only for that esoteric mini-faction of the world's population that invests serious consideration in the study of literature and even more narrowly in the development of English tragic theater. Even Shakespeare, the towering achievement of the age who briefly appears here, is trivialized in a discussion between Hunnyman and Alysoun on the woeful condition of contemporary theater. They concede he will continue to write, of course, but not out of any burning need of the artist but rather to help pay for his new lodgings, specifically the new tax on fireplaces (his new home has ten).

The imagination, then, compels our emotions, stuns us by its architecture, moves us by its uncanny ability to explicate the rush of event into plot, but it is ultimately a most desperate divertissement. At one point, Barfoot's Dutch whore offers that, for her, the most compelling narrative is the fairy-tale story of transformation, the magic tale of turning "dirty straw" into gold (127). Imagination, which compels both history and fiction, imposes narrative on raw event, fashioning from harsh contingency the stability of pattern and symmetry. It comforts us amid an otherwise terrifying immediate world. But Garrett reminds us that the ultimate fairy tale, the ultimate gesture of magic transformation that we accept in our naiveté, is not straw into gold but rather event into plot.

II

You that say, today or tomorrow we will go into such a city, and continue there a year, and buy and sell, and get gain. Whereas you know not what shall be on the morrow. For what is your life? It is even a vapour that appears for a little time and then vanishes away. You ought to say, If the Lord will, we shall live and do this or that. But you rejoice in your boastings; all such rejoicing is evil. —Epistle of James (4: 13-15)

We are left, then, with a deeply conflicted text—one that appears to celebrate, even encourage the imaginative exuberance that reclaims history and fashions from its bone and ash the liveliest games of invention—but, on the other hand, one that leaves a disquieting sense of frustration, that appears to remind us coldly of the limits of such human endeavors. To find resolution, we must listen to the voice that dominates the work, the voice of the controlling narrative conscience, the failed poet Paul Cartwright, the man who speaks at energetic length with the vigorous argumentation and unbending didacticism of a preacher; a man whose frequent allusions, whose diction, whose logic bespeak a mind informed by Scripture; a man deeply convinced of the reality of Satan (as "near as a shadow" [283]) and grimly anticipating the fast-approaching apocalypse at the hands of a justifiably angry God; a man who looks back bitterly on a life wasted pursuing earthly satisfactions that have only left him empty, who disparages the sorry folly of sufficiency and argues rather the darker Christian wisdom of submission; a man who turns most frequently to the logic and vision (and writings) of his namesake, the apostle Paul, whose Epistles are themselves conceived (much as Garrett's novel) as exhortation and as instruction to a blasted secular world to remember the foolishness of investing faith in any but the vertical vision of faith; a man whose heavy limp testifies to his painful education, whose admitted alcoholism testifies to his too-human weakness; a man who argues that dignity is available only within the calming wisdom of the sole written artifact not generated by the fallible human imagination.

We are in the hands of a failed poet who no longer invests his faith in the fragile if appealing baubles concocted by the imagination. Quoting James, Augustine, Paul, Ezekiel, he speaks with unapologetic sternness; his face, we are told, is as "thin and hard as an ax blade" (103). In a passage from James' Epistle, which Cartwright quotes, James understands that the world teems with those who know the Bible and yet who turn from its wisdom like a man who turns from a mirror. Cartwright, however, has learned the limits of the human endeavor. He confesses to an earlier zeal for fame, a willingness to whore his meager talent to produce shoddy works for the stage. He now rues such involvement with the immediate, such consuming egotism, with the same zeal with which he confesses his onanistic fantasies about Alysoun, who printed his poems (largely at his own expense). But unlike Barfoot and Hunnyman, whose stories he tells, Cartwright has reformed, has righted his cart, much as Paul and Augustine so dramatically did. And he brings to his tale a clear agenda. In a narrative so heavily crossed by uncertainties, Cartwright's indictment is as unambiguous as a lightswitch. He will not stomach the human craving for immortality, our hunger to cast a favorable light on our lives for posterity—he understands the ambition, the pride, the folly of energy wasted on the horizontal.

The critical tension, then, is not between fact and fiction or between history and narrative—they are ultimately the same energies—but rather between the secular and the sacred, between the burgeoning Renaissance with its soaring assumptions of human sufficiency and a most Medieval resolution: the significance of humility and joyful dependency, which have always been the simple gifts of a complex God. Like his apostolic namesake (and Garrett draws attention to the name by having other characters keep getting it wrong: he is Paul, as in the proselytizer; not Peter, as in the betrayer), Cartwright uses the medium of language here as encouragement to call to discipline an audience despoiled by secularism and hence largely unwilling to accept its limits. Like Paul (indeed, like Jesus Christ), Cartwright is nevertheless drawn by the hopeless—by the stupid, the blind, the hungry—not merely in his own avid age but, in the spirit of such religious writing, to a vastly larger readership: he talks to our age, which has, by his Christian interpretation, lost the respect for the authentically spiritual, lost all touch with humility and limitations. For all of Garrett's protestations, his

London of 1597 is one strikingly familiar to any contemporary reader: it is our sad, thin secular landscape, denied its privileged status as creation, as a deliberate act illumined by intentionality. The sacred world offers resolution. It accepts mystery as its first principle; it demands mystery and truth coexist without irony; it draws its stability from the reassuring power of an unsearchable, inscrutable master designer; and it demands our accepting limitations as an opening premise. Through his narrator/apostle Paul, Garrett closes his trilogy admitting the human imagination is damned by its own adjective.

Cartwright tells the stories of men and women who attempt to satisfy themselves by accommodation to the immediate without reference to the transcendent—it is as if Paul relates the story of Doctor Faustus. Cartwright's characters hunger for uncomplicated satisfaction and are, in the end, each punished by ignoble death or, ironically, by a surfeit of material comfort. Barfoot, a tormented hypocrite who publicly denies his deep-rooted Catholicism and serves the military designs of a Protestant queen, enjoys the easy comradeship of the tavern and the safe harbor of a night's rest between his two Dutch whores, all the while trembling at the notion of his soul's approaching judgment. Denied expression, his soul has become a burden; it brings him only nightsweats and black guilt that he assuages by visits to comfort those in Elizabeth's jails, those devout Catholics who stood tall without fear for their beliefs. His hypocrisy is underscored by his odd fondness for heavy cologne. He will die, we are told, in a bloody encounter suppressing Catholic rebels. And Hunnyman, the actor, finds most fulfilling the scattered applause he earns on the stage or the sweaty lovemaking, the "sheet dancing," with the beautiful Alysoun, either one the very exercise in the ephemera premised by the horizontal vision. After all, he admits, he "loves this tired world" (27). He pays only scant attention to any afterlife, preferring a sort of *joie de vivre* that finds its highest expression in a bearhug of the immediate, a non-examined refusal to despair. Hunnyman's highest wish is to live forever and not grow old, a most damnable concession to the thin consolation of the immediate. Cartwright damns Hunnyman the only way he can—with prosperity. He imagines Hunnyman married off purely for material gain to an aging widow who conveniently dies and leaves him grand master of a fine hall, dancing to visiting minstrels and tupping servant girls—the very embodiment of the allegorical figure of damnation.

If characters do hunger for more than the crushing cycle of dust and lust, they find ways other than traditional Christianity to infuse the physical with a sense of the transcendent. In a striking subplot, we follow Alysoun's obsession with the paranormal. She would seem unlikely for such interests. A most accomplished materialist, supremely hard-edged and pragmatic, coldly negotiated while quite young into a loveless marriage to a much older stranger, she manages upon his death to take over his printing business and succeeds with cool entrepreneurial savvy. More to the point, she is most captivating, her body "white and gold," her skin "fine sugar and shine" (50). In bed, in long afternoon sessions with Hunnyman, she is passionate (and boldly physical) without the higher complications of commitment or love. (She admits a telling fondness for the mythical Circe.) At the height of their sheet dancing, Alysoun coolly discusses the printing business with Hunnyman. When, at the close of the narrative, she is pregnant from Barfoot, she calmly dispatches Hunnyman and selects with an eye for the gently stupid one of her printshop apprentices to fill the public role as husband and father. In short, she would seem the sadly toughened by-product of the secular world, an engaging form (she is the object of desire for all the three male characters) quite emptied of principle (she publishes tracts of any fanatic sect without regard to content—if her price is met), a woman whose regular attendance in church is little more than part of her public role as widow.

Of course, Cartwright must undercut the comforts of sweat and muscle offered by the erotic Alysoun. We note, even as Alysoun and Hunnyman primp for their public appearance at Accession Day, the chipped and faded design on the back of Alysoun's handmirror that shows a naked Venus and Mars "locked in the wrestle and shudder of love" (238), while the crippled Vulcan, the cuckolded, furiously looks on. The story of human relationships is the ancient story of hot attraction and cold betrayal. The flesh ultimately, necessarily disappoints. There is Hunnyman's painful adolescent memory of being sold for the pleasure of decrepit sodomites who traveled with the acting company; or Alysoun's repeated and quite open infidelities; her own early marriage negotiated by her parents; or Barfoot's Dutch whores who in the end are dispatched by Cartwright in a moralistic pique—one dragged from the Thames, bloated and rotted, the other cut up and disfigured by a knife-wielding maniac. Even the higher expressions of the sexual attraction—the institutions of marriage and family—offer only problematic comfort. Hunnyman's loving family is destroyed in the plague; Barfoot's family is ruined by the religious persecutions of the queen he now serves. Hunnyman dies childless; Barfoot dies never even knowing he has a son. It is Cartwright's point (in echo of Paul) that secular love is utterly insufficient, doomed by the logic of unavoidable disappointment.

Alysoun's damnation, however, takes a different and far more bizarre turn. She pursues inexplicably an extraordinary course of investigation premised on the most eccentric assumptions about the viability of the paranormal. Sparked by an encounter as a child with an old witchwoman in her village who prophesied while staring into dying coals a bright (if sadly materialistic) future for Alysoun that involves a throne and jewels, Alysoun believes herself "touched by the inexplicable, a power beyond the body and mind and spirit" (194), an empowerment she compares (heretically) to Pentecostal inspiration. Like Marlowe's Faustus, she traffics in the spooky world of the paranormal, a sorry substitute for the higher argument of Christian transcendence. She comes to believe her dreams are authentic spiritual experiences that require interpretation, that significant ghosts haunt her sleep, that exotic potions will stimulate lovemaking (it actually numbs Hunnyman). She visits the shadowy shop of Simon Forman (whose allegorical name indicates how he services only the immediate), a notorious apothecary who reads her horoscope, interprets her dreams, dispenses magic salves—all for a glimpse in the privacy of his candlelighted chambers of her naked body. In a most bizarre twist, Alysoun comes to believe that the restless ghost of Marlowe inhabits her body until its hunger for uncompleted business is satisfied. That satisfaction comes, she intuits, when she gets herself pregnant after a most passionate session with Barfoot. Her conviction, born equally of egotism and animal desire, that she has access to the spiritual world indicates her hunger for a realm vaster and more luminous than the sad, sorry world of the immediate that she has so coldly mastered. But in Cartwright's knowing hands, she is offered to us (much like Barfoot and Hunnyman) as cautionary lesson. Alysoun, we are told, is claimed by the plague and left in a common grave.

Entered from the Sun, then, is that most unicorn figure in the contemporary literary bestiary: a parable, made all the more eccentric, of course, by the striking lack of any widespread faith community interested in such message-fiction.[3] Cartwright has come to learn that the role of the poet is not merely to enthrall and enchant but "to learn and teach" (152). In a novel so heavily crossed by intelligencers, the ultimate spy is Jesus Christ, the sacred messenger who moves unnoticed, unsuspected, untouched within the vast self-important complicated machinery of the secular system; He is the ultimate secret agent within the immediate, His presence felt but never secured. Cartwright reminds us again and again that the simple message of the Christian gospel is readily available yet wholly ignored, save by what he terms "the precious few" (163), the adjective serving to suggest both the scarcity of such believers and their privileged status. Even institutional Christianity, as revealed by a documentary interchapter that quotes from the era's prominent theologians, cannot help; it has soured, turned into a fierce force of intolerance, bogus fealty to secular authority, vicious persecution, fascistic self-interest, and virulent campaigns to exterminate dissent. It has left an age that hungers and thirsts, conditions cited by Cartwright (28) as a Scriptural shorthand for spiritual need. Characters here frequently minister to the raw itch of hunger and thirst— they eat to excess, they drink to excess. It is Garrett's point, of course, that such quenching of the purely physical urge is paramedic at best, much as when Barfoot recalls a campaign where, driven by desperate thirst, he quenches his with the "scum and slime" (28) of a fetid ditch. It is our lot within Christian logic to live with the hunger and thirst these characters so ruthlessly attempt to satisfy.

III

FAUSTUS: How comes it, then, that thou art out of hell?
MEPHISTOPHELES: Why, this is hell, nor am I out of it.
Thinkst thou that I who saw the face of God
And tasted the eternal joys of heaven
Am not tormented with ten thousand hells
In being deprived of everlasting bliss?
0 Faustus, leave these frivolous demands
Which strike a terror to my fainting soul.
                    —*Doctor Faustus*

Listen, we are each half-mad. And all that can be said for certain is that

we live in a poor time for simple souls. But what a golden age for
fantasticks!
Show me a simple soul, if one is left anywhere in England; and I shall
kneel down in honor and offer up all that I have and all that I am.
        —*Entered from the Sun*

But what sort of parable does Garrett tell? Like Marlowe's
Faustus, Entered from the Sun is perhaps best approached as a
parable of temptation. Both Hunnyman and Barfoot are approached
independently by conniving strangers to investigate the murder of
Marlowe. Both resist, citing inappropriate background. Both are
seduced to enter the agreement by the offer of significant renumer-
ation, payments, oddly enough, that increase even as their respective
investigations lead nowhere. Both dutifully investigate—Hunnyman
through contacts in the theater; Barfoot largely through court
records. Hunnyman and Barfoot—as well as the agents who secure
their services—hunger for knowledge, for certainty, much as the
Marlovian code hero who damns himself by a heroic resistance to
the limited lot of mortals. They are tempted to fashion truth. Neither
investigation ultimately leads anywhere.

But Cartwright, as Christian moralist, is interested in far more
than taunting us with an unsolvable mystery. He regularly intrudes
into the narrative of the investigations to make sure that we
understand what Hunnyman and Barfoot miss in their busy hurry to
find solution. We come to see that both characters inhabit an immediate world that is itself fiercely riven by uncertainties, a world
that provides Cartwright's most emphatic endorsement of the saving
commitment to the wisdom of Christian humility, the wisdom to
accept the world as mystery. Put simply, we are given a plot that
flounders, one that is wholly unable to settle even the most basic
questions. Why (and for that matter who might) select a retired
soldier and an itinerant actor for these very sensitive political
investigations? Why investigate Marlowe's death, now four years
passed? Why is Ralegh, introduced in the closing pages as a sort of
anti-*deus ex machina*, interested in Marlowe? Was Marlowe an
atheist? A sodomite? How does the stranger in the bar know that
Hunnyman had killed a man once in self-defense—indeed, we are
never given a clear answer whether that murder even took place.
Who is it watching Hunnyman at the Royal Exchange? How does
the anonymous clerk, who gives Barfoot valuable information on

Marlowe's arrest for treason, even know that Barfoot is investigating the murder or, more stunning, that Barfoot is a closet Catholic? Why does that clerk simply hand over that valuable information? Why does the Dutch whore, who chances to visit Forman, volunteer critical information about Barfoot within Alysoun's hearing? Why is Alysoun, convinced she is inhabited by Marlowe's ghost, curious about Marlowe's sisters? Why does Barfoot visit the Catholics in the London prison despite his elaborate efforts to keep his faith a private matter? Who mutilates Barfoot's whore? Why does Cartwright get his throat viciously cut? Why does Hunnyman decide not to confront Alysoun with the evidence of her infidelity with Barfoot? Indeed, why is Alysoun so swept into a passionate stir over Barfoot? The narrative past is similarly fraught by the anxiety of interrogation. Why did Alysoun ask Hunnyman, then a stranger, to sell her books as part of his traveling repertory company? Why did Cartwright select Alysoun to publish his poems? Who was the old lady who saved Barfoot from a nasty death in an open grave during the plague? The list goes on and on.

Characters themselves are frustrating matrices of contradictory impulses, what the knowing narrator terms "the tugging and wrestling of contraries" (95). For instance, Barfoot, a pious Catholic, is as well a seasoned (and heavily scarred) career soldier for a Protestant queen; a man hardened by the horrific experiences of clumsy, brutal warfare, he is as well the most deeply spiritual, the most emotional, the most aesthetically turned of the characters, a man most enthralled by the catharsis of the theater; a career soldier whose muscled bulk commands respect in the most dangerous London taverns, he moves somehow with the precious grace of a "small girl" (15); a man of boundless courage who evidences in long (poignant) letters to his brother a most profound sensitivity to the priorities of the spiritual world, he nevertheless cannot muster the courage to embrace publicly his own faith; a loner, taciturn and stony faced, he is given nevertheless to extravagant camaraderie and drunken affection and animated reminiscing; generous and sensitive to his constant companions, the Dutch whores, he remembers as well military campaigns that involved the brutal raping of "helpless, terrified bodies" (285); humbly rural, he impresses tavern patrons as a cosmopolitan, worldly and traveled; a gentle man who visits jailed Catholics, he dies thrusting steel into the bellies of Irish Catholic rebels even as he murmurs a Hail Mary. We cannot find a simple formula for accounting even for this central agent within the narrative. He is a savage gentleman, or perhaps a sensitive monster; a pious heretic or perhaps a blasphemous Papist. And should we decide to bestow the responsibilities of narrative hero on Barfoot (or on Hunnyman for that matter) we do so at our risk; we do so as an exercise in the human capacity to speculate and draw conclusions, a capacity here openly questioned for its fallibility and its bias.

Such a complicating overlay of contradictions and lingering questions is perhaps the stuff of the general interpretative contract with any alert modern reader—it is our job, after all, to conjecture. Yet here such questions come with contrary responses or with simply no discernible answer at all. The plot knots into deliberate inexplicability and, in turn, compels even the most daunted and imaginative reader to collapse with the exertion of effort. Unlike Faustus, we must accept limits. This is a novel that will not brook the question why—despite teeming with characters abuzz on missions to provide a reliable response to exactly that question. We cannot afford to end like Barfoot, who closes his investigations satisfied with a best guess, a concoction of his own probing imagination that is reassuring—even as it denies its own reassurance.

At narrative's end, then, we are left in a world where event resists plot, where cause does not lead to effect, where characters are inexplicable, where behavior is errant and eccentric, where events are inelegantly compelled by chance, where why cannot be answered with any reliability. We are left either with a remarkably sloppy novel or a remarkably astute simulacrum of the terrifying confusions of the secular world, the mist-ery. We are left helpless within event, much like Hunnyman, who opens the novel enjoying the conviviality of a tavern but quickly departs that cozy atmosphere and steps out into the dark night of the City where he is abducted from behind at knifepoint, suddenly pitched into helplessness and confusion and vulnerability, the necessary definition of the Christian condition since the abrupt exodus from the Garden.

Garrett's proper subjects here are those accommodations and negotiations we undertake to make the immediate sufficient. Politicians, monarchs, poets, actors, necromancers, whores, soldiers, alcoholics—the entire sorry cast Cartwright assembles busy themselves with the immediate, coax themselves through the kinesis of the imagination that the earth is somehow an end in itself. In her Poem 415, from which Garrett takes his title, Emily Dickinson (surely another writer who felt the compelling conflict between the imagination and the soul) argues quite heretically that heaven will be like a house without a door where we will be closed in without chance of escape. Ironically distracted by an eternity of the unchanging, we will fashion recollections of bits of life on earth. Surely it is just such secular arrogance and sorry presumptiveness that compels Cartwright's parable, that sense of earth's sufficiency, that Faustian pride that limits the horizontal as the farthest scope of our vision. Dickinson's poem, after all, closes with a ringing affirmation of the ultimate, inescapable sway of God.

Cartwright warns us early, "There are no saints in this story" (25). Indeed, none cast the simplest glance upward. That would be to accept limitations—to drink the bitter wine, Cartwright suggests in his gloss to Proverbs, that is finally the sweetest draught. Our finest efforts—whether poems, histories, monarchies, or love—are finally, sadly fragmentary, much as when Hunnyman and his mysterious employer talk in the open at the Royal Exchange and part of this critical exchange is blotted out, left unintelligible, by the noise of the Exchange bells tolling. It is reinforced by Garrett's stylistic device of stringing fragments. The picture can never be complete— only mesmerizing.

Although Cartwright has learned much about the world's vanity, Garrett does not offer him as saint. His education has left him joyless, "bitter as brown myrrh"(167). "Who among us," he darkly intones, "if he could sprout wings and fly would not shit upon all those beneath him" (52). The closing, he offers, therefore, is problematic—he ends not in prayer but rather in a last indulgence of the imagination, a splendidly empty show of authority: projecting futures for his characters. He even tempts the unwary reader. We may perhaps enter into the invitation extended by the narrator to fashion our own endings, to assume the false authority necessary to dole out destinies, to provide neat and tidy closure, thus intriguing via the inexhaustible energy of our imagination. In a parable of temptations, this call is ours.

It is, perhaps, Garrett's larger wisdom that we might step from this last temptation, to see the distressing egotism of pretending we might design fates, to see that the only way to close this novel appropriate to the Christian vision is to close in ignorance, accepting that certainty is simply not our lot. From Marlowe's splendid tragedies to Garrett's own magnificent trilogy, from the Warren

Commission's voluminous study to our own hastily structured endings (even to this essay, for that matter), the artifacts of the imagination are finally as glittering and as dead as seashells. The intriguing imagination promises what Faustus burned after—power without the interfering need to acknowledge any greater authority. It is, perhaps regretfully, gloriously (in)sufficient. After all, it makes bearable and clear the radical mist-ery and confusion that must be the lot of the Christian believer in an (im)perfect world that is at best a pilgrim state where certainty and truth are promised then as now only to those "precious few," to those simple souls humble enough to submit and devout enough to trust.

Notes

[1]Garrett, writing of the earlier volumes, speaks of his resistance to using history for satiric reference to contemporary events ("Dreaming"); Spears writes of the gorgeous rendering of Elizabethan times that has no particular relevance to contemporary events, to "the real world" (264); Whalen speaks of Garrett's ability to immerse us in the sights and sounds of the lost era; Sullivan sees the sole tie to the present in the inevitable question of why our age has not produced a Marlowe or an Elizabeth.

[2]Garrett, speaking of the earlier volumes, points out that "the proper theme of the work . . . is the imagination, the possibilities, the limits and variety of imaginative experience" ("Dreaming" 416). Robinson cites the earlier works as an "aesthetic achievement," that history lives via the exertion of the imagination, both Garrett's and the reader's; Betts sees the imagination as the vehicle for finding stability in the rush of historic event—although he never questions such confidence within any larger Christian perspective; in Spears' review of *Entered from the Sun*, he relishes the vividness of the imaginative achievement, although he finds the novel quite gloomy. Indeed, the conventional approaches to the novel have set up alternatives: Borgesian readings (see Dillard's work on the earlier volumes) that delight in the open-endedness, but ignore the frustration; and Kafkaesque readings (see Whalen and Goreau) that rue the ambiguity, but ignore the fun—the Christian reading offered here presents a possible via media.

[3]It is all too easy to ignore or to minimize Garrett's steadfast interest in the relevance and argument of Christianity. Dillard is really alone in placing such religious backdrop firmly behind any understanding of Garrett. His study, of course, does not treat *Entered from the Sun*. It is a matter of

conjecture to draw lines from *Entered from the Sun* to an earlier Garrett work that is specifically Christian, his 1965 *Do, Lord, Remember Me*, which also features a character named Cartwright. In that case, Cartwright is a most repulsive, thorough-going materialist, a man who fantasizes of acres of naked women to pollinate. Perhaps in recycling the name, Garrett shows the imperfect struggle to self-educate the damaged ego, which Cartwright, in *Entered from the Sun,* claims is the highest and subtlest work demanded by Scripture.

Works Cited

Betts, Richard A. "'To Dream of Kings': George Garrett's *The Succession.*" *Mississippi Quarterly* 45 (1991-92): 53-67.

Dillard, R. H. W. *Understanding George Garrett.* Columbia: U of South Carolina P, 1988.

Garrett, George. *Do, Lord, Remember Me.* Baton Rouge: Louisiana State UP, 1994.

_____. "Dreaming with Adam: Notes on Imaginary History." *New Literary History* 1 (1970): 407-21.

_____. *Entered from the Sun: The Murder of Marlowe.* 1990. New York: Harcourt, 1991.

Goreau, Angeline. "Who Killed Marlowe?" Rev. of *Entered from the Sun. New York Times Book Review* 16 Sept. 1990: 7.

Robinson, W. R. "Imagining the Individual: George Garrett's *Death of the Fox . . . .*" *Hollins Critic* Special Issue 8 (1971): 1-12.

_____. "Trilogy Completed, a Past Recaptured." Rev. of *Entered from the Sun. Virginia Quarterly Review* 67 (1991): 146-51.

Spears, Monroe K. "George Garrett and the Historic Novel." *Virginia Quarterly Review* 61 (1985): 262-76.

Sullivan, Walter. "Elizabethan Glory: George Garrett Rests His Case." Rev. of *Entered from the Sun. Sewanee Review* 99.2 (1991): ii-vi.

Whalen, Tom. "Eavesdropping in the Dark: The Opening(s) of George Garrett's *Entered from the Sun.*" In *To Come Up Grinning: A Tribute to George Garrett.* Ed. Paul Ruffin and Stuart Wright. Huntsville: *Texas Review* P, 1989. 90-99.

Joseph W. Reed

Settling Marlowe's Hash

George Garrett's three historical novels, *Death of the Fox* (1971), *The Succession* (1983), and *Entered from the Sun* (1990), constitute at the same time a departure from the rest of Garrett's fiction and an affirmation of what the rest of his fiction has accomplished.

Historical fiction is generally held to be an idiot-second-cousin genre supposed to sell well in hard times: Kenneth Roberts, the late Depression. Historical fiction ripped bodices before we even knew that Romance was such a powerful force. The lowest examples of the genre are bottom-feeders, gratifying and disgusting by turn as regular as clockwork: they please and distress on cue, like horror fiction.

Of course historical fiction was not just written by Roberts or Shellabarger or Thomas B. Costain. It was penned with pride and a bit of snobbishness by William Makepeace Thackeray and William Faulkner: *Vanity Fair* and *Henry Esmond, Barry Lyndon,* and most of *Absalom, Absalom!,* all of *The Unvanquished*; Stephen Crane and William Styron and Norman Mailer, Robert Louis Stevenson and Joseph Conrad and Thornton Wilder and Paul Horgan and Thomas Hardy all wrote historical fiction.

Now writers such as these did not flock to this low-rent district out of a desire to increase their revenue: they were writing historical novels for very good aesthetic and formal reasons. Faulkner saw the South and wanted to get at what he saw as its roots in the past; Thackeray wanted to try out this or that historical alienation; even Kathleen Winsor had the sense to want to get close to the fictional Plague. Styron wanted to write about what he thought made the Slave Rebellion. There were quite good fictional reasons for inhabiting the past. Historical novels let us tread where they trod.

Every writer has the freedom to change his stripes or at least try out a temporary paint job. So it is not to blame him that we identify Garrett as a very adept writer of historical fiction. Garrett's historical fictions are among the higher examples of the genre—more

Vanity Fair than *The Silver Chalice,* less Lloyd C. Douglas than Mary Renault. They frequently read like contemporary fiction, like his other novels. Probably he is fighting shy of the excuse of the self-fulfilling prophecy: if you write historical fiction you can't be a serious novelist. So Garrett will resort to overt narrative devices—sometimes willfully interrupting the reader in the act of what he takes to be devouring historical fiction by the numbers, doing anything he can to interrupt the smooth flow of the past. As John Kirkpatrick once said to one of his piano students, "A piano ought never to sound like a piano." Each of Garrett's three novels is historical in a powerful way but is also twentieth-century fiction: sounds like a piano not sounding like a piano. None is limited to what the "novel" could have been in the sixteenth century or to what it has become since. Of the three, *Death of the Fox* most engages us as readers of historical fiction, *The Succession* perhaps best engages our critical historical consciousness, but *Entered from the Sun* is most dependent on our binocular vision: right eye sixteenth century, left eye twentieth.

Garrett has always believed that readers are there to be pleased, and he has pleased them; he has also frequently pleased himself. These books are a particular kind of pleasing of others and self. Garrett is writing three historical novels (pleasing himself), but he is also writing something more. Each novel has experiments in structure, narrative strategy, character, and finish. The three historical novels join our life to the life they embody in profound mediation between our time and theirs.

Finish is important to Garrett, and tied up with his other experiments here is a concern for finish. He wants the novels to have participational immediacy. But in its strong similarity to modern private eye mysteries, *Entered from the Sun* has formal immediacy. Of the three it is maybe the most dependent on later fictions—the seeming accidence of a covert narrative strategy, good mystery-by-omission structure, disarmingly immediate twentieth-century style. And characters. And magisterial artifice enclosing (and helping to conceal from us) all this up-to-dateness.

Its formal immediacy is conveyed in part by that force Elizabethans knew so well, the surface attraction of deliberate artifice: the construction of an obvious artifice that suspends verisimilitude but still gets the reader properly talked to. In the hands of an Elizabethan—most *any* Elizabethan—or of *Entered from the*

Sun the reader is never in danger of thinking this is all clipped out of some newspaper or, worse yet, "made-up."

Entered from the Sun turns on (but is not *about*) the great reckoning in a little room, the death of Christopher Marlowe, a poet long-dead and in the years of the novel, little lamented.

> Thus it is not surprising, at least from your point of view, that you date your involvement in this matter, matter of the late Christopher Marlowe, which is what chiefly concerns us here, from a particular time and place.
>
> For you the time begins on the afternoon of October 11, in the year of our Lord 1597. (76-77)

Garrett is carefully positioning us in the narrative: in a way it forbids us to assume time is rigidly consistent. Time is in this novel made to be played with, as is character—the comings and goings of the friends we meet—some left doubtfully for dead, others surviving the Plague.

> Somehow I heard, not without meaning but with the utter indifference of a ghost, the doors axed and smashed open and thieves came in to loot. To steal the coins in our purses, the jewels off our fingers (thank God my rings hung loose; for when a ring was tight they cut off the finger to take it), and the clothes off our backs. I felt myself lifted and turned like a log of wood as they stripped me naked and dropped me again to the floor. And I remember how I saw the blue-black swellings on these thieves themselves. Would have grinned then, if I could have. For here they were, dead men already, risking much for what little they could steal from us. (128)

And "somehow" we can't help connecting "dead men already" to the barely born state of a fictional character. Barfoot lives as Garrett wills him to, and as he wills it, lives on. Barfoot's survival takes some of its color from the rags and tags of the Holocaust. This works on our reader's subconscious, tugging at a soiled and guilty string: we have been here before and then everybody was wearing a different sort of costume. But stripped in the charnel house, dumped into a mass-grave in a way they are no different.

The structure of mystery-by-omission puts in our way two persons charged to find out about Marlowe's death. We know from the start that each investigator is likely to come to different conclusions and that each may be working for a different agent, or both the same, one backing up the other, but above all that their free-agentry is most significant. We are not in the world of the Elizabethan intrigue but rather in the slimy and conspiring underworld of the American private eye of the 30s or 50s. This is a sunken world, not a musty one, an underbelly of the subconscious. This world rocks beneath our feet and each chapter persuades us we have come farther and farther from the world of Samuel Shellabarger.

Private-eye fiction (see Philip Marlowe's bookstore visit in *The Big Sleep)* loves the clever interrogation, question-asking that doesn't give away anything, asking questions without tipping the hand. Although the private eye, the Continental Op, doesn't risk his life as Barfoot and Hunnyman do: he'll just get beat up, will probably get beat up whether he tips his hand or not.

"Next day, if he had been particularly obstreperous, he would come by, on the way to or from Scadbury, and bring me some presents, some herbs or some flowers, a fine bottle of the best sack, the sweet kind I have always favored."

"Perhaps if he had lived through this occasion he would have given you a fine jewel. Or even married you on the spot."

"Shame on you, sir!" With a laugh that showed that sack and sugar, among other things, had left her with teeth like the toppled and crumpled crenellations of an old castle. "I do not believe Kit Marlowe was likely to be a husband."

"Pity . . . for him."

"It pains me to speak ill of the dead."

"To be sure." (137)

Do Garrett's historical novels constitute a trilogy? If a trilogy is three connected novels, that's what this is. If our sense of trilogy is more like the structure of a television miniseries, that is, mutually supportive of a common structure, then no, Garrett's is not a trilogy. If it is something like Nordhoff and Hall's *Bounty* Trilogy, a series formed of a novel and two sequels, it is perhaps a near thing. I find the example of Faulkner's trilogy *Snopes* useful here. Faulkner wrote a novel *The Hamlet* (1940). He added a segment to *Snopes* called *The Town* (1957) and another, *The Mansion* (1960). In a foreword to *The Mansion* he summed it up:

This book is the final chapter of, and the summation of, a work conceived and begun in 1925. Since the author likes to believe, hopes, that his entire life's work is a part of a living literature, and since "living" is motion, and "motion" is change and alteration and therefore the only alternative to motion is unmotion, stasis, death, there will be found discrepancies and contradictions in the thirty-four-year progress of this particular chronicle; the purpose of this note is simply to notify the reader that the author has already found more discrepancies and contradictions than he hopes the reader will—contradictions and discrepancies due to the fact that the author has learned, he believes, more about the human heart and its dilemma than he knew thirty-four years ago; and is sure that, having lived with them that long time, he knows the characters in this chronicle better than he did then.[1]

Garrett wrote no such note because he thought what he was doing was self-evident: the novels had some revisited characters and a narrow range of years in common, common ambiance, some continuity book-to-book, no common structure.

If they were to have these, very likely it would weaken them as novels: as they stand each is subject to its own structure, force, and strategy. This makes each of them more of a piece with Garrett's other novels. In fact, I should be hard-pressed to say anything in particular in any of his books is Garrettesque *except* that it's all done anew each time and with care. That is, I know what sort of fictional experience it will be if I read a novel with his name on it: this is less a matter of structure or substance than of the feeling of a whole Garrett book. But as to habits of novel-making, look to each book, because each is its own map. Sufficient unto the book is the structure thereof.

There are, of course, in *Entered from the Sun* (and in the others) set pieces, and these seem the most characteristic passages in the book. As in an Elizabethan book, *Entered from the Sun* finds everything an excuse for a conceit. Knowing as we do the private-eye's high level of abstract ratiocination, allegory is just around the corner. None of this is done without a customary appeal to the historical fiction reader in us all. The seemingly separate piece on

Robert Greene is typical: playing with our hobbyist's sense of the sixteenth century, Garrett gives us more by seeming only to annotate what we know already (146).

Entered from the Sun is Garrett's best writing. He works at the stuff of the story in prose cut free (except for a nod at the Tilt-yard) from the narrative, an overarching metaphor for both termini of the straddled centuries.

And long before first light, all over London and Westminster and the suburbs around them, gentlemen and ladies (false and true) are busy preparing to dress themselves for the pageants and shows at the Tiltyard. Truth is, they must *be dressed,* clothed with the aid and comfort of others. For other hands are needed to take care of the buttoning and snapping and lacing into tight, hidden places of the many parts that are the fashion these days. Clothing calling by its intricate artifice and design for others to help. And unlucky is that man or woman who has the benefit of the services of nobody else but an ancient, weak-eyed, stiff-jointed servant who has forgotten where all the parts come together and how. If she ever knew. Or perhaps only a loutish, heavy-handed, turnip-fingered apprentice lad, grinning and well-meaning but hopelessly inept. Or maybe a sour-faced scullery maid, as dirty as she is ignorant. Will take more than these to dress and send master and mistress forth into this day's daylight world. Unlucky ladies and gents who will go forth, in spite of the riches of the materials (the silks and satins, taffeta and damask and velvet, finest leather, and lace so fern-fine and delicate that it must certainly have blinded the strangers who bent and squinted to make it), in spite of all fans and furs, jewels from slippers to top of curled and frizzed hair, in spite of all these things, even the least costly of costumes being worth the price, perhaps, of a fair-size farm, with farmhouse and barns and outhouses, with pasture and pond and woodlands; and the most expensive and elegant, being worn by the truly great and by those wishing to be mistaken for the like and same, costing as much as some lord's estate with its mansion and part, village and parish, tenants and sheep—unlucky the lady and gent sent forth, dressed carelessly by careless hands, without each and every thing precisely in its perfect, casual place. Why, no matter how grand your clothing, how cut to the latest fashion, you might as well be a scarecrow or a country clown, the survivor of a shipwreck or a siege. (230-31)

Clothes make the courtier, the age, and the historical novel. To paraphrase Melville, the velvet glove but conceals the remorseless and corrupt hand. The prose for this is like the prologemena to *Bleak House*, incantatory prose that measures up to be more than Dickens had in mind because of that twentieth-century overtone. The hall of a very old house is novel, trilogy, the novelist in hiding. The way of getting next to the past, treading where they trod. And of making synthetic life.

Picture the hall of a very old house. Many torches and smoky candles toss brightness and make huge shadows. Large fireplace at far end and where half a tree could burn and, indeed, huge logs are now aflame sputtering and sparking. Once there was only a smoke hole at the center of the hall. You can see where it has been patched and covered over on the high roof. And on the stone floor of the hall you can also see darker stones where fires were laid and burned in times beyond the remembering of anyone alive now.

It is night and, outside, the wind blows in hard gusts rattling the windows. Where once there was nothing but air; then dull sheets of horn; now leaded glass. Snowflakes in the air, in the wind, sticking to the windows. (344)

Notes

[1]"Conceived and begun in 1925": evidently a reference to "The Peasants," a story not surely traced, supposed to be about the Snopeses. The note quoted appears in all editions of *The Mansion* I have examined. It clearly represents Faulkner's rather limber-jawed attitude to formal structure.

Walter Sullivan

Time Past and Time Present: Garrett's Entered from the Sun

"Turn your eyes to the immoderate past," Allen Tate wrote, and probably no past era in modern history is more immoderate than the age of Elizabeth. Then you could see a new play by Shakespeare or Jonson or, until his untimely death, George Garrett's hero Marlowe, and not long thereafter, you could be dead of the plague, your body dumped with scores of others into a common grave. When the queen needed money to fight her wars, she would raise your taxes. If she thought you were seditious or an atheist or a Catholic, she would have you beheaded or drawn and quartered according to your state in life. If you were a common criminal, you would be executed too, and anyone could be confined to prison or put on the rack or left to rot in an oubliette. In spite of all this, the received wisdom, even in what Garrett calls our own "bitter, shiny century," is that the age of Elizabeth was an age of glory, and all the bad things that happened—the poverty, disease, and occasional famine—were mere counterpoint to a grand and expansive time when people, by and large, were happy, and art and science flourished, and England stood on the brink of a political hegemony that would last for centuries to come. Perhaps the deep uncertainties of life, the intrigues played out for high stakes, the specter of untimely death, injustices, all the vicissitudes summed up in Hamlet's familiar soliloquy, endowed the lives, even of the most lowly Elizabethans, with a sense of dramatic urgency that gave purpose to their existence and joy to their days.

Nobody knows more about all this or has rendered it better than George Garrett. I said that Marlowe was Garrett's hero, but that is true only in *Entered from the Sun*. Garrett's real hero is Walter Ralegh, soldier, poet, explorer, courtier, victim, finally, of political machinations, himself a kind of avatar of all that we mean when we speak of Elizabethan life. Garrett uses Ralegh's last words, which come at the end of *Death of the Fox*, as the closing paragraph of *Entered from the Sun*, and Ralegh is a character, albeit a minor one, in that novel. When Ralegh enters to play his cameo role, the tone of *Entered from the Sun* lifts slightly as if to reflect Garrett's joy at being reunited with his old companion. But the controlling figure of *Sun* is Marlowe, the facts of his life and of his death uncertainly known, his very being shrouded in mystery. Was he homosexual? Was he an atheist? Was he a secret papist, a spy, a double agent? Did Ingram Frizer stab him in self defence, or was Frizer a hired killer in the pay of Walsingham, whom Marlowe once had served? Garrett believes the latter, but within the parameters of the narrative, we never know. Here is a riddle without an answer, a story built on an unsolved mystery. This works, because like most good novels, *Sun* is driven not as much by plot as by the depth and angularity of the characters, the complexity of their motives as they interact with each other, the sense of inevitability in their pursuit of their own fates. Marlowe is not one of them, but even so, he is the force that sets the other characters in action, and in his moral ambiguity, the inscrutable facets of his personality, the vastness of his literary talent he, like Ralegh, can be taken as a different, but equally valid, image of the age itself. The subjects he pursued in his writing, Tamburlaine's vast ambition, Faustus's thirst for knowledge and power that were denied him by his very nature, are reflections, distillations perhaps, of the temperament of the English Renaissance.

Also images of their time are Captain Barfoot and Joseph Hunnyman, the soldier and the player, who are enlisted separately to seek the truth about Marlowe's death. Barfoot is one of Garrett's most brilliantly drawn characters. So ugly by nature that the scars he has received in battle improve his appearance, so fierce looking that his coming into a room can impose a silence, he is, unless challenged, companionable and generous. He wears ladies' perfume, moves with the grace of a dancer, is kind to the Dutch whores whose company he favors, and appears to have, should he ever settle down to use them, domestic gifts. A Catholic who fights for a Protestant queen, he has spent a good part of his life recuperating from injury and illness. He is London agent for his land-holding brother, he helps priests come and go from the continent, and he dies at the hands of Irish tribesmen, as much a victim of his incompetent fellow soldiers as of those who strike him down. Like Marlowe, like the queen, he is bigger than life, heroic in his concept of himself and in the role he plays in the novel.

Hunnyman is smaller, a thinner character than Barfoot, but not, perhaps, as small as he at first appears to be. His trade is fantasy, to create a world that does not exist, to pursue an art in which pretense becomes reality for the space of the performance, after which the dead rise, the lame are made whole, the thwarted lovers dry their tears. Hunnyman is a good actor. But he knows as well as Barfoot does that life and art, though intimately connected, are not the same. His career with itinerant companies has brought him scant profit, and in one of his absences from London his wife and children have died of the plague. On the stage, he can mimic sorrow or gaiety according to the demands of the script, but dealing with his own failures and losses is another matter. Still, in the end, his fortune may be better than that of Barfoot. Though he loses Alysoun, whom he loves, he marries a rich widow, inherits her estate, and passes his last years as country gentleman and patron of small theatrical companies similar to those in which he once was employed.

Given the difference between Hunnyman and Barfoot and the fact that the essential qualities of both seem to combine to form the character of Marlowe, *Entered from the Sun* might be taken as another thrust at the dialectic of art and life, of imagination and reality, and, in a way, it is. Barfoot is the man of action, Hunnyman is the artist, but neither of them rests easily in his role. Although Hunnyman's trade is that of creating fantasy, his bereavement is real, and the circumstances of his quotidian life have often left him hungry and cold. Barfoot's scars testify to his comprehension of the brutally concrete aspects of human existence, but his perfume and grace, his sentimental attachment to his whores, and the dandified way in which he dresses on holidays disclose a delicate aspect of his character. He has sufficient imagination to conjure up, sometimes with mild regret, a more peaceful life that he might have lived: he can fancy himself gathered with a family beside a rural fireplace.

But the story that seems to define Barfoot and in some ways to define Garrett's book is anything but peaceful. Posted as a soldier to a town in France, the name of which he cannot remember, Barfoot is struck by the plague, robbed by burglars who are themselves sick while on his apparent death bed, hauled on a cart full of corpses and dumped with them into a mass grave. He is rescued from what he later calls his "bed of flesh and bones" by an old, old woman, hideous to behold and with stinking breath, who takes him to her hut and feeds him bitter broth. Through his long recovery, she nurses and cleans him and speaks to him in a language that he has never heard before and never hears again. She is not French and not, insofar as he can determine, a Gypsy. She is a giver of life who looks and smells like death. Or she is death who has decided, for a time, to spare him.

The moral of this story may be only that Barfoot was not meant to die in bed, and Barfoot does not insist on our finding a deeper interpretation. Others, he surmises, have survived the plague. Still, his own experience lives in his memory, and the crone, appearing to be even uglier and more foul breathed than she actually was, haunts his dreams. In his dreams, she asks him to kiss her, but whose are these unsavory lips toward which he leans? Is she a witch? Is she an enchanted princess waiting for his kiss to restore her youth and beauty? Agent of death or life, disguised maiden or evil sorcerer, in her physical presence, she is the witch of Elizabethan drama, a representative of the supernatural which was a further dimension of Elizabethan life.

The crone who saves Barfoot, the *memento mori* of the novel, has a counterpart in the sorcerer Simon Forman whom Alysoun consults. Forman, who styles himself a doctor, sells poisons and potions, aphrodisiacs and salves and abortifacients; he casts horoscopes and predicts the future and interprets dreams. Alysoun herself may have supernatural gifts. At least she is a dreamer, has been one since before the printer and bookseller, who has left her a rich widow, took her from her rustic home, brought her to London, and taught her the secrets of his trade. Her dreams now are of a man with a wounded face, a man whose soul is adrift, seeking, she believes, a woman's body to inhabit: while Barfoot and Hunnyman search for the truth about Marlowe's murder, she encounters the dead man in her dreams. Forman is of little help to her, but her dreams of Marlowe, her belief that she is haunted by his spirit cast her in a role both alongside and beyond Barfoot and Hunnyman. Like the crone and the sorcerer, she penetrates the supernatural world.

The introduction of the supernatural into the story—a practice more common in Elizabeth's time than in our own—enhances the dialectic between life and art. Which is it? To what realm, art or reality, does the supernatural belong? To visionaries and to certain dedicated believers, the supernatural is the most intense of all realities, the most vivid experience of life itself. For others it is purely a construction of the imagination. For still others, the vast majority of us if we trust our social statisticians, it is embraced as a vague hope, an antidote against the fear of death. Still, the idea of a dimension of reality not fully seen or understood nags at us. In our time, it is the stuff of a specialized literature, novels that sell millions of copies, movies that play to vast audiences. But it is not integrated into the main thrust of our literature in the way that it was in the Elizabethan age. Nor are the two views of the supernatural quite the same. For most Elizabethans, the supernatural was as real as the sun, and they conceived of it in terms of the theology of the time. Marlowe knew this. Whatever his personal beliefs might have been, he chose the story of Faustus, with all its supernatural elements, as his subject, and he developed it according to a Christian philosophy that conformed to what both Papists and Protestants believed. He furnished his play not only with the satanic Mephistopheles, but with good angels who are messengers from God. In the literature of our own day, we are likely to find only demons. Unlike Pinky in Graham Greene's *Brighton Rock* who believes in the existence of hell and grudgingly admits that logically a belief in hell postulates the existence of heaven, most of our present writing deals with a supernatural that is rooted in no theology of good and evil. Our ghosts and devils threaten and cause harm, but both they and what they do are random: they serve no single master; they are defined by no system. They live outside the context of either the visible or an invisible world.

All this is important, I think, because the historical novelist operates in two realms: his own and the one he is reconstructing. As Garrett himself has said, the writer, being of his own generation, knows what he knows, and most of what he knows is also known by his readers. Neither the writer nor the reader can evacuate his modern sensibility—a circumstance that the writer can attempt to suppress insofar as he can, or try to use as a means by which to enhance the ancient story. For example, the opening image of William Golding's *The Spire* establishes the spire that Jocelyn intends to add to the cathedral as a phallic symbol which alerts Golding's readers to the Freudian thrust of the novel. That the characters in the novel do not see their own story in the terms in which we see it, that they will have been dead for centuries before Freud is born, does not prevent Golding from putting a modern twist on a medieval story and enriching the novel thereby. We understand his characters and their motivations not only according to their own philosophy, but according to our own as well.

For those of us who take literature seriously, Garrett's choice of Marlowe, the author of work that we still read and perform, as the controlling image of his novel strengthens the connection in *Entered from the Sun* between present and past. Writers seek enduring literary fame as a means of achieving immortality, which is to say, of cheating death. Thus they create a dialectic separate, but not totally different, from those of art and reality, of body and soul, of human death and eternal life. This is no small matter. James Joyce was by no means alone in deciding that trying to create great literature, trying to write better than anyone else had ever written, was worth, if need be, the loss of his own soul. Whether Marlowe shared this view, I do not know, but there can be no doubt about his fidelity to his literary vocation. Without an absolute loyalty to his art, he could not have written so well. Whatever he believed, whatever the motives behind his death, he remains alive in our century. In human terms, he has won out over Ingram Frizer, over Walsingham, if Walsingham were the instigator of his murder, over the great majority of his Elizabethan contemporaries of whatever degree.

Under the shadow, not of Marlowe himself, but of his image, Garrett's characters pursue and endure their own fates. One of the ways in which art impinges on reality is that the artist is not alone in his desire to do what he does well. Marlowe's ambition was doubtless more elevated and more sharply focused than that of Alysoun, who wanted to be rich and to be a lady, but she felt other longings that she could not define. She is fulfilled, at least on a physical level, by being made love to by Barfoot and being impregnated by him. This is the incident that defines her life. Her death from the plague is subordinate to it. Hunnyman lives his last days still engaged with his art, sponsoring performances, sometimes mouthing the lines with the players. He is reconciled to his fate, to the fact that the greatness he set out to achieve as an actor has eluded him. Barfoot's death may be the best culmination of all, to die as he has lived. Or more than that: to die still in the service of death itself, to become one with those who have died at his hand; to enter into what T. S. Eliot called a "constitution of silence."

In novels, as well as in life, the characters are measured against each other. We judge them to be good or bad, weak or strong, wise or foolish according to what they do within the ambiance of the novel. But the ambiance matters. I read recently that many, if not the majority, of college students who study Albert Camus's *The*

Stranger conclude that Meursault does no wrong, that his murder of the Arab is justified by the circumstances under which it is committed. He has just buried his mother; the day is hot; the sun is bright; he is disoriented. His friends are eager to forgive him. This should come as no surprise, given the strict, existential parameters that are established in the novel. The plot, the characterization, the bleak tone of the story combine to deflect all metaphysical interpretation. The ambiance denies the supernatural.

Certainly, the world of Elizabethan England is larger, richer, more various than Camus's twentieth century Algeria. But the enveloping action in every work of fiction is a cooperative venture between the facts of the time and place and the author's rendition of them—another dialectic. As I have said, the author is free to bring the learning and the moral and ontological principles and prejudices of his own time into his creation of the world of his narrative. In some cases, as in that of Golding, to do so adds depth to the novel. But to do so can also distort the ambiance of the fictional world. For example, in his characteristically gentle way, Garrett has pointed out that the historical novels of Barry Unsworth are damaged by the author's furnishing his characters with twentieth century minds, a flaw that is endorsed and encouraged by contemporary criticism that judges ancient authors by ethical standards that did not prevail when the authors wrote. In his Elizabethan trilogy, Garrett has taken the opposite course: in being faithful to the world about which he was writing, he has shown us a society in which all levels of reality combine to create its spirit and its conscience. By enabling us to share the world of Elizabeth, of Barfoot and Hunnyman and Alysoun, he makes it possible for us to see ourselves in a new perspective. In the centuries that have passed since Marlowe was killed, courage and faith have diminished. Something of our humanity has been lost. We are indebted to Garrett for showing us that.

Contributors

Richard A. Betts is assistant professor of English at Penn State University, Delaware County Campus. His interests center on the use of historical materials in contemporary American fiction. He has published articles on Styron, Barth, and Berger.

Nicholas Delbanco is Professor of English and Chair of the Hopwood Awards Committee at the University of Michigan. His seventeenth book, the novel *Old Scores*, was published by Warner Books in the fall of 1997; that year he also served as Chair of the National Book Awards Fiction Panel.

Joseph Dewey, Associate Professor of American Literature at the University of Pittsburgh, Johnstown, is the author of *In a Dark Time: The Apocalyptic Temper in the American Novel of the Nuclear Age*. His essays have appeared in *The Mississippi Quarterly*, *The Hollins Critic*, *Modern Fiction Studies*, and *Review of Contemporary Fiction*, as well as other publications. He has recently completed *Locked in Magic Kingdoms: Spectacle Realism in the Novels of Reagan's America* and is co-editing a collection of essays on the short fiction of Henry James.

R.H.W. Dillard is a Professor of English and chair of the creative writing program at Hollins University in Virginia, where he edits the journal, *The Hollins Critic*. He is also a poet and novelist and was awarded the O.B. Hardison, Jr. Poetry Prize by the Folger Shakespeare Library. Among his books is the critical monograph *Understanding George Garrett*, from which the essays in this collection are taken.

Thomas Fleming is a classical philologist, poet, and editor of *Chronicles: A Magazine of American Culture*.

Reginald Gibbons was born in Houston, Texas, and educated at Princeton and Stanford. His most recent book of poems is *Sparrow: New and Selected Poems* (LSU Press, 1997), and his most recent fiction is *Sweetbitter* (Penguin, 1996). From 1981 till 1997 he was the editor of *TriQuarterly* magazine. He teaches at Northwestern University.

Laurence Goldstein is the author of three books of poetry, most recently *Cold Reading* (Copper Beech Press), and three books of literary criticism, most recently *The American Poet at the Movies: A Critical History* (University of Michigan Press). He is Professor of English at the University of Michigan and editor of *Michigan Quarterly Review*.

Steven G. Kellman is Ashbel Smith Professor of Comparative Literature at The University of Texas at San Antonio and film critic for *The Texas Observer*. His recent books include: *The Plague: Fiction and Resistance* (Twayne, 1993); as editor, *Perspectives on "Raging Bull"* (G.K. Hall, 1994); and as co-editor, with Irving Malin, *Into the Tunnel: Essays on William Gass's Novel* (University of Delaware, 1998).

Joseph W. Reed is Professor of English and American Studies at Wesleyan University. His books include *Three American Originals* (1984) and *American Scenarios* (1989). He is married to Kit Reed, the novelist.

Monroe K. Spears, retired from his position as Moody Professor of English at Rice University since 1986, lives in Sewanee, Tennessee. Among his books are *The Poetry of W.H. Auden* (1963), *Dionysus and the City* (1970), *American Ambitions* (1987), *Countries of the Mind* (1992), and *The Writer's Reality* (1996).

Walter Sullivan is a fiction writer and critic. His books include *In Praise of Blood Sports and Other Essays, A Time to Dance*, and, most recently, *The War the Women Lived: Voices From the Confederate South*. He is professor and director of the program in creative writing at Vanderbilt University.

Tom Whalen has published fiction, poetry, criticism, and collaborative translations in numerous journals and anthologies. He directs the creative writing program at the New Orleans Center for Creative Arts and teaches American Literature and film at the University of Stuttgart, Germany. His recent books include *Roithamer's Universe* (Portals Press) and *A Newcomer's Guide to the Afterlife* with Daniel Quinn (Bantam Books). *Light on Glass* (poems) is forthcoming from Red Dust.

Allen Wier is the author of three novels, *Blanco, Departing As Air*, and *A Place for Outlaws*; also a collection of stories, *Things about to Disappear*. He has edited a collection of essays on contemporary fiction and an anthology of short fiction. In 1997 he received the Robert Penn Warren Award for Fiction from the Fellowship of Southern Writers. He teaches at the University of Tennessee in Knoxville, and he has just completed a new novel.

The Editors

Brook Horvath is co-editor (with Irving Malin and Paul Ruffin) of *A Goyen Companion* (University of Texas Press). He is the author, most recently, of *Consolation at Ground Zero* (Eastern Washington University Press) and an editor with *Review of Contemporary Fiction*. He teaches American literature at Kent State University.

Irving Malin is the co-editor of critical essays on Gass's *The Tunnel* (1998) and *Leslie Fiedler and American Culture* (due out in 1999). His reviews have appeared widely in journals, newspapers, and magazines.

107-109, 112, 113, 116, 129, 130, 141
Robert Devereux: see Essex, Second Earl of
Robert Dudley: see, Leicester, First Earl of
Robert Greene (*Entered from the Sun*): 141, 167, 185
Robert Penn Warren Talking (Watkins and Hirs): 47
Roberts, Elizabeth Madox: xi
Roberts, Kenneth: 180
Robinson, W.R.: 30, 178n2
Robocop (film): 98
Roland (*Chanson de Roland*): 92
The Romantics: 44
Rome: 92, 101
Rome Prize: 140
Rose tavern: 165
Royal Exchange: 174, 177
Rubicon: xiii
Rubin, Louis: 139
Ruffin, Paul ("Interview with George Garrett"): 156
Russell House: 102
Russia: xii, 58
Rutherford (Charles Johnson, *Middle Passage*): 99

Sabattini, Rafael: xii
Sacred Hunger (Unsworth): 100
Saint Catherine's Castle: 104
Saint Cuthbert's Church: 109
Saint Martin's Lane: 102
Salome (Garrett, "Salome"): 131
Sartre, Jean-Paul: 39
Satan: 168, 191
Scadbury: 183
The Scarlet Letter (Nathaniel Hawthorne): 46
Schliermann, Heinrich: 90
Scotland: 46, 51, 52, 72, 78, 86, 88, 92, 102, 113
Scott, Sir Walter: xii, 46, 92-94, 114
Settle, Mary Lee: 100
Sewanee Review: 102
Shakespeare, William: 50, 55, 62, 92, 93, 94, 101, 116, 127, 130, 134,

135, 141, 151, 163, 167, 187
Shellabarger, Samuel: xii, 180, 183
Shiloh (Foote): xi
Sicily: 52
"Signs and Symbols" (Nabokov): 10
Sigurd (Scandinavian mythological hero): 92
The Silver Chalice (Costain): 181
Simon Forman (*Entered from the Sun*): 135, 172, 175, 190
Sly (*The Succession*): 73, 82
Snopes trilogy (Faulkner): 183
Socrates: 25
The Sot-Weed Factor (Barth): 99
The Sound and the Fury (Faulkner): 50
Sounding Brass (magazine): 102
The South (American south): 38-39, 101, 180
South Carolina Review: 102
South Carolina, University of: 140
Spain: 63, 86
Spears, Monroe K.: 9, 84n, 108, 109, 141, 151, 152, 158, 178n1, 178n2
Spengler, Oswald: x
The Spire (William Golding): 191
Stapledon, Olaf: ixi
Starmaker (Stapledon): xi
The Steel Glass (Gascoigne): 15
Steenie (*Death of the Fox*): 28
Stein, Gertrude: 19, 22, 106
Steiner, Wendy: 64
Stevens, Wallace: 30, 35
Stevenson, Robert Louis: 180
Stone, Oliver: 130, 160, 161
The Strand: 102
The Stranger (Camus): 192, 193
Stratford: 127
Strauss, Leo: 97
Stubbs, Philip: 151
Styron, William: 180
Sullivan, Walter: 178n1
Syndicate: 161

The Tale of Genji (Murasaki Shikibu): 98
Tamburlaine (Marlowe): 130
Tamburlaine (Marlowe, *Tamburlaine*): 188